VINTAGE NBA BASKETBALL
THE PIONEER ERA (1946-56)

A Mostly Oral History

Neil D. Isaacs

A Division of Howard W. Sams & Company
A Bell Atlantic Company

Published by Masters Press
(A Division of Howard W. Sams & Co., A Bell Atlantic Company)
2647 Waterfront Pkwy. E. Dr., Suite 300
Indianapolis, IN 46214

Published 1996

Printed in the United States of America

10 9 8 7 6 5 4 3 2 1

Library of Congress Cataloging-in-Publication

Issacs, Neil David, 1931-
    Vintage NBA basketball: the pioneer years (1946-56) : a mostly oral history / Neil D. Isaacs.
        p. cm.
    ISBN: 1-57028-069-X (trade)
    1. National Basketball Association--History. 2. Basketball--United States--History. I. Title.

GV885.515.N37183 1996
793.323'64'0973--dc20   96-4790
                                                                            CIP

To Sylvia Lichtman
and to the memory of Joe Lichtman

dear friends, devoted sports fans,
and (not least) Ellen's parents

with love and appreciation

Acknowledgments

Bill Tosheff has been a kind of godfather to this project and deserves much of the credit and thanks for its being nurtured to completion. Also generous with their time, friendly support and welcome suggestions, beyond their own contributions to the text, were Tom King, Wally Osterkorn, Whitey Macknowsky, John Ezersky and Fuzzy Levane. Special thanks to Dutch Garfinkel because, one summer in the mountains, he gave me my first mesmerizing glimpse of what pro basketball could be, and I've stayed tuned-in ever since. Jack Russell has been a constant source of laughs, leads and memories. Harold Rosenthal and Lenny Lewin helped this fellow writer by providing good, productive leads. I am also indebted to other writers who walked parts of this beat before: Leonard Koppett, Zander Hollander, Terry Pluto, Sam Goldaper and (again) Phil Berger. When I discovered Zelda Spoelstra at NBA headquarters, I happened upon a most welcome ally whose guidance and fulfilled promises are much appreciated. Thanks also to Evelyn Miller for her prompt and efficient transcriptions, to Kim Heusel and Holly Kondras for their editorial expertise, and to Tom Bast, a publisher whose handshake is as good a contract as a writer ever had. Special thanks to Elizabeth Badavas for her gracious and patient assistance; and to her leader (and mine), Senator Bill Bradley, whose unfailing sense of rightness, timeliness and teamliness made his manifold basketball skills more valuable, and whose enlightened contributions to public life have enriched the body politic and its discourse. Finally, as always, thanks to my wife Ellen, a fan after my own heart, who nursed this one home, too.

Credits

Cover Design by Suzanne Lincoln
Photo reproduction assistance by Terry Varvel and Scott Stadler
Edited by Kim Heusel
Editorial Assistance by Holly Kondras

Foreword by Senator Bill Bradley

As a member of the World Champion New York Knicks of the 1970s, I learned that you have to give up a little of yourself for the team to win. That's what the fans often missed. Enlarged egos and slick individual moves alone could not ensure victory. Red Holzman told us we were as good as any team and that potentially we were the best, yet, in the same breath, he reminded us that "Everything done today was done 20 years ago; you guys just do it better."

Nobody could dispute these words of wisdom, coming as they did from a pioneer in professional basketball's backcourt. Whether it was "seeing the ball" on defense or "hitting the open man" on offense, Red had learned the fundamentals of team basketball in the early '40s, playing guard for the National Basketball League's Rochester Royals in a memorable lineup that included the likes of Fuzzy Levane, Dutch Garfinkel, Al Cervi and Bobby Davies. I therefore consider myself a beneficiary and direct descendent of these pioneer players, and I welcome Neil Isaacs' book as a fitting tribute to the pioneers' lasting impact on professional basketball.

For me growing up in Crystal City, Missouri, in the '50s, the St. Louis Hawks, rather than the Royals, were the team of my childhood fantasies and the Boston Celtics were respected rivals. Emerging at the conclusion of the Pioneer Era as a part of the young National Basketball Association, the Hawks challenged my imagination, made my interest in the game burn and provided me with examples of individual moves to develop. I learned my set shot – the staple shot of the pioneer years – from "Easy" Ed Macauley, the Saint Louis University All-American who later starred with the Boston Celtics and the Hawks, and I spent endless hours in the high school gym perfecting my free throw by recreating the game as played by Bob Pettit, Bill Sharman and Bob Cousy, as well as by Elgin Baylor.

Described here in vivid detail by the pioneers themselves, the years from the Andrews Sisters to Elvis (1946 to 1956) were a time of transformation that ushered in what most label the modern age of professional basketball. With the birth of theBasketball Association of America in 1946 – the immediate precursor of the NBA – professional basketball came to America's cities. However, its players were no match for the barnstorming teams of America's small towns – Fort Wayne, Sheboygan, Oshkosh and Syracuse – which made up the older National League, and neither professional league could compete with college teams for the loyalty of the fans.

Although the professional game had evolved since the Depression and prewar periods, game scores still lagged at around 40 or 50, with the two-hand set shot, the hook and the layup dominating offensive play. Jumpin' Joe Fulks of the Philadelphia Warriors had just introduced his revolutionary offensive weapon – the jump shot – but that was not to take root until the end of the Pioneer Era. Instead, the game was dominated by big players who could muscle their way into position under the basket.

At the same time, 1946 was the first year in which professional basketball, with its bigger arenas, bigger money and bigger players, could really employ full-time players. With the improved conditioning and offensive strategy that accompanied full-time play, scoring began to open up as the decade progressed, reaching almost 80 points per game by 1954. Play also gained interest as the lane width was increased to 12 feet (on its way to the present 16), forcing the big man to get out from under the net.

However, as former NBA President Maurice Podoloff reminds us in *Vintage NBA Basketball: The Pioneer Era,* his young league was barely scraping by, even with the infusion of talent from the National League, which he had effectively raided in 1948-49, and cash from lucrative television deals after 1953. Fan and cameraman alike threw up their hands in disgust as excessive fouling and stalling techniques lengthened playoff games to more than three hours. As Podoloff explains, "To me everything was threatened with death. The NBA, the TV deal and me, also."

Predictions of the NBA's early demise were premature, however, and two significant rule changes – limits on team fouls and the 24-second shot clock – allowed the NBA to prosper and mature into the fast-paced, high-scoring game fans recognize today. The pioneers are quick to point out that the credit for the latter and more crucial of these rules must be given to Nats operator, Danny Biasone. His contemporaries are equally eager to point out that, like many innovators of the Pioneer Era, Danny has not been given due credit for his contributions. Biasone is hardly a household name; however, with the efforts of basketball historians and scholars such as Dr. Isaacs, the achievements of professional basketball's pioneers will be remembered and celebrated well into the 21st century.

In *Vintage NBA Basketball: The Pioneer Era*, Dr. Isaacs points out that a crucial part of the pioneer players' efforts to gain such recognition is the inclusion of all survivors of the Pioneer Era, including three- and four-year veterans of the NBA and its predecessor leagues, in professional basketball's pension plan. Despite the fact that professional sports has become a worldwide, multibillion-dollar industry, the day-to-day business of its franchises – details of ownership, player contracts and retirement benefits – remain obscure to the public. All the while, those pioneers of basketball whose military service limited their professional careers to a couple of years less than the five required for vesting in the NBA pension plan receive none of the fruits of their early labor which helped to build the NBA of today.

Believing so strongly in the pre-1955 NBA, Dr. Isaacs has committed a third of the royalties from this book to aid the efforts of pioneer players to gain pension benefits. As a player who benefited from the growth of a players union in the 1960s and 1970s, and from the subsequent collective bargaining agreements which loosened the owner choke-hold on player movement and provided players with per diem money, severance pay, disability insurance, medical insurance, increased pension benefits, better playing conditions, first-class air travel and moving expenses, I am pleased that Neil Isaacs has recognized the unique contributions of the pioneer players and has called for their inclusion in the NBA's pension plan.

— Bill Bradley, U.S. Senator and
former player for the New York Knicks

Contents

Introduction: The Pioneer Era of NBA Basketball

Historical Context

With the clarity of hindsight, the historian may see that in 1946 the time was ripe for a new professional basketball league. The elements were present and conditions cohered to produce what we now know as the NBA, emblematic of basketball at its best and a model of professional sports operations. From the vantage points of those who lived through the emergence of the league, however, the situation was chaotic, turbulent, unpredictable and almost completely random.

Mobility or fluidity was the order of the day. The whole spirit of the immediate post-war era was characterized by openness. Conversion to peacetime was not a matter of a search for order nor was it a retreat to the status quo ante nor a yearning for hibernation. Instead, where standards had been loosened by the war, a mind-set of laissez-faire pervaded civilian society. The values that dominated the reconversion processes were the traditional camp followers of wartime values: opportunism, relaxation of moral standards, permissiveness as opposed to repressiveness and an ends-justify-all-means philosophy.

Sports had been protected and preserved throughout the war years. Not only had they been kept going on the home front despite travel restrictions and the draining of the talent pool, but also they were actively sponsored all over the world by service teams and performers. A national commitment to athletics became justified or demanded as a bulwark of morale – public and military. Athletes themselves comprised a substantial cadre of "special services."

The State of the Game

Basketball had evolved from a game of a few regional hotbeds to the status of a major national and international sport. Forty years into its history, the college game had received a promotional boost when Ned Irish began to bring elite teams from around the country to play in doubleheaders against the best of New York's teams in the 1935 season. The National Invitation Tournament, starting in 1938, grew naturally from that success, and though the NCAA began its own postseason tourney the following year, it was often played in Madison Square Garden, too, while the NIT remained at least equally prestigious up until the '50s.

Two other tournaments, however, countered the notion that basketball was exclusively, in Pete Axthelm's phrase, "The City Game," with New York as the city of record. These were the annual AAU tournament in Denver and the World Professional Tournament in Chicago. The latter was played for money, the amount of the payoff determined by final placement in the tournament, the former for glory, the winner laying claim to bragging rights as the nation's best. Many former college stars played in these tournaments, though the lineups included many players who had for one reason or another not been collegians.

Throughout most of the '30s, there was little formality in the organization of leagues. The AAU teams had regular rivals and regional play, the most prominent pro teams were touring groups who took on all comers, and weekend pro and semipro circuits were largely geographical conveniences with constantly shifting components.

Two developments changed all that. One was the formation in 1937 of the National Basketball League, which brought together major industrial teams in the Midwest, drew crowds to some of the larger arenas in the heartland and began actively recruiting collegiate stars. The other was the full-scale mobilization of World War II, which made service ball the outstanding player in the world of organized basketball. The armed forces had an enormous player pool to employ, and they exploited it, with every branch, training station, fort, base and hospital fielding a team or teams. They played each other, they played the surviving AAU clubs, they entered tournaments against the pros, they played the colleges and they played all-star exhibitions for fund-raisers.

The personnel of service ball was naturally in a constant state of flux, except for those special service squads that toured together for the entertainment of the troops. Many trainees played for different colleges, when their training took them from campus to campus. Many stateside players were able to play service ball during the week and moonlight for pro or semipro clubs on weekends. But the most significant result of all this was the taking of regionalism out of the game. Distinctions were dulled, styles consolidated, and no player or coach or club remained a stranger to the rest.

In two senses of the word, theater plays a leading part in the establishment of the Basketball Association of America: the performance that provides entertainment and the venue for the performance. With post-war audiences hungry for entertainment, metropolitan arenas had too few ice shows, rodeos, circuses, prize fights, basketball games, hockey, and other spectacles and sporting events to fill all the dark dates. The NBL had, arguably, the three best basketball teams in the world, but the major cities of the East had the empty houses and seats.

Formed mostly by hockey and arena owners, the new league organized with 11 franchises in 1946. Arthur Wirtz and the Norris family were key players, with their holdings in Chicago, Detroit and St. Louis, along with Al Sutphin with his underused Cleveland facility; but Boston (Walter Brown), New York (Ned Irish), and Philadelphia (Eddie Gottlieb) provided the necessary clout in the East. Providence, Washington, Toronto and Pittsburgh completed the original lineup.

Toronto and Pittsburgh were through after one season, along with Detroit and Cleveland, while Baltimore completed an eight-team league and went on to win the championship, succeeding Philadelphia. The regular-season play had seen the Washington Capitols lead the league the first year, the St. Louis Bombers the second, as short playoff series tended to produce upsets. Max Zaslofsky, Joe Fulks, Stan Miasek, Ed Sadowski, Bob Feerick, Ernie Calverley and Fred Scolari were standout performers, while Buddy Jeannette, as player-coach, led the Bullets to the title, succeeding owner-coach Gottlieb of the Warriors.

All eight teams survived into the third season though many suffered financial losses. But President Maurice Podoloff successfully raided the NBL and corralled the best pro teams into the league. Minneapolis and Rochester, along with Fort Wayne and Indianapolis, swelled the ranks of the BAA; the schedule was expanded from 48 to 60 games (reducing the exhausting preseason schedule of exhibitions), and the divisions were rearranged so that all six teams in the East were old BAA teams and one would survive to the finals in the playoff system. It was Washington, but the decisive matchup to produce the champion was the semifinals in which the West was won by the Lakers of George Mikan, Jim Pollard and Arnie Ferrin over the Royals of Bob Davies, Bob Wanzer, Red Holzman and Arnie Risen.

The quality of competition gained ground, while box-office losses continued. Providence folded, and so did the Indianapolis Jets. Indianapolis, however, was to accommodate the great Kentucky collegians with a team-owned franchise that would renew the old NBL. Instead, because the Alex Groza-Ralph Beard-Wah Wah Jones entity was seen as the most promising gate attraction in the game, the BAA expanded to include seven teams from the NBL in a 17-franchise amalgam. It was newly named the National Basketball Association, it had all the greatest teams in the land and most of the great players, and yet it still struggled for identity, security, stability and even survival.

The 1949-50 season demonstrated conclusively the superiority of the NBL teams. In an awkward three-division setup, the new kids on the block in Indianapolis beat out the Anderson Packers in the West, Minneapolis and Rochester dominated the Central in a dead heat, and in the East the NBA establishment was overwhelmed by the Syracuse Nationals, newly arrived from the old league. In a clumsy playoff structure, five of the six divisional finalists were originally NBL clubs, and the Lakers took the Nats for the title.

It was less a matter of dilution of talent than the fact of inadequate facilities that reduced the number of teams for the following season. And it was less a matter of media markets than of meeting expenses of long road trips. Chicago and St. Louis shut down, and Washington followed midseason, so that only Boston, New York and Philadelphia were survivors of the charter BAA members. In fact, they were the only three franchises to last through the whole Pioneer Era. The West was also reduced to a five-team division, with the departure of Anderson, Sheboygan, Waterloo and Denver. It was as if the show had benefited from a long period of out-of-town tryouts and was now streamlined and ready for a prime-time opening.

The Evolution of Distinction

The NBA had trimmed down and turned a corner. Two contrasting happenings had significance far beyond the actual play, in which Rochester wrested the title from Minneapolis and the Knicks extended the Lakers to seven games in the finals. One was the brainchild of Haskell Cohen: the first NBA All-Star Game, played in Boston, a triumph of Walter Brown's optimism and largesse over the dispirited naysayers around the league. It was a showcase for proud and inspired talent: Fulks, Paul Arizin, Dolph Schayes, Ed Macauley, Bob Cousy, Dick McGuire and Andy Phillip leading the East over Groza, Vern Mikkelsen, Pollard, Mikan, Davies, Frankie Brian, Beard and Fred Schaus. At a time when the promotional ingenuity of the league seemed to be restricted to the notion of having the Harlem Globetrotters perform their showbiz antics as a preliminary event before a real professional basketball game, the showcasing of the game's elite talent was a giant step forward.

The other significant happening was the explosion of the college basketball scandals. A tragic event for a number of young players, it exposed the commercialization of the college game and created a vacuum in public support which the NBA was prepared to fill. Podoloff adopted a firm policy of banning for life any player implicated in point-shaving or betting on games. This led to some injustices against certain players guilty only by association or inference, but it shored up the public faith in a sport with a severely tarnished reputation. No NBA game was ever shown to have been fixed, and the appearance of integrity was preserved.

The policy exacted a heavy toll. In some cases unjustifiably, enormous talent was lost to the league for years to come: Bill Spivey, Sherman White, Floyd Layne, Jack Molinas, Roger Brown and Connie Hawkins. And yet it could be argued that the policy was the saving of the game and the making of the NBA as a premier sports attraction. The biggest loss was in Indianapolis, where the arrest of Groza and Beard ended enormously promising careers and in time led to the failure of the whole franchise that had looked, going into the 1951-52 season, like long-term championship material.

Meanwhile, yet another development with far-reaching long-term consequences had already begun to take place. In the 1950-51 season, Chuck Cooper signed with the Celtics, followed in short order by Nat (Sweetwater) Clifton with the Knicks and Earl Lloyd with the Capitols. They were joined as the NBA's black pioneers by Don Barksdale and Davage (Dave) Minor with the Bullets the following season. As several of the contributors to this book say, racial integration came smoothly and unremarkably to pro basketball, in sharp contrast to baseball. What is not often acknowledged is that, while no blacks played in the NBA until 1950,

Dolly King and Pop Gates had played in the NBL even before an all-black squad of former Rens came into that league to finish out the 1949 season.

In basketball, there had been few observable racial anomalies or animosities outside some die-hard collegiate conferences. The Rens and the Globetrotters had regularly played against and toured with all-white teams for decades. More significantly, the leading AAU and service teams were more likely to be racially integrated than not. As far as basketball's pro players were concerned, this was the most natural thing in their world, hardly worth noticing, never mind getting excited about. Nevertheless, all acknowledge that over time it was a development that changed the face of the game considerably.

In its quest for stability, respectability and continuity, the NBA still had to upgrade both its product and its packaging. Podoloff credited two people for being instrumental in the league's survival and ultimate achievement – Haskell Cohen, less for the college draft and the All-Star Game than for his role in securing a TV contract; and Danny Biasone, less for his leadership of the Syracuse franchise and the consolidation of the big leagues than for his generation of the 24-second rule.

Rules changes came with annual persistence. Deliberate and excessive fouling destroyed the game's inherent virtues of action, pace and excitement. The concept of "team foul" limits made a significant contribution to the product, and so did both the widening of the lane and the tool of the "technical foul" for officials to have some control over players' and coaches' sometimes barbarous or outrageous behavior on court. But it was the advent of the 24-second clock that permanently altered the nature and image of the NBA game.

Those changes upgraded the attractiveness of pro basketball for televised packaging. Podoloff was prophetic about the importance of TV for pro sports, and not only vigorously pursued contracts but was a vigilant presence to guarantee the commercial viability of the product. He worked hard at cost containment, but his major concern was always the maintenance of the image of integrity. In these regards he was sometimes thought to be excessive or even eccentric, but he took great satisfaction in later years that his vision was fulfilled to such an extent that the NBA's achievement exceeded even his own fondest dreams.

In the last five years of the Pioneer Era, the streamlining continued. Nine franchises remained after Indianapolis folded, and then Baltimore's departure left them with eight. Eight it remained until 1961-62, when a new Chicago franchise entered, initiating a gradual growth up to the present. But geographical change was a feature that remained unchanged. The Milwaukee Hawks (once the Tri-Cities Blackhawks) moved to St. Louis in 1955 en route to Atlanta in 1968, and in 1957 the Pistons moved from Fort Wayne to Detroit, the Royals from Rochester to Cincinnati. The NBA map changed dramatically in 1960 when the Lakers moved to Los Angeles, and when the Warriors followed them west in 1962, the Syracuse franchise could move into the Philadelphia vacuum the following season, when Baltimore reclaimed its place in the league with the transplanting of the latest Chicago franchise.

Those Lakers in Minneapolis had continued to dominate the league in the early '50s. Their two-year reign having been interrupted by Rochester, they came back with three titles in a row. Schayes and Cousy became fixtures on the all-league teams, while Mikan's teammates, Pollard, Mikkelsen and Slater Martin, joined him on the annual squads. Arizin and Neil Johnston of the Warriors were leading scorers, Foust and Harry Gallatin leading rebounders, and Phillip, Davies, Paul Seymour, McGuire, Wanzer, Jack George and George King rivaled Cousy as playmakers.

Mikan's retirement in 1954 (and his misguided comeback to play half the 1955-56 season) ended the dynasty. Fort Wayne, with Foust, George Yardley and Mel Hutchins won the West both years but lost in the championship series, first to the Nationals of Schayes, Seymour, Kerr, Lloyd and Red Rocha, and then to the Warriors of Arizin, Johnston, George, Joe Graboski and rookie Tom Gola. But these two years constitute an interregnum, and as the era ends a new dynasty ascends.

The End of an Era

The end of the Pioneer Era is clearly demarcated by the initiation of a new and wholly distinctive age with the arrival of Bill Russell in 1956. In a period in which Bob Pettit, Elgin Baylor, Wilt Chamberlain, Oscar Robertson and Jerry West (a starting all-time basketball five according to some analysts) come to prominence, it is nevertheless Russell at the center of a Boston team dominating the whole league that gives his name to the era. Not only was he surrounded by a deep squad of talented players, not only did his presence make better players of all of them, but the style of play that he imposed on his team and that prevailed over the rest of the league gave identity and distinctive quality to the game as played in the NBA. The Bill Russell-led Celtics showed that the game had ascended to new heights on the floor, above the rim, and in the eyes of media and fans alike.

The succeeding eras, relatively shorter in duration but perhaps no less distinctive, bring the NBA to its golden anniversary this year. It is golden in the sense of its 50 years, but also in the sense of its financial achievements and the glories of its game as spectacle, as arena for enormous athletic talent, and as goose that lays ancillary eggs of unlimited potential in images, endorsements, products and "properties." As the recent contract disputes fade to their own indistinct place in the NBA's dramatic history, it is worth reflecting on the contributions of the pioneers.

Underrecognized and largely unrewarded, survivors of the early years deserve the attention of those who have benefited from their struggles. That an all-star team of Mikan, Pollard, Schayes, Zaslofsky and Davies could in their prime have competed with the stars of any other era seems to me arguable if moot. But that the players who competed with and against them throughout the league's pioneer decade, many of whose stories appear in the following pages, deserve inclusion in an NBA pension plan seems to me *inarguable*. That the league has so far excluded many of the pioneers is penny-wise but pound-foolish, not to say shortsighted in

Max Zaslofsky was among the top five scorers in the league in its first four seasons, and led the league in 1947-48. PHOTO COURTESY OF JIM SEMINOFF

terms of how public, media and posterity may regard the value, values and attitudes of the NBA.

What comes through most clearly in the following pages is that these men loved the game. They had to, because for the most part that love was the only reason to play. Their comic anecdotes about travel and facilities make light of their conditions, while all they went through was justified by what Marty Glickman calls the "sheer joy" of what they experienced on court.

What remains unheard in their recollections are references to the Korean War, which apparently had little impact. The names of McCarthy and MacArthur, the Rosenbergs and J. Edgar Hoover, Milton Berle and Lucille Ball do not impinge on their collective memory. If the Eisenhower Era is a fitting title for the '50s, and if the society's confidence in its achieved stability in the face of the Cold War is mirrored in the NBA's achievement by the end of its first decade, those are the judgments of history or hindsight, not of the contemporary participants in the league's composite memory.

Their focus is on basketball and its context, where they played and how they lived, not on the great world at large, and that focus is what makes their reminiscences entertaining and enlightening. Podoloff and Gottlieb, Kerner and Biasone and Irish, those are the executives that figure in their world, not Eisenhower, Dulles, Warren and Kefauver. The careful reader, however, will be rewarded by the amusing appearance of Adlai Stevenson at a remembered banquet in Moline, Illinois.

Method

This is basically a work of oral history. Every one of the 40 contributors has his spoken words appear in the text, but with some variation. Eight chose to record their reminiscences on tape; they were then transcribed, edited and modified in follow-up conversation. Seven were interviewed live, followed by similar transcription, editing and follow-up. For 19, the primary interview was by telephone, followed by the usual three-part process.

The written word came into play along with the spoken in many cases. Five contributors chose to write their recollections, but they too were edited and followed up like the others. Finally, the posthumous contribution of Mr. Podoloff is based on a series of interviews/conversations with the author over a period of years, and augmented by a detailed narrative in a 1981 letter to the author. In the cases of Whitey Macknowsky and Jack Russell, I was able to use their books, *The Dynamics of Basketball* (1991) and *Honey Russell: Between Games, Between Halves* (1986), to supplement the oral material; another dozen of the contributors supplemented their tapes, interviews and conversations with follow-up correspondence.

There is a rough chronological order to the arrangement of entries. Some of the players and coaches who were there at the beginning were still around when the Pioneer Era passed into the Russell Era. I have arbitrarily spaced them out. I have tried to keep together contemporary teammates, and I have attempted to bracket entries of contributors who have differing perspectives on common events. A pair of pioneer writers and the son of a pioneer coach stand first, a pair of pioneer referees and the pioneer president are last, and the premier broadcaster takes center stage.

Remembered events have the virtues of vividness and illustrative, defining details. What they may lack is accuracy of historical data. Wherever feasible, I have chosen on the side of the compelling qualities of narrative rather than the verifiable fact. Where several versions of the same material were rather redundant than complementary, I have exercised editorial taste in choosing the best version, and so for example the Green Parrot Cafe, a treasured setting in many memories, is rendered here only in Marty Glickman's play-by-play.

Two or more conflicting versions of events that have taken on the aura of legend are instructive in their very variety. Once again, the clarity of hindsight may confer a procrustean grid upon a "history" of protean material. What did Big Ed Sadowski and Dutch Garfinkel say to each other in the visiting locker room in Chicago? What and who precipitated the "Boston Massacre?" Who broke the bronze bison's tail in the Buffalo train station? In insisting that the BAA-NBL merger was a "raid," was a 90-year-old Podoloff confusing the negotiations of 1948 with those of 1949? Answers to such questions may be inferred by reader or historian, but the individual answers recorded here are at least equally valuable in terms of what they say about the processes by which the past becomes fixed in history, legend, lore and memory. They are also instructive about the character telling the tale.

So I have often corrected correctable errors of fact – scores, statistics, verifiable dates and rosters, and the like. For the rest, I have erred on the side of what the contributor remembers or believes rather than what concurs with my own or others' historical research. The result is a record less encyclopedic than entertaining.

Harold Rosenthal

When professional basketball came to New York in 1946 it was all nickels and dimes. To keep writers happy, they'd pay for a piece in the program that sold for 25 cents. But they wouldn't pay you 25 bucks for the piece, it was 20.

Here's another example, a story I got from Jim Heffernan who covered the Warriors for the *Philadelphia Bulletin.* One of the original promoters in the league was Eddie Gottlieb, a basketball guy back in gymnasium days with the South Philadelphia Hebrew Association, the SPHAs. Now he had the Warriors in the Philadelphia Arena. When they came to New York they wouldn't take a bus or train, they'd pile into three cars and drive up. But they timed the trip so that they'd get to the Garden on the day of a game just before six o'clock in the afternoon, when the parking restrictions ended, so they could park on the street. Heffernan and Gottlieb would be in the first car, with one of the players driving, and one night they got to Eighth and 50th too early, about a quarter to six. The player said, "Let's park in a garage," but Gottlieb answered, "Drive around the block a couple of times."

My paper, *The Herald Tribune,* was a big basketball paper at that time, even though Stanley Woodward and Red Smith didn't care for it. Woodward called it "round ball" and Smith called it "dump ball." But Irving Marsh and Everett Morris were interested. They invented the six-column box score for basketball, an innovation that first appeared in the Trib.

It was largely because of Ned Irish's friendship with Marsh and Morris and a lot of other writers in the City that basketball got the kind of coverage it did. Marsh said to me, "Go do a story on this new league." Walter Kennedy was their press agent, and he was delighted. He had been the Stamford, Connecticut, correspondent for *The Sporting News.* I went over there and he said, "Let's go to lunch — there's a nice little place around the corner." I'm expecting one of those fine French places in the neighborhood, but he had in mind a luncheonette where each of us takes a stool at the counter where we had sandwiches, and I did the first interview with Maurice Podoloff about the Basketball Association of America. That's the kind of shoestring operation it was then.

Maurice Podoloff, the league's first president, got involved because he and his brothers owned the New Haven Arena and he had been president of the American Hockey League. Podoloff and his brothers were involved in a lot of real estate, and they acted as "beards" for the Catholic Church in New Haven. You know, when the church wanted to acquire property without attracting any attention, the Podoloffs would do it under their name.

OK, now Maurice Podoloff shows up in New York as president of this new league, and not too many people know him. They get him a little office not too far from the Garden – even though that first year they didn't play much in the Garden. Most New York Knicks games were in the 69th Regiment Armory, where they put down a new floor.

I was on the Knicks' first road trip to Cleveland. It was pitiful – there were about 50 people in the seats. Joe Lapchick came along. He was the Knicks' coach-in-waiting. Neil Cohalan was the coach, a wonderful man and coach but an alcoholic. He had been given the job as a favor from Ned Irish to Cohalan's brother, who was a district attorney in the days before Frank Hogan. It was understood that Lapchick would take over when Cohalan couldn't continue.

Another coach I remember that first year was Red Rolfe, the great third baseman of the Yankees, who took over the Toronto Huskies, after three of their players – two of them from Seton Hall, Ed Sadowski and Dick Fitzgerald – tried their hands.

Freddie Scolari was the player I remember best. He had the most magnificent hands I ever saw, a magician with the ball. They called him Fat Freddie because he had this tire of baby fat around his waist, but he was a favorite of the girls. Bud Palmer was a big attraction, too, a good-looking guy who brought some Ivy League class along with his jump shot from Princeton to the Knicks.

You know what the editor would say when he sent you out to cover a pro basketball game on the road, his final words? This will tell you what importance it was given: "Call me night press rate collect, and keep it short."

After 35 years as a reporter and columnist for the New York Herald Tribune, *Harold Rosenthal moved into sports public relations with the Continental, American and National football leagues. He has written a dozen books, including* The Ten Best Years of Baseball, Fifty Faces of Football, *and (with Johnny Unitas)* Playing Pro Football to Win. *He lives in Boca Raton, Florida.*

Lenny Lewin

This was a league created with a minimum. There's a lot of talk about salary caps now, but in 1946 the agreement was that you couldn't pay a player more than $5,000.

Arthur Wirtz, who had the Chicago Stadium, was the chief motivator behind the organization of the league. He was aware of events that filled buildings. He had the Sonja Henie tour, the Globetrotters were a major attraction, and like most of the big-city arenas (New York, Philadelphia, Boston, Buffalo) he had great success with college basketball doubleheaders.

So he went to other arena owners, many of whom owned hockey franchises, and persuaded them to come in, that they would get more dates for events in their buildings. But Ned Irish said that he couldn't afford to spare the dates for Madison Square Garden. They were solidly booked, not only with college basketball double-headers but with the rodeo, the circus and boxing, all of which drew good crowds.

Wirtz sold Irish on the urgency of New York being in the league. It's a New York game anyway, and the New York fans were deeply involved with the players, knew the names and the guys, mostly because of their Madison Square Garden exposure. All the great college players were getting media attention, and there had to be a team in the media capital of the world.

Irish finally agreed, but he could only provide eight dates in the Garden in the first couple of seasons. The other home games were to be played in the 69th Regiment Armory. Even playoff games against the Lakers, as late as 1952, were played there.

The league opened with the Knicks on the road at Toronto, against the Huskies. Red Rolfe, the great Yankees third baseman, was general manager of the Toronto franchise, which lasted only that one season. It's weird that Toronto is just now getting back into the NBA after 50 years.

For the first playoff game, Lester Scott, who came from the *World-Telegram* to be publicity director for the Knicks, took a large media entourage from New York to Cleveland. In fact, there were so many of us that there weren't enough tickets for us at the press window. Les had to buy some more to accommodate us.

As an attraction, the pro game suffered in comparison with the college game. College basketball was the fever, the number one event in New York. It was hard to get a ticket in Madison Square Garden. Most of the outstanding players had played in the Garden either in doubleheaders or in tournaments. But when they came in as pros they were scattered among all these new teams. For the fans then, the teams and the league lacked meaning and credibility.

From the moment the BAA began, two players jumped out as stars. There was Max Zaslofsky, a great ball handler and set shooter out of St. John's, who played for Wirtz's team in Chicago, and Joe Fulks, a great outside jump shooter for Philadelphia, who easily led the league in scoring. They were the singular standouts.

Dolph Schayes would have been the third, but Ned Irish didn't sign him for the Knicks because of the salary cap. An extra five hundred dollar bonus would have done it, but Irish wouldn't break the league rules and Schayes signed with Syracuse in the NBL.

In the BAA's third season, four clubs came over from the NBL – Minneapolis, Rochester, Fort Wayne and the old Indianapolis Jets. This brought in Red Holzman, Bob Davies, Bob Wanzer, and Rochester's owner-coach, Les Harrison. It also brought in George Mikan, basketball's meganame. The league was still floundering, but Mikan and the Lakers gave new momentum to the pro game in New York.

Ironically, the scandals that killed interest in college ball gave impetus to the pro game. We all knew about the scandals before they broke. It was purely coincidental and a little weird that I wrote a column about Kenny Norton, the coach at Manhattan, who was about to be fired. I said, 'How can you place the blame on the coach when his two best players, Hank Poppe and Jack Byrnes, are so erratic?' When Junius Kellogg, Manhattan's next star, reported a bribe attempt, it turned out that Poppe and Byrnes had been accepting bribes. The next time I saw Kenny Norton, he said, "That column you wrote saved my job."

The officials back then were a different breed. They grew up with the game, and they had an awareness that seems lacking now. Of course, it's the most difficult game to officiate, because every play's a foul. But they traveled together, they knew each player's idiosyncrasies, and they knew the game and the way it should be called. I'm talking about guys like Pat Kennedy, Sid Borgia, Mendy Rudolph, Johnny Nucatola and Chuck Solodare.

Knowing Charlie Eckman as I did, I didn't consider it odd that a ref would become a coach. That was because he was an oddball anyway, who might do anything. Besides, Fred Zollner found it very economical. Eckman didn't command a high salary like big-name college coaches, and in those days many coaches were hired for name recognition alone.

Zollner, by the way, fought hardest of all against the union. He told his players that anyone who joined the union wouldn't play on his team. And he had some clout in the league. He had some Fort Wayne games played in Miami because he had a home there.

Among the coaches, Joe Lapchick was the greatest talker. He never went home after a game. He'd keep me up talking basketball and philosophy till five or six in the morning.

Lapchick was still coach of the Knicks when Walter Dukes came in from the Globetrotters. But he was gone by the end of the season, when the Knicks made a terrible mistake. They could have drafted Bill Russell. Les Harrison had the first draft choice for Rochester. He offered to use it for Russell and trade him to the Knicks for Dukes and $15,000. Ned Irish turned him down because he didn't want to spend the money. Russell ended up in Boston, of course, and led the Celtics to 11 NBA titles.

Dukes was a character. He once had his car broken into, and when he was asked what had been taken, he said he had a hundred raincoats in the trunk. In the summer of '55 I traveled to Europe with the Globetrotters in their chartered plane. We were leaving from Paris to come home, and there's no Dukes. The plane had to leave without him, and he ended up having to pay his own way home. When I saw him, I asked him what had happened. He said, "I had to go to the cleaners to pick up my suits."

In those days, the basketball writers used to have a regular luncheon at Leone's. The one I remember best was after the NBA had adopted the 24-second clock in 1954. Maurice Podoloff, still president of the league, was our scheduled speaker. There was a balcony right over the dining room, and we had installed a 24-second clock. As soon as Podoloff had been speaking for 24 seconds, the clock went off and we had a great laugh. That innovation saved the game, but unfortunately it has no effect on after-dinner speakers.

Lenny Lewin started at the Daily Mirror *in 1937 and covered basketball and all sports from 1943 to 1963, then wrote on basketball and all sports for the* New York Post. *Since 1993, shortly after being enshrined in the Basketball Hall of Fame in Springfield, he has been Executive Director of the New York Knickerbockers Alumni Association.*

Honey Russell. PHOTO COURTESY OF JACK RUSSELL

Vintage NBA: The Pioneer Era

Jack Russell

Back in the summer of 1946, I was with my family in Rutland, Vermont, because my father had been given the baseball job managing the Rutland team in the New England College League. The previous year he had been the coach at Manhattan College, both basketball and baseball. When it turned out that the NBA, or at that time the BAA, was being planned, someone had told Walter Brown, who had the Boston franchise, about my father. He was told that Honey Russell would be a very good asset to the league and also that he happened to be in the area at the time.

When Walter Brown got in touch with my father about the Boston job, he felt he had to decline. In the first place, he was committed to finishing the baseball season with Rutland. In the second place, if he were going to leave Manhattan College, he felt he would have to make provision for adequate replacements. Mr. Brown was willing to wait, probably admiring that kind of integrity himself, and so my father became the first coach of the Celtics, but he started at a disadvantage because of his personal code of behavior.

The men organizing the league were mostly hockey magnates, so they were depending on the coaches they hired, mostly college coaches or player-coaches who had the best sense of available talent, to put together their teams. Because my father had to finish out the baseball season in Vermont and also provide for his replacement at Manhattan, he missed out on players he might have garnered had he been able to start his recruiting earlier. It was the kind of thing that put him and the Celtics management in a situation where the odds were against them.

For example, he thought he might be able to build a team around Ed Sadowski, who had played for him at Seton Hall and was the best center in the league that first year. But Toronto had beat him to Sadowski, made him player-coach of the Huskies at the start of the season, and paid him $10,000, the highest salary in the BAA. The next year, after Toronto folded, Sadowski did come to the Celtics, and so did Eddie Ehlers, an outstanding football player just out of Purdue, and in baseball, having been a nemesis to my father as the league-leading hitter of that Vermont summer. It was only after the season that my father learned that he was also a fine basketball player.

In 1946, a lot of athletes had not checked in yet because of the war, but he was able to assemble a somewhat makeshift squad. On that first Celtics team, my father had an excellent player in Dutch Garfinkel, a fine all-around athlete in Al Brightman, the Simmons brothers – John and Connie, and Kevin Connors, better known as Chuck, or the Rifleman, who had also played for him at Seton Hall.

I have a particularly fond remembrance of Dutch Garfinkel. In October of 1945, when I was a high school senior, I had the good luck to see my father play his last game as a pro, in his 28th pro season. He was pushing 44 and already coaching at Manhattan, but was trying to organize one last American League club. His team of the moment was called the Jersey Reds, and they were playing an exhibition game against the Brooklyn Visitations, both teams with just six players.

The Reds won, 34-26, my father playing most of the game and scoring 10 points to lead them, with two-for-two from the free-throw line and four-for-four from the field. The first three field goals were two-hand set shots from outside. The final shot, the vintage Honey Russell play, was on a backdoor cut set up by the earlier outside shooting. Played too close now, he cut to the basket and took a perfect pass for an easy layup. The passer was Dutch Garfinkel. It was my father's last bow; one year later his newly dragooned Celtics would be led from the bench.

Connie Simmons and Al Brightman would head up the team in scoring and assists, but it was baseball that directly or indirectly brought them onto my father's basketball team. Perhaps because he had played three sports professionally himself he often favored athletes who played more than one sport. Brightman showed up in Boston, unrecruited, from the West Coast. And as good as he was that year, it was just a way to occupy himself between baseball seasons, and he didn't come back to the game.

Connie Simmons was just a kid out of high school. My father had recruited John Simmons, whom he knew as a baseball player at NYU. He, too, stayed with pro basketball only that year, stuck with baseball, and made it to the majors for part of one season with the Senators. But he left a basketball legacy in his brother, after suggesting that my father take a look at the kid. Connie was tall, but skinny, and he could take the outside shot but couldn't take the rough stuff inside. My father was dismayed once during the season when Connie called timeout on the court, saying he had to go the bathroom, when what he really wanted was to get out from under the physical beating he was taking. "Dismay" might have been the key word to describe my father's reaction to the events he weathered through the Celtics' haphazard first season.

The most vivid scenes of that year, in my memory and I believe in my father's, too, centered around Kevin Connors. "I made a millionaire out of him," he used to say, "and he made a pauper out of me." He would always name Kevin as his best "discovery," pretty much a surprise to those who knew that he had coached Bob

Davies, Bobby Wanzer, Walter Dukes and Richie Regan. "Sure," he'd say, "who else played two sports in the major leagues and then made good in the movies?" It was Connors who shattered the backboard during warm-ups on opening night in the Boston Arena, costing the franchise its first home crowd, who quietly sidled out of the building, and it was Connors he had to get out of jail in Buffalo for climbing up on the bronze bison in the train station and breaking off the tail. On the road or at home – it hardly mattered where the high jinks occurred, while major-league basketball suffered.

At Seton Hall, Kevin had been a scrupulously clean player. In 1943, when he was a tank instructor stationed at West Point, my father got him to play weekends for a Brooklyn Indians team in the wartime American League. For his first game, my father asked him to sit out the first half and study the play of Mike Bloom, the Trenton center and probably the best player in the about-to-fold league, who later joined him in Boston at the end of the second season.

Bloom, at 6 feet 6 inches, was a slick, finesse-type player, who liked to face the basket from the corner rather than play the pivot with his back to the basket. At halftime, my father told Kevin to forget everything he'd seen and, as the ball was tossed up for the center jump, to sock him on the jaw. Connors was shocked and at first refused, but my father told him he wouldn't play another pro game if he didn't do it. The idea was first to make Bloom worry about the madman he was facing and then to strengthen Kevin's reputation as a pro player to be reckoned with.

Well, it worked in the first instance, and they won the game. But the second result failed to come to pass. A week later, without being told, Kevin started a game against a Philadelphia team by trying the same stunt against Irv Torgoff. Torgoff didn't go down and, in this rebaptism of fire for Kevin, righted the wrong. Kevin came off the court at halftime a badly beaten and sadder but wiser man. "What in the name of God possessed you to hit *him*?" my father asked at halftime. "You told me to, Honey," he said, and then heard, "Christ, Kevin, that was last week."

My most vivid image of Kevin, though, comes from early in '47-48, Boston's following season, before he was finally released from a now better team, and it is associated with the name of Jackie Robinson. I know it was the second season because Eddie Ehlers was there, and he and Kevin were always talking about baseball. The scene in my mind is from October of 1947, with the Celtics in pre-season training at the Boston Arena. Jackie Robinson had broken the color barrier in baseball, playing first base his first year in Brooklyn (with Gil Hodges still a part-time young catcher), and Kevin had recently learned that he was to be brought up to Montreal, the Dodgers' chief farm club, to be a first baseman the next season.

Ehlers and some of the others were sitting on a bench courtside when Kevin came running out on the floor wearing a sweat suit with a first baseman's mitt on his right hand and a new basketball under his left arm. He flipped the basketball up in the air, came down in the position of a first baseman stretching for a throw and caught the ball in his glove while grimacing at his teammates. They were already laughing when he broke them up with his punch line: "The new white hope."

The more things change, the more they stay the same. At the chalkboard, coach Russell diagrams a play for (l-r) John Simmons, Ed Ehlers, Ed Sadowski and Art Spector. It's a three-man weave off the high post, while a weakside forward sets a baseline screen for the center. Note the use of numbers of 1-5 to designate players by position. All this is to be found in any offense today. But note the size of the lane.
PHOTO COURTESY OF JACK RUSSELL

Vintage NBA: The Pioneer Era

Sometimes the second season gets confused with the first in my memory, and I hate to sound like Wordsworth but I can remember that sometimes during those seasons my memory would drift back to my boyhood days when my father was coaching Seton Hall, probably because so many of his former players and those I had seen them play against were in the league. For example, whenever I saw the Celtics play Rochester with Bobby Wanzer or Syracuse with Whitey Macknowsky, I couldn't help but reminisce about being on a train in 1942 with the Seton Hall freshman team traveling to a road game at West Point, and seeing Wanzer, always a clever one on or off the court, play a trick on gullible Macknowsky. (Incidentally, the five starters on that freshman team all went on to play in the NBA – Tommy Byrnes, Bob Fitzgerald and Mike McCarron, along with Bobby and Whitey – something no other frosh team ever did in the sport's history.)

Whitey became engrossed in a *Life* magazine article that was being passed around the private train car, about a thief who had had his fingers filed or sanded so that he'd never be detected through fingerprints. The New Jerseyite Whitey wondered if it could be true, and Wanzer convinced him that it was not only a useful procedure for thieves, especially in Queens, but that it was common for ballplayers because they could handle the ball much better if they got the treatment on their fingertips. For weeks afterwards, Whitey kept after Bobby Wanzer to arrange for him to get the treatment, and Wanzer, to the amusement of the rest of the team, never let him in on the joke.

The Celtics in their second year became a mirror of the transition that was taking place in professional basketball, because my father felt that he had the talent to alternate two five-man units, each playing a different style. The veterans, with Sadowski in the middle and Dutch Garfinkel handling the ball outside, teamed up often with Mel Riebe, Mike Bloom and Art Spector, to run a vintage pro offense, effective and reliable but plodding and predictable.

The other five, led by Ehlers, with George Munroe, a future Rhodes Scholar from Dartmouth, Gene Stump, who had been the number two man at DePaul on the great George Mikan teams, and speedy Cecil Hankins, who had played second banana to Bob Kurland on the great Oklahoma A&M teams, were all used to a wide-open, full-speed, all-over-the-court freelance game. It was the popular college style, exciting and unpredictable, and was to lead to the prevalent up-tempo style of the NBA to come.

In one particular game I remember, against Providence, the veteran unit started and opened up a lead, which the scrambling youngsters quickly lengthened at first, only to fall apart and blow it all in the second quarter, when my father rushed the starters back in to bring them back close by halftime. He spent most of the halftime demonstrating defensive measures for what the Steamrollers were doing and seemed to be talking only to the veterans. I recall thinking that I didn't like his mood and as the interval went on I was seething, feeling that his neglect of the younger players, whose heads were hanging at the periphery of the group, was unjustified and would make things worse.

The old pros were already moving toward the door when he turned to the others, the subs who were hanging back, ignored for the whole halftime, especially Stump, Munroe and Ehlers, all of whom coincidentally wore contact lenses, a fact my father took advantage of. I can remember only some of the phrasing but the sound and tone of what he said is unforgettable.

"What in the name of God are you stalling around back there for? You're starting this half. Take your 18 eyes and get out on the damned court. Get the hell out of here and win the game, for God's sake. Get off your tails, get out of here, get up on the court."

That psychological strategy certainly worked, Ehlers and Stump especially playing their spirited game for most of the second half, and they came back to win. The two-unit strategy, however, did not survive the season; they could not rise from third place in the division, and Chicago took them out of the playoffs in the first round two games to one, when Andy Phillip, who was injured, rose to the occasion, scoring 10 consecutive points to show the way in the initial game and reveal the die was cast.

My father continued to feel that the material was there for a more competitive team, and for a time he had the feeling that Sadowski was the central problem. He was a commanding figure in the middle, looked more like the Swedish Angel, a popular wrestler of the time, than a basketball player. But too often, when the ball came in to him, usually from a clever pass by Garfinkel, the offense stalled.

My father harbored a suspicion that Big Ed, having had a taste of being player-coach at Toronto, hoped to take over the club after, that is, if my father failed. I think Dutch agreed with him, because there was friction between the two old pro players during the season. They came close to a confrontation at one point, but it seemed to clear the air, and they all finished the season more harmoniously. Meanwhile, Doggie Julian from Holy Cross, not Big Ed, became the successor coach.

By the end of the season my father and Sadowski had become good friends again, to a degree where they were teammates on the Long Island Sportscasters softball team, led by Don Dunphy and Stan Lomax. At one point this stellar group went up to Sing-Sing to play an exhibition against the prison's all-stars. My father was the third baseman, Sadowski the overpowering pitcher and his catcher was the great middleweight Jake LaMotta, who blocked Big Ed's pitches with his chest as joyfully as he took Sugar Ray Robinson's punches.

These gifted sports figures all just loved to play, whatever the game. Anyway, after they won, the team was seated on the dais in the mess hall where they were honored guests. My father could never tell without laughing in mock surprise about the remarks that Sadowski happened to make when addressing the prison population. He began by saying, "It's nice to see so many of you here," at which point a row went up; they began thumping their tables till Ed began his closing line, "I don't want to take up too much of your time." Now he became confused when some of them spilled out into the aisles. And Big Ed himself could never understand the laughter that greeted his remarks. Signing off, he walked up to the edge of the stage and pulled out a cap to wave at the convicts – one of them who had played in the game had given Ed an inmate's cap when it was over, and his swinging that at the diners was his way of getting out of the situation. He went back with a big smile to settle down next to LaMotta, who followed suit applauding.

My father didn't talk very much about NBA basketball after his two years in the league.

There was very little in the way of scouting and virtually no assistant coaches at that time, but what did open up for him was the chance of a second tour of duty at Seton Hall, which brought him in the early 1950s to field a superlative sequence of college teams, as good as any the country had to offer.

My father was known as a defensive coach. Eddie Ehlers, whose high school coach was John Wooden, told me that my father was the best defensive coach he had known. But the style of play that evolved in the NBA tended to move the game away from him, with its emphasis on up-tempo offense – and not much defense. He felt that the 24-second clock was a necessary development for the game, though it changed its nature from what he'd known as player and coach all along (and he's a Hall of Famer in both categories). Still, when the Celtics made the playoffs the second year, he was disappointed to be let go, competitor that he always was, and contributor, since the 1920s, to the development, with pals like Nat Holman, Dutch Dehnert and Bennie Borgmann, of professional basketball in its infancy, and afterwards, starting in 1946, to its future maturation.

Jack Russell, Honey's son, is John D. Russell, professor of English emeritus at the University of Maryland, College Park, and the author of Henry Green: Nine Novels and an Unpacked Bag; Anthony Powell: A Quintet, a Sextet and War; Style in Modern Fiction, *and* "Honey" Russell: Between Games, Between Halves.

Jack (Dutch) Garfinkel

My idol when I was growing up was Mac Posnack of the St. John's Wonder Five. I always loved basketball. I'd take my G.O. card from school and 25 cents and go to the Arcadia Hall to see the Jewels play. In 1934, my first year in high school at Thomas Jefferson, I came out to play our first game against the alumni, who included Allie Schuckman and Rip Kaplinski, and whom did I have to cover but Mac Posnack. I just kvelled.

They may have called me Dutch because I didn't look Jewish, had a kind of German-looking face. But probably the real reason was that as a kid when I'd climb over the fence to play ball in the school yard, three-on-three, I'd play with my back to the basket to pass off to teammates cutting by me, just like Dutch Dehnert used to do for the Original Celtics. He invented that style and they called it "playing Dutch," and so they called me "Dutch," too.

Clair Bee used to run tryouts for metropolitan-area high school kids, where they'd be recruited for colleges. I played, but nothing came of it. Then, I was supposed to meet someone from George Washington University at a hotel in New York. They were supposed to be interested in me, but the guy didn't show up. So I ended up at St. John's with the attractions of playing for Joe Lapchick and getting to play in Madison Square Garden.

I had always considered playing in the pros, certainly as early as 1941. While I was still at St. John's, I was recruited to play for the Goodyear team in an industrial league, but then I was drafted. I was ready to play anywhere. John Donlon, who coached the Baltimore Clippers in the old American League, called me. All he had to do was say "play" and I went. He paid me $25 a game and I had to pay my own travel expenses. I remember getting down there the first time, showing up at the hotel and finding the team gathered around the pinball machine, guys like Albie Esposito and Herb Gershon. I asked if we shouldn't be upstairs, resting up for a game, but I was told that real pros did what they wanted and just showed up to play. In the Army I would play ball on the weekends, when all the American

Dutch Garfinkel. PHOTO PROVIDED BY DUTCH GARFINKEL

Vintage NBA: The Pioneer Era

League games were played. I played some for the Trenton Tigers, and for two years I played for Eddie Gottlieb's Philadelphia SPHAs. I also got to play in a War Bond All-Star game in '44 and in another fund-raiser in the Polo Grounds that year on a court set up between first and second base. While I was still stationed at West Point in 1944, Dutch Dehnert came up and recruited a bunch of us to play on a squad called the Brooklyn Eagles he entered in the World Professional Tournament in Chicago. Chuck Connors, who could talk almost anyone into almost anything, got our commanding officer to give us 15-day passes, and we went all the way to the finals.

Basketball was a rough game then, in the old American League. You didn't leave your feet on a layup, because if you did you might end up in the stands. In the American League, the price of admission included a ballgame and a dance afterwards, so we played on very slippery floors. The game was the same all over – college ball, service ball, all the pro leagues – with set shots and give-and-go plays. And everywhere you played, there were all these New York ballplayers you'd always played with and against.

Once I was out of the service, through Fuzzy Levane I got to play for Les Harrison's Rochester team in the NBL. They were overloaded in the backcourt, though, with Al Cervi, Bob Davies, Red Holzman and Fuzzy, so I didn't get much playing time. Cervi, Davies and Holzman played 40 minutes a game. But then, when Cervi was out with an injury, I got to play and we won a streak of games. But when Cervi came back, I sat again.

Les Harrison was a good judge of talent, but not much as a coach. As an entrepreneur, though, he was the best. He had Otto Graham on that team, a good ballplayer and great athlete even before getting the call to report to Art Modell's Cleveland Browns for $15,000 a year. He had Del Rice, not much of a player and flatfooted, but a local favorite when he played baseball for the Rochester Red Wings before going to the St. Louis Cardinals. And he had Chuck Connors.

Chuck didn't play much, but Les always wanted him around, at least until he had to report for spring training in February. He was tall, good-looking, with gleaming teeth, and wherever we were, whether in the Seneca Hotel where the team stayed, or anywhere else, if they had a microphone, forget it. He had the gift of gab and loved to perform.

We always played a lot of exhibition games, and in Schenectady we represented the town with their own uniforms. We'd get off the train, get our Schenectady uniforms on, and play – the Rens, the Globetrotters or whoever came to town. We traveled strictly by train and I enjoyed the nickel-dime poker games. Les had a guy at the Rochester terminal, Tiny, who weighed 3-400 pounds. Les would call Tiny and say, "I need a dozen sleepers to wherever," and he'd pick up the tickets. We'd take a couple of dark shirts, we'd be given about four bucks a day meal money, and usually after a game we'd be rushing to catch a sleeper to another town.

The Fort Wayne Zollners were a great team in that league, but the Royals came along to replace them as champions. They never beat us. The Rochester media people were fantastic and the fans were a family affair. They packed 4,000 people in the Edgerton Arena, and after the season they had a benefit for us where the fans would throw money in a blanket spread out on the floor.

The following season the BAA was getting started. Honey Russell contacted me about playing for Boston, and I was glad to play for him. Honey was great, and I loved him. The Celtics played at both the Boston Arena and the Boston Garden. At the Washington Capitols' Uline Arena, we played on a floor that was laid over the ice. I could never work up a sweat. In the locker rooms there and around the league, there were no individual cubicles, just nails on the wall. You'd come in and grab a couple of nails to hang your clothes. And there were usually just one or two showers. We had no equipment, no oranges, no trainers, though Harvey Cohn sometimes taped us.

We only flew once in my time, a trip from Chicago to Boston with a layover in New York. Between Chicago and New York, we dropped 400-500 feet in an air pocket that the pilot said was the worst he'd ever seen. Luggage went flying, and guys were hitting the ceiling. We landed in New York, and Honey was saying, "Let's go, we've got to catch the plane to Boston." I said, "I don't think so. Art Spector, Connie Simmons and I are taking the train. We'll see you in Boston."

We had a tough guy from the West Coast on that team, Al Brightman, one of the toughest I remember, who reminded me of Al Cervi when he would get in Bobby McDermott's face and harass him all over the court. We had Connie Simmons, with that great two-hand set he shot from over his head. I didn't think it was a good idea when he was traded to Baltimore for Mike Bloom, though Mike was good, too. And best of all, for me, I was teamed up with Chuck Connors again.

Chuck was a crazy bastard, and I loved him. We always kept in touch. Even after he was a big star, he'd call me up from Hollywood and say, "I'm lonely out here, I wanna get back to Bay Ridge." We were roommates and would always try to get good food to take on the trains with us, unlike guys like Ed Sadowski and Mel Riebe, who had a feeling for smoked fish, and for their suppers on the train they'd take along a hunk of bread and some smoked sablefish.

Chuck once pulled a stunt in a hotel on Art Spector and his roommate Jerry Kelly. He went down to the office and got the stenographer to write a letter on hotel letterhead stationery, that said, "During your stay in our hotel, the cleaning woman found a sum of money in a bureau in your room." He had them address one copy to Art and another to Jerry. For days after they got those letters they kept it secret from one another while each one tried to figure out how to get the money without the other one knowing about it. The rest of us all knew about it and got a good laugh out of it, but no one let on until Chuck told them.

On one train trip from Boston to Toronto we had a long layover in Buffalo, and the guys were drinking pretty good. Not me, one or two beers was all I ever wanted – I usually went for malted milks. All of a sudden the railroad police came into the bar and confronted us because someone had climbed up on the bronze buffalo in the station and broken off the tail. Actually it was Charlie Hoefer who had taken it, and he hid it behind the juke box in the bar. The police got right on the train with us, rode 30 or 40 miles escorting us toward Canada, but never found out who the culprit was. Everybody who heard that story assumed it was Chuck, but that time it wasn't – he wasn't even on that trip. Honey was pissed off at us. "Not only are you losing ballgames," he said, "but you're getting into trouble with the police, too."

The second season in Boston, we had a better team. We had Gene Stump from DePaul; George Munroe, a future Rhodes Scholar from Dartmouth, who later became CEO of the Fortune 500 Phelps-Dodge Company; and Saul Mariaschin from Brooklyn, who had gone to Harvard on a Navy program. Saul was a fine player, who wrote music and played great piano. He ended up on the West Coast in the furniture business, and died a couple of years ago of a heart attack while skiing in Colorado.

In all fairness, the team was improved because we had Ed Sadowski in the middle, even though one of the good reporters who covered us in Boston once wrote a lead that went, "Ed Sadowski is playing like the first three letters of his last name." A lot has been written about a confrontation between me and Ed, but this is the true story. We were in Chicago playing the Stags, and during the game the ball was going out of bounds when I dove and flipped the ball back to Ed, who laid it in. Later in the game, I fed him in the pivot, and the pass wasn't perfect. Admittedly I often threw hard passes, broke Jackie Goldsmith's finger one time and Mel Riebe's another. But this was a catchable ball, and he made no effort to get it, so it went out of bounds.

At the next timeout, I said to him, "I break my neck trying to get you the ball – when I throw you a pass, why don't you try to catch it, extend your arms at least."

"Aah," he said, "all you wanna do is shoot and score points."

He actually said this to me, when I would take three, maybe four shots a game, and everybody knew it. So after the game I was still needling him in the locker room and he started to chase me. The guys stopped him, and nothing more came of it, except that some reporters saw it and it got in the papers in one form or another. Honey got very annoyed. He called me aside and said, "I'm gonna have to fine you."

"Why me and not him?" I said.

"Because we're getting ready for playoffs," he said. "Don't do or say anything like that to that big lummox, or the big son of a bitch will sulk and go home."

The most exciting event of the following season came two days before the season started. Nine of us lived in a dorm behind the Boston Arena, and I was awakened by the smell of smoke early on the morning of November 2, 1948. One of the papers credited me with saving everyone's life, but in any case we all got out of there with most of our stuff, though there was $75,000 worth of damage and the Celtics lost all four sets of new uniforms to start the season.

Doggie Julian had come in as coach, and we got off to a hot start through nine or 10 games. We were leading the league, and Gene Stump was leading the league in scoring. He was getting about 20 points a game, and we had a good thing going with me hitting him with passes in the corner whenever he was free for his set shots. Then, without warning, Doggie released me and Hank Beenders. Walter Brown, the owner of the Celtics, one of the finest men I ever knew or played for, took me aside and said, "Dutch, I'm terribly sorry you're being released." He didn't have to do that.

I watched the scores after that and saw that Stump's scoring went down to three or four points a game and the team went on a long losing streak. Anyway, I went home, and Honey called. He was coaching the Schenectady team to fulfill the last year of his Boston contract. He and I both knew I was nearing the end, but I just wanted to play ball. He asked me to come up and play weekends, and I did.

I also went back to school, getting my degree in physical education and then a master's in safety education from NYU. I taught at Junior High School 166 in Brownsville-East New York until I retired in 1977. But I wasn't finished with basketball. I refereed for 30 years, mostly in the PSAL and the ECAC, but also many weekends in the Eastern League in Pennsylvania where Mendy Rudolph's father, Harry, was the commissioner.

From my playing days, the officials I remember best are Johnny Nucatola, Natie Messenger out of Chicago, Pat Kennedy, Hagen Anderson, Lou Eisenstein and Ed Boyle from Boston. The two things that guided me as a referee were that I stayed in shape and that I always tried to be consistent.

I didn't have to become an official to be aware that there was always a lot of betting on basketball. I knew about it when I started out at St. John's. One summer I worked at the Nevele (so called because it began as a boarding house whose first customers were eleven – nevele backwards – nuns) as a busboy responsible for six tables. I'd get off work at 9 or 10 at night and go play ball. I was 19 years old and that's when I really learned how to play. When we played over at Grossingers, the betting was wide open, with craps games prevalent and pools on the ballgames and a lot of man-to-man betting. In that period, 1937-39, there were odds on the games, not point spreads. I think the real trouble started when the points came in.

Anyway, the guy who ran the gambling up there took a liking to me. And when I was starting as a sophomore at St. John's, I got a call from him. I may have been naive, and I was shocked when those scandals broke later on, but it was clear to me what this guy wanted. "It was nice knowing you up there," I told him, "but I don't think we'll be talking anymore. I'm not interested."

I still follow NBA basketball, but to tell the truth I'm kind of tired of it. The play seems very repetitious. There's a sameness to it. When I watch at all, I'll turn on the last five or 10 minutes of a game, unless it's something special like Hakeem Olajuwon playing against the Knicks.

Dutch Garfinkel's five seasons in the NBL and BAA are only a part of his basketball saga and legend, as demonstrated by the company he kept when enshrined in the New York City Basketball Hall of Fame in the same class as Marty Glickman, Willis Reed, Joe Lapchick, Sonny Hertzberg, Richie Guerin, Tom (Satch) Sanders and John Isaacs. As St. John's captain in 1940-41, he won the Frank Haggerty Award as outstanding college player in New York City and in November 1941 was MVP for the College All-Stars in Chicago Stadium. In 1986 he was inducted into the St. John's University Hall of Fame.

Eddie Ehlers. PHOTO COURTESY OF JOHN EZERSKY

Eddie Ehlers

In 1946 I came back from four years in the service and went back to Purdue where I participated in football, basketball and baseball. I became very disenchanted with college life after being gone that long, even though I always wanted to have a degree. No one in my family had ever gone on to college. My mother and father, who were wonderful people, had perhaps gone as high as the eighth grade. My disenchantment with college life was that, after the seriousness of service, I just felt that I ought to be out doing more than that. I held on to a burning desire to get a degree, and fortunately that did happen, but not at that particular time.

I was pleasantly surprised when I was drafted by the Chicago Bears and the Boston Celtics. But my big thing was that I wanted to be a professional baseball player. The Yankees approached me, as well as the Boston Braves and some other clubs, but the end result was that the Yankees paid me $10,000 to sign with them, an awful lot of money at that time. As far as the Bears were concerned, Mr. Halas offered me a minimum salary of $5,000 and told me I could only play one sport. I didn't feel that I was that good of a football player anyway, and so I went the other route with baseball and basketball.

It was 1947, the second year of the NBA, and the bottom teams drafted first, as they do now, but the Toronto and Cleveland franchises had folded after that first year, so Boston, which had the next pick, drafted first. It was the first year the draft had taken place and being No. 1 didn't mean much at the time, but if you mention it on the cocktail circuit now it raises a few eyebrows. I felt fortunate to be drafted in all three sports and have the opportunity to play professionally, but really it wasn't that big a deal. I had other things on my mind in regards to athletics and a career.

After I finished my first year in the Three-I League with the Yankees, who assigned me to Quincy, Illinois, I received a call from Honey Russell. I had known Honey because I had played up in Vermont, with Bennington in the old Northern League, where he was running the Rutland club, so we became knowledgeable about one another. I know that he came out and scouted me when I played in the College All-Star Game in Chicago Stadium, and as a result of that he drafted me.

I took his call in the locker room at Quincy, and he said, "We'll give you $500 to sign plus $4,000 for the season." That sounded good to me. I needed a winter job, I was getting married and I told him I'd be out. He knew I wanted to continue my education and had me signed up at Boston University. Joyce and I were married after the baseball season and we arrived in Boston before the rest of the team. We stayed at the Lennox Hotel, headquarters of the Celtics, where they had their training table, and it was a wonderful experience. Honey had given me a ball and Joyce and I would work out at the Boston Arena. She'd go into the pivot, and I'd pass in to her and cut off her.

I was in respectable shape from baseball, but there's quite a difference in the demands of the two sports. The first time I walked into the gym to meet the veterans, the first person I saw was Big Ed Sadowski. He looked like anything but a basketball player, more like someone you'd see on television today rasslin' Incredible Hulk Hogan. I'll never forget the scene. Here he was out there, 6-foot-6 or 6-7, with this enormous chest, a chop haircut, wearing a gray sweat suit with no top, smoking a cigar and shooting hook shots.

Big Ed probably had one of the best hook shots anyone ever had in basketball. It was incredible for such a big man that he had such a wonderful touch. Outwardly he had a gruff manner but in reality he was a big puppy dog inside. We had played against each other in service ball and I knew him slightly, but as the years went on we developed great mutual respect. He was a wonderful person.

John Wooden had been my high school coach, and now I had Honey Russell. Both were wonderful men and coaches. Honey was different from coach Wooden in that he was the best defensive coach I ever experienced. He was the first one that ever took me aside and said, "When you take a look at your man, study him, find out does he go to the right, does he go to the left and how are you gonna beat him." As a result I learned and enjoyed defense. Coach Wooden was the all-around greatest coach I had in any sport, and he was the biggest influence on my life.

The Celtics played a slower style than Wooden's teams, lots of pick-and-roll and shots from outside, but basketball was basketball where it's always a matter of motivation. Both of those coaches were good at that. Honey was just exactly what I was looking for after spending four years in the service. He treated us like men. I never drank, but he had beer at the training table. Most important, he always would take you aside and tell you absolutely what was going on.

Once we were playing the Knicks in Madison Square Garden on Saturday afternoon, and we both played hard because we were playing for first place. We didn't play a bad ballgame, but we lost, and I came in the dressing room thinking he was going to come storming in and chew us out. He walked in and said, "You men played a good ballgame, and we should have won. Here are your tickets back to Boston. Have a good weekend. I'll see you at practice Monday."

I respected him for that because we had played hard. We lost but it wasn't because the effort wasn't there. That's the way Honey was. I was sorry to see Honey go, and I know he was very depressed about being let go. I ran into him later on at the World Series, when he was scouting for the Braves. He told me he still felt bad that Walter Brown had let him go. We had finished in the playoffs, and he thought he deserved another year. I thought so, too. I would have loved to play for Honey for at least another year.

Walter Brown, the owner of the Boston Celtics, was one of the nicest and most sincere men in pro sports. He treated us with a lot of empathy and respect. Some people tried to take advantage of him, but he handled it very well. One night, we played Philadelphia in Boston, and we were so terrible we left a lingering odor over the court. He came in storming, said, "You're the biggest bunch of overpaid crybabies I've ever been exposed to," slammed the door, and went out.

We were all kind of shocked, because we liked Mr. Brown. Next day he called a team meeting and we all came in, and I'll never forget what he said. "I have a little girl, ten years old, my daughter. She's usually pretty good, but every once in a while she gets kind of bad and I have to discipline her. And then she comes to me and she looks me in the eye and she says, 'You know, daddy, I'm really sorry.' And I'm looking at all you people in the eye, and about last night I'm really sorry." And he left.

Here's a man who pays our salary, who really owns us, and he has the humbleness to come in here and apologize to all of us. He was a real class act, and I was happy the Celtics came around, not for the players' sake but because of Walter Brown. He deserved it.

The league was started originally to fill up vacant spots, open dates, in the arenas. We needed to generate crowds before television. The floors were terrible to play on because they were on ice. Every night in Boston Garden, my wife and I would see something different – a fight, a man rasslin' an alligator, a rodeo, and we'd play, and the Bruins would play. You were always hesitant to run out there, because you'd get out past the canvas and you'd hit ice. Still, the Celtics had the best floor in the league. That parquet floor, it was solid. Most of the floors, like Madison Square Garden, you'd go down and hit a weak spot on the floor and the ball would just go down.

We traveled by train most of the time. A little later we got into flying, but the airlines didn't have as much sophistication, as far as instrumentation and approaches and so forth, as they do now. Once, after playing at home Sunday night, we got up early Monday morning to fly to St. Louis for a Tuesday night game. We were forced down in Albany because of bad weather, got on a train, and ran into a blizzard. Everything froze up on the sleepers by the time we got to Buffalo, and they moved us out to the coaches.

There was a fine if we didn't show up for a game, and we were frightened we weren't going to make it on time. We jumped into cabs at the station, dressed and taped up on the way to the arena, and got there just in time to play a triple-overtime game and lose. The next night we had to be in Minneapolis to play the Lakers, so it was difficult.

The ballgames themselves weren't tough. What killed you was the traveling. You never had a decent meal. I drank Pepto-Bismol all the time, trying to keep my stomach in shape, because we'd be eating at Nedick's or someplace like that, standing up while catching a plane or train or bus.

On that team we had Dutch Garfinkel, an excellent outside shooter of the old set-shot type, though he couldn't make a free throw to save his life.

I'll never forget one night playing Chicago in Chicago, where for some reason we could never beat them. But Dutch had a heck of a night. He knocked in 10 straight set shots and beat Chicago at Chicago. The reporters came in after the game and one reporter was talking to Ed Sadowski.

Big Ed said, "We was lucky to win tonight with that gunner out in front."

Dutch heard that remark and said something back. Ed had a kind of Polish accent and there was an expression he always used that he repeated now: "Listen you sum-nabitch, I'm gonna give you the back of my hand."

Dutch says, "If you're gonna swear at me, at least learn how to pronounce the words." We all laughed, and nothing came of it.

We didn't win as much as I would have liked, but we had pretty good *esprit de corps* on that ballclub. Honey was good at that. Then Doggie Julian came and he was a different kind of coach. He rubbed our heads before we went in. He had a set type of offense, the old give-and-go type of thing, and it worked good the first time around the league. But then they caught on and we finished with a very mediocre season.

Chuck Connors was on the ballclub my first year, a big fella, 6 feet 6 inches, but extremely left-handed. He was not a good basketball player, an excellent baseball player, though. I played against him in the International League. He was so left-handed that as the game became more of a finesse situation, Chuck didn't make it the second year. We all enjoyed him. He was a terrific entertainer. On the road, in airports and train stations, he'd put on an act. He'd do *Casey at the Bat, The Face on the Barroom Floor, The Charge of the Light Brigade.* Laraine Day, who was married to Leo Durocher, heard him at spring training and encouraged him to try out for the movies. Chuck and I became very close friends. I can remember when he'd come over to our house and burn our broom or throw our little girl's doll out the window. He was a real character, but he had a lot of talent.

Another beautiful person was Howie McHugh, our publicity director, a red-faced Irishman who always kept us laughing and happy. And then there was Jock Semple, our trainer, who later put on the Boston Marathon. He ran us continually and kept us in good shape. One more memorable guy was Eddie Powers, our comptroller. Many years later, Joyce and I drove out to Boston for a business meeting when we hadn't been back there for a long time. Our four children, three girls and a boy, joined us there, meeting us at Back Bay Station. We showed them around Boston and New England, winding up at Boston Garden. We saw Red Auerbach, Milt Schmidt, Howie and Jock, and then walked into Eddie's office.

"You bring back a lot of memories," he said and started talking about how poor the Celtics were in my time. "When you were playing, the IRS came in. We hadn't been paying our taxes, and they said they were gonna shut us down. I said to them, 'Fine, just go ahead, shut us down, and I'd like to show you our list of assets. We have 10 basketballs, 12 jocks, two sets of uniforms. If you want to go ahead and shut us down, shut us down. My advice to you is to let us keep going because I think we're gonna make it.'"

And he was so right. I had never heard that story but I knew we were – the whole league was – on thin ice. But a lot of people had the intestinal fortitude and the vision to make it go and as a result the NBA is what it is today. I don't like to sound resentful, but sometimes I hear people talking about the old NBA who weren't even around and have no idea of what we all went through. I'm not looking for any plaudits or sympathy. I was very appreciative to have played. But these people just have no idea what it took to get that league started.

The real godsend was television. When that came around it really took off. The NBA today is impressive. The athletes in that league are probably the finest group of athletes in any sport any place in the world. With their size and agility, they do things that we couldn't dream of back when I was playing. Too bad their intelligence hasn't kept up with their bodies in some instances. Overall, NBA basketball is a tremendous spectacle.

The last time I was with coach Wooden, I asked him what he thought of the game today and what he would change. He went into detail. He didn't like the roughness. He didn't like playing on Sunday. But when he got all through, he looked at me with that great twinkle in his eye, and he said, "Yes, but it's still a great game."

That's true. It is a great game. It grew up here in America and out here in Indiana where it's almost a religion. It's a wonderful game, but don't ever lose sight of the fact that it is a "game."

There were a lot of great ballplayers in the league in my time. The Lakers were a great team. John Kundla was a good coach. Their big gun was George Mikan, who was great because he was not a selfish ballplayer. Every time he got the ball, he'd look for the open man to pass off, and that's why he was so effective. You couldn't get on him because he'd pass off. He was only 6-9 but had a good hook shot and he passed off – that was the real asset. They had Slater Martin, too, and Jim Pollard, who was a thing to behold, a great ballplayer. And they had a good old friend of mine, Arnie Ferrin.

Rochester was also a great ballclub, with Red Holzman, Arnie Johnson, Bob Wanzer, and of course Bob Davies, who really was a magician. The Knicks had a good ballclub. I used to marvel at Butch Van Breda Kolff and the way he could drive. And they had Bud Palmer and Sid Tanenbaum. The Caps had a good ballclub when Red Auerbach was coaching them. They won the first league championship with Bones McKinney, Fred Scolari and Bob Feerick. Those guys were good.

Providence had Kenny Sailors, Chicago had Andy Phillip and Gene Vance, and Philadelphia had Howie Dallmar and Joe Fulks, who led the league in scoring. Every night was a real thrill to play against a group of athletes such as that. It was downright fun, a lot of work as far as the traveling was concerned, but a good league that continued to get stronger.

At the time, I looked at professional athletics as a means to going on. I wanted my degree and Purdue wouldn't accept eight hours of lab work from Boston University, so I went back to Purdue, took Joyce and our little daughter Sally, and went back and lived on campus and got my degree. I've never regretted that. Fort Wayne wanted me to come and play for them. But I had played five years of baseball, and as the family came along it became more difficult. Our decision was to move back to South Bend, buy a home and go into business.

I'm extremely appreciative of professional athletics for what it did for me. A few years ago at the Special Olympics, Patrick Ewing said to me, "How much did you make?"

I told him, "$4,000."

"A game?" he said.

"The whole season," I said, and he fell over laughing.

I made $4,000 the first year, and the next year I made six, pretty good money back then in '48, when I was also playing baseball and making $800 a month in the Yankees chain. Now I'm afraid that pure greed is going to ruin professional sports, especially baseball.

Joyce and I have been blessed. God has been good to us. We chose South Bend as a good place to raise a family, with a good school system and park system. At the time, not knowing what I wanted to do, I went to a psychiatrist and a psychologist who directed me into the life insurance business. I became a general agent for Lincoln National Life and at one time had 50 agents in a territory of three states, flying around in my own plane to keep it all in order.

We have four children and 16 grandchildren, 13 of them right here in South Bend. One granddaughter is playing volleyball for the United States in the World Games. One grandson is a linebacker at Kentucky, another a quarterback at Michigan. Our son Tommy played six years in the NFL with the Eagles and the Bills, and he now runs our company, Ehlers and Ehlers. This is a story of middle-class America in the Midwest, and it's not at all bad.

In his two seasons with the Boston Celtics (1947-9), no one scored more points or had more assists than Eddie Ehlers.

Jim Seminoff

In 1946, when the Stags management telephoned me in Los Angeles and asked me to play on their team, I was given 72 hours to reach Chicago. My wife, Rosemary, and I loaded our luggage and two young children (a third was expected soon) into our 1942 Chevrolet coupe, and we headed east, driving day and night to reach our destination on time. Some of our belongings, such as a playpen and stroller, were roped to the top of the car.

Right in the middle of Albuquerque the load shifted and was about to fall off. We had to unload everything onto the sidewalk right on the main street of town. Fortunately, there was a Montgomery Ward store nearby. We bought a small trailer, repacked and once again started off to the "windy city." Our 3½-year-old daughter put her head out the window of the car and for all passersby to hear, called out, "Let's go get 'em Stags!"

When we first arrived in Chicago we stayed at the Midwest Athletic Club not far from the Chicago Stadium where the Stags played. Fortunately, I had a clause in my contract which said the club would pay to house my family and me at a hotel until suitable apartment housing could be found. Housing wasn't easy to find in those post-war days. A couple of years later when I was traded to the Boston Celtics, my family and I drove east and stayed at the old Lennox Hotel for about five weeks until the owner of the club found us an apartment in Winthrop. Not all of the players had a housing agreement with the owner, and I was thankful that was part of my agreement.

In 1946-47 the starting range of salaries was $4,000 to $8,000. George Mikan joined the league two years later and reportedly started at about $15,000. My most memorable moment that first year was beating the Washington Caps, coached by Red Auerbach, in the playoffs, though we went on to lose the championship to Joe Fulks and the Philadelphia Warriors. During the regular season the Caps had beaten the Stags five out of six games, but in the playoffs we beat them four out of five games. Playoff money then was all of $2,000 per player. But that paid for our

Jim Seminoff. PHOTO COURTESY OF JIM SEMINOFF

Vintage NBA: The Pioneer Era

new car and the hospital expenses incurred by the birth of our youngest son who was born near the end of the season.

I found that the main differences between college and pro ball were that the pro players were more talented, played more games and made more road trips. In one game they decided to experiment with four 15-minute quarters. I played all 60 minutes. Thank goodness, they decided to go back to 12-minute quarters.

Almost all of the players wore low-top basketball shoes. I chose to wear the same Sam Barry high-tops which I was used to wearing at USC. My coach at SC, of course, was Sam Barry. In the pros, we actually had a dress code, and were supposed to wear coats and ties on trips.

In the early days of pro basketball the "Player of the Game" was usually awarded a felt hat. A few of them came my way. A cap with earmuffs would have been more practical. While traveling by train from Chicago to New York, for a game between the Stags and Knicks, we arrived at Penn Station in the midst of a record-breaking, 27-inch, one-day snowstorm. No taxis were on the roads. We were lucky to get the last bus to leave the train station. After slipping and sliding through the snow we made it to the game on time. We were freezing cold and didn't have time to warm up before the game started, but we won!

Some of the arenas where we played, like where I remember playing the Anderson, Indiana, team, were high school gyms. We didn't have the luxury of million-dollar stadiums such as they have today. But I can't blame the facilities for the time when I threw a long pass to a player at the other end of the court, and instead of the ball being caught by my teammate, it went through the hoop. What a surprise!

Another surprise, when I was with the Celtics, was to see one of my teammates, Tony Lavelli, playing the accordion at center court in the Boston Garden during the halftime. I suppose that gave added entertainment in case the game wasn't exciting enough.

We traveled by train to most of the cities in the league. My one and only suit became a bit threadbare at the knee where my leg rubbed against the side of the Pullman car. Those were long, boring, uncomfortable train rides. We passed the time playing bridge or other card games, but Pullman cars weren't made for 6-foot-2 plus ballplayers.

While a member of the Chicago Stags team in 1946-47, I found myself aboard one of those trains traveling with my teammates from Chicago to Boston. I was awakened around 3 a.m. by a conductor or porter who told me coach Olsen had been taken off the train and hospitalized for medical treatment. Olsen left word that I was to coach the team until he returned. With me as acting coach we played Boston and New York and won both games. As far as I know, I am the only undefeated "coach" in the BAA. Of course, a record of 2-0 isn't much to brag about.

That brief experience convinced me coaching would probably be too stressful for me as a lifetime career. Hence, when Walter Brown, owner of the Celtics, approached me about coaching the Celtics team, I turned him down. Luckily for the Celtics, Red Auerbach took the job, and we all know what a fabulous job he did for the team.

After retiring from pro ball, I refereed for the Pacific Coast League for about 16 years. During that same period of time I was associated with Western Lead Products, Inc. which later became Quemetco, Inc. I served as vice president of that company for 27 years before resigning to start my own company, Semco Enterprises, Inc., a zinc alloy business in City of Industry, California. I am presently CEO of that company.

Although I have had three artificial hip operations, quadruple heart bypass surgery and colon cancer, I enjoy good health and am able to work every day. Sports and travel are my hobbies. Life has been good to me, and I attribute part of that to the fact that I had an opportunity to play professional basketball.

Jim Seminoff came east from USC for four years in the NBA, two with the Stags and two with the Celtics in Boston, where he led the club in assists both seasons.

Tom King

I grew up in East Lansing, Michigan, where my father served as line coach for the Michigan State football team. In high school I was captain of the football and basketball teams and earned all-state honors as an end in my senior year. Unfortunately, our record in these two sports was only mediocre, though in baseball we won the state championship.

Since these were the war years, I went to Michigan State, although I had always hoped to play football for the University of Michigan. After I won two letters at Michigan State, the Marine Corps transferred me to Michigan, where I met the Michigan end coach, and head basketball coach, Bennie Oosterbaan, who said to me, "Tommy, come out, but you're not gonna play football at Michigan."

"Why?" I replied.

"Because you're gonna play basketball for me."

I did and was voted MVP in 1944. In November, 1945, I played in the College All-Star Game in Chicago. We had a fine team, with Eddie Ehlers (Purdue), Dike Eddleman (Illinois), Harry Boykoff (St. John's), Bruce Hale (Santa Clara), Murray Mendenhall (Rice), Arnie Ferrin (Utah), Sid Tanenbaum (NYU), Paul Cloyd (Wisconsin), Fred Lewis (Eastern Kentucky), Milo Komenich (Wyoming) and Big Bob Kurland (Oklahoma A&M). The all-star program described me as the "shortest and lightest member of the squad" at 5 feet 10 inches and 155 pounds. Unfortunately, Fort Wayne, the professional champions, handled us pretty easily.

Dike Eddleman was a great player who had a famous "kiss shot," where he'd put the ball in front of his nose and shoot it with two hands. During the first quarter, Ehlers lost one of those hard contact lenses he wore, and while we were searching for it I suddenly realized that Eddie was just trying to slow down the tempo of the game so we wouldn't get crushed.

During my tour with the Marine Corps I had the opportunity to play with the nationally ranked Camp Lejeune team with Bob Smith of LSU, Frank Carswell of

Tom King from Falcons program. PHOTO COURTESY OF TOM KING

Rice and John Kelly of Notre Dame. When I was discharged, I still had a year of eligibility left at Michigan, but Arthur Wirtz, who had seen me play in the old Chicago Stadium, invited me to join the Chicago Stags. Mr. Wirtz was also co-owner with James Norris of the Olympia in Detroit, and I agreed to play for the Detroit Falcons in the initial year of the BAA.

When I reported to the Falcons training camp, it was obvious to me they had a coach and a gym and the uniforms were ordered. But they didn't have a publicity director or business manager. Since I majored in business administration at Michigan, and in high school I'd been a stringer for the *Lansing State Journal* and the *Detroit Free Press*, I asked Mr. Norris for the jobs of publicity director, business manager and traveling secretary for the Falcons. Arthur Wirtz had agreed to pay me $8,000 as a player and gave me a $500 signing bonus. Jim Norris paid me another $8,000 for the other jobs, making me the highest-paid player in the league. I certainly was not the best player.

I carried my typewriter to all the games and filed wire service stories for the AP, UPI and INS. I remember being impressed by Ernie Calverley of the Providence Steamrollers. Ernie was an unbelievable little player who could shoot from anywhere on the court. Later, Ernie became coach at Rhode Island State University. I also recall labeling Joe Fulks "the Babe Ruth of basketball." He could jump and shoot while falling away from the basket and was the top scorer in the league.

One of dumbest things I ever did as traveling secretary was after arriving in Toronto the first time. I jumped off the train, leaving my gear with the other players, and ran out to line up taxis to transport the team to our hotel. Well, I arranged the taxis and was steering the team to them when one of the cab drivers informed me that the Royal York Hotel, where we were staying, was right across the street from the station.

I wasn't always such a fool in Canada. I married their Olympic gold-medal figure skater, Barbara Ann Scott. This September we will celebrate our 40th anniversary.

A major problem that first year was the travel, which was my responsibility to arrange and mostly by trains. One time the team was forced to take a 30-day road trip because the ice show was booked into the Detroit Olympia. My traveling wardrobe consisted of one gray suit, a single black knit tie, two shirts and two sets of skivvies, which I washed out every night.

The Falcons were not a very good team, although we did have an excellent player in Stan Miasek, who was a first-team all-star that year. Another teammate was Grady Lewis, a 6-6 guard with a keen basketball mind. Grady was a marvelous person who moved on to St. Louis and Baltimore as a player-coach and later became president of Converse All-Star Shoes.

The Falcons finished the season with Cincy Sachs, a well-known semipro coach in the Detroit area who had a good record in the '30s. Cincy took over from Glenn Curtis, who fell ill halfway through the season.

Coach Curtis had been an outstanding college coach at Indiana State and was a nice man who tried to keep everyone happy. Before every game he gave a little speech: "Now men, I want you to remember two things. First, when you have the ball, have poise and confidence. Second, when they have the ball, be like cats and dogs. Poise and confidence with the ball, cats and dogs on defense. Now here's the starting lineup..." One time he announced six starters.

As a Falcon I started about half of our games and averaged only a fraction over five points – not very impressive. My most memorable game was at the Chicago Stadium in December, when I scored 27 points in a 60-minute game that was one of Mr. Maurice Podoloff's experiments. As president of the league, he was an astute businessman and was always helpful to me.

I also admired and respected his successor, Walter Kennedy. As the league's publicity director, Mr. Kennedy called a meeting of the publicity directors of the teams early in the season. I recall I had to leave the team right after a practice to travel to the meeting in New York City, and when I showed up, Walter said, "What are you doing here?" He had known me only as a player up to that point. He took me under his arm and we became good friends.

When the Falcons folded after that first year, I was assigned to the Chicago Stags, where Harold "Ole" Olsen was the coach. We knew each other since I had played against his Ohio State teams while I was at Michigan. The Stags' publicity man, Lou Diamond, had recently died, so that job was open, and Coach Olsen advised me to take the sure thing rather than try to play any more. Ben Kerner invited me back to play with the Hawks in Milwaukee, but I turned the offer down and remained working for Mr. Wirtz for seven years.

I really appreciated the opportunity to play basketball in stadiums like the Boston Garden, Madison Square Garden, the old Chicago Stadium and the Olympia in Detroit. Frankly, I would have paid to play.

Looking back, the triangle offense was only a dream and the trap defenses today are much more technical than the ones we employed. Most offenses in the pioneer days were "pass and go to the ball." Today the flow is away from the ball, which puts more pressure on the defense.

The players in today's game are much more skilled than in the formative years of the league. However, in my opinion, today's players, despite their great ability, do take steps and palm the ball. Another thing that has me baffled is the inconsistent foul shooting by some of the quality players. Just hard for me to understand.

In 1955 I went to work for the Kennedy family and eventually became president of the Merchandise Mart Properties in Chicago and Washington, D.C. After 20 years plus I decided to go into my own commercial real estate company and am now owner and chairman of Seay & Thomas, Inc., a 60-year-old Chicago firm.

I have kept a keen interest and valued friendships in basketball, and I was proud to serve on the President's Council for Physical Fitness along with Dr. Ernie

Vandeweghe, the former New York Knicks star, who I played against in the initial year of the league.

Tom King may have been one of the smallest players in the new league in 1946-47, but he had the biggest salary because not only was he a starting forward for the Detroit Falcons, but also their business manager, publicity director and traveling secretary.

Brooms Abramovic. PHOTO COURTESY OF JOHN ABRAMOVIC

Vintage NBA: The Pioneer Era

John Abramovic

We loved the game and played from the heart in those days because there sure wasn't any money in it.

I got my nickname, "Brooms," from the family business. We had started manufacturing corn brooms in 1921 in Etna, Pennsylvania, where I graduated high school in 1937. For two years I worked in the plant, and then through my old high school coach I was offered a scholarship at Salem College in West Virginia. It was a small school but played a big-time schedule. We played against Duquesne in Pittsburgh and West Virginia University at Morgantown. After my freshman year, Cam Henderson wanted me to transfer to Marshall, but I didn't want to sit out a year; I wanted to graduate on schedule, which I did in '43.

Then came two years and eight months in the service with the Gene Tunney V7 program, and when I got out I was invited to play for the Pittsburgh Ironmen. I hadn't given any thought to playing pro ball, but it was the local team so I thought I'd give it a shot.

There were some tough players – Jumpin' Joe Fulks, George Senesky and Howie Dallmar for the champs in Philadelphia, Al Brightman, and of course George Mikan. The first seven-footer I saw was Elmore Morgenthaler in Providence. He was always chewing a big wad of gum. When he was fouled he'd stick the gum behind his ear while he shot his free throws. He didn't last long.

Early in the season, Toronto came in, and as I was going for a loose ball I got kneed in the head and went down hard. But I came up looking to get even and took after the first guy I saw, who happened to be Ed Sadowski, probably the biggest man in the league at the time. Fifteen years later, at some function, I bumped into Harry Miller, who said, "Brooms, you remember that time you got kneed in the head? Well, I was the guy who did it, and I'm sorry."

We played under adverse conditions that first year, with 12-minute quarters instead of 20-minute halves, on portable floors over ice rinks, with dead spots and so much condensation you couldn't get any traction. I had probably my best game in New York, at the 69th Regiment Armory, 29 points against the Knicks in a game we lost in overtime. I had gotten cramps in the third period and missed several minutes or we might have won in regulation. Another time in New York, I won a foul shooting contest with Stan Stutz and made an extra 10 bucks.

Once, before a three-game road trip, I caught my hand in someone's loose jersey in practice, and it swelled up. They said it was a sprain and I played those games, mostly using my other hand because I was pretty ambidextrous. When we got home I found out I had played with a broken hand.

It was always a lot of fun to play against Boston and Chuck Connors, a rough guy, always arguing with the refs. But I used to enjoy hearing him ream out the officials with his very foul mouth.

It was in Boston that they brought in Coulby Gunther to play center for us. He was a pivot man who hooked with either hand, but if you passed the ball into him and cut to the basket you'd never get the ball back. Our coach, Paul Birch, started pulling guys one by one and asking us what happened. And he'd get the same story from everyone: you pass the ball into the pivot and the ball never comes out. At halftime Birch was so mad he took a heavy wooden chair and threw it across the locker room. If he'd hit anyone it would have killed him.

I remember another time when Moe Becker from Duquesne got into a locker room fight, and when we went to break it up coach Birch stopped us and said, "Let the Jew protect himself."

We didn't win many games, had no size, and by the end of the season the owner, who was a hockey man, had given up on the franchise. By this time it was obvious to me that there was a lot of betting on the games in Pittsburgh. The only people left in the stands were the gamblers, who would be yelling derogatory things at players when they were losing their bets.

Before the next season, I learned that Boston had picked up my rights, but I didn't want to go there. I signed with St. Louis, played a few games and went over to Baltimore. But Buddy Jeannette didn't use me very much, so I went up to Syracuse in the old National League. Incidentally, I had roomed with Paul Seymour in Baltimore and it was partly on my recommendation that they picked him up later.

The play was a little rougher in the NBL than the BAA. I think we got away with more. The officiating was inconsistent, just like it is today. It was fun, a good experience, but the train travel was difficult. By the end of that season the novelty had worn off. I was 28, I was getting married and I came home to the family business.

I kept my hand in basketball for another 20 years, coaching some in high school and college, but I have no regrets that I saw that my career was in the business. Now I'm retired, enjoying my children and grandchildren in Florida, and working two days a week as a starter at a local golf course. But I still get a kick out of being recognized, asked for autographs and hearing other people reminiscence about my All-America days at Salem College.

I don't care to watch the game anymore. There were more set plays in our day; today it's mostly alley ball. The science in the game is gone.

Brooms Abramovic played in Pittsburgh, St. Louis and Baltimore after making his reputation with scoring records at little Salem College. For the Ironmen, he holds the all-time record for field goals attempted and is second in free-throw percentage and scoring average.

Paul Cloyd

I started at the University of Wisconsin in Madison in 1939 and was second-highest scorer on the freshman team. I was one of the first, if not the first, of the one-handed shooters in Wisconsin. I shot all free throws with a one-hand push shot as we called it in those days, and it was accurate, too. Most of the field goals I made would be three-pointers today.

I got married after my freshman year, and we went out to California. At that time there were no pro basketball teams west of the Mississippi, but there were a lot of teams out there playing in the AAU leagues. I got a spot on the Cliftons Cafeteria Club and after a scrimmage with the 20th Century-Fox team, I was recruited to play for them.

That was the team that was chosen to represent the United States on a goodwill tour of the Far East – Japan, China, the Philippines and Hawaii – in January and February of 1941. We sensed no animosity toward us from the people in Japan, and enjoyed riding on their fine trains from Yokohama to Kobe. There were about 21 uniformed Lieutenant J.G.'s with us, though, and their military questioned the hell out of them. Our ships were also followed by what we learned later were their midget subs. Then, our departure from the Philippines was delayed three or four days because they were afraid we were going to be sunk. We had gone out with the *USS Coolidge* and the *Cleveland*, one of which was the first American naval vessel sunk in World War II.

We got back in time for the national AAU tourney in Denver, and we won it. In the finals we beat the San Francisco Olympic Club with Hank Luisetti. We moved back to Wisconsin after that, and in the '42, '43 and '44 seasons I played for the Allen Bradley AAU team in Milwaukee. We won our state title each year, but got no farther than the quarterfinals in Denver in '44, where we were beaten by my old Twentieth Century-Fox team.

For the '45 season I was assigned to Great Lakes. I went into the Navy on a one-man draft to play basketball, and I was a dry-land sailor for two years. I joined

Dick McGuire and Walt Budko as starters on the Great Lakes team that went 33-5. Coach Anderson was coach of the year. In our best game, we beat DePaul with George Mikan when Luke Majorsky and I had 20 points each.

Dick McGuire and I were chosen for the college all-star game in Chicago Stadium that fall against the pro champions from Fort Wayne. What a team we had! We were coached by Dutch Lonborg and Hank Iba, and we started Bob Kurland, Fred Lewis, Eddie Ehlers, Bruce Hale and myself. Besides McGuire, we also had Harry Boykoff, Dike Eddleman, Milo Komenich, Sid Tanenbaum and Arnie Ferrin. We were facing a great team, though, with Buddy Jeannette, Big Ed Sadowski, Chick Reiser, Bob McDermott and Bones McKinney. They beat us, but we played them tough, 63-55. I led the all-star scorers with 10 points and Milo had nine.

I played some that season of '46 in Bainbridge, Maryland, and then for the Chelsea Naval Base Hospital in Boston. I was contacted by the Dow Athletic Club in Midland, Michigan, and I joined them in midseason after mustering out. We played about 70 games, including all the NBL teams, and went to the World Professional Basketball Tournament in Chicago. We lost in the quarterfinals that year and again in '47, but I made the second all-tournament team. A highlight of that '47 season was a plane trip to Los Angeles, where we played against a team featuring Jackie Robinson, who that year had become the first black player in the major leagues. Whatever problems they had with integration in baseball, it went very smoothly in pro basketball.

This was a hectic time in pro basketball, with different leagues vying for ball-players. The players were jumping around to different teams and different leagues. It was kind of a mess. Buddy Jeannette wanted me to come to the Baltimore Bullets where he was going to be player-coach, but I signed with Doxie Moore's Sheboygan Redskins for the same money. When I was playing basketball in those days, we were not too concerned with the remuneration, although we all wished we would make more. In Sheboygan it was $11,500, just about the same when I was with Dow Athletic Club, though they were not yet in the NBL. I really did not see too much difference in the game played in either league or in any of the leagues.

We often drove to games in large Chrysler wagons that would hold eight or nine, with the luggage on top. Driving from Chicago to Sheboygan one night we ran into a blizzard. The weather was blowing in from the Lake Michigan waters and the snow was coming down in buckets. We got past Milwaukee and it kept getting worse, until finally the cars couldn't move at all. A good-natured farmer came out with his snowplow and tried to make a path, but eventually he couldn't go any farther either. All the players had been out in the wet with their warm-up outfits, and we ended up spending the night sleeping on a farmer's floor with clothes lines hung up all over the house. The snowplows were out the next morning and we finally made it home to Sheboygan.

Sometimes we took trains out of Milwaukee and Chicago, but the schedules were such that sometimes we'd have to fly. One time we were supposed to fly out of Chicago to play in Syracuse, but the weather was too bad. The trainer and one of the players volunteered to drive some of us to Syracuse, and the rest of us waited for the weather to clear so we could fly. The Chrysler wagons got there ahead of us, and those guys didn't even know if the rest were going to make it. By the time we got there, they had been partaking of a little nectar. It was quite an evening.

I was 24th in NBL scoring and made the all-star team, but my teammate Mike Todorovich was rookie of the year. The '49-50 season was very unsettled, with teams folding, leagues folding and ballplayers jumping all over. There were no rules governing these actions, no union and no insurance. I refused to sign a contract with Sheboygan, signed with Jeannette in Baltimore, then left for the Waterloo Hawks. And after that season I signed as player-coach of the Kansas City High Spots of the new NPBA (National Professional Basketball Association), but they folded after one year.

I wasn't quite through with pro ball. Dutch Dehnert, the original pivotman for the Original Celtics, hired me for the Boston Whirlwinds, one of the two white teams that toured with the Globetrotters and another black team. We crossed the South, played a number of games in Florida, and then went on to Cuba. In a game there, I was undercut by one of the Trotters in a way that seemed deliberate. The injury to my back was pretty serious, and I was temporarily paralyzed. The team was so upset that they went out and beat the Globetrotters in the next game, and that was one thing they were not to do. Abe Saperstein had become a good friend of mine, and he paid for my travel home to Madison and all my hospital and medical bills.

Now at 75 I really don't watch too much basketball except some high school games. I really don't understand why they have three refs in NBA games since they don't call anything. Running, charging, hanging on, palming the ball, dunking the ball and then knocking down several players, all that is not basketball. Evidently people like the blood-and-guts type of play. They pay for it, so that's their choice. I dislike that type of so-called play. But I have a twin granddaughter on scholarship at Wisconsin, and I get down to Madison to see her play as much as possible.

One of the original world travelers of basketball, a veteran of the Pioneer Era, Paul Cloyd has for many years been proprietor of the Paul V. Cloyd Insurance Agency in Beaver Dam, Wisconsin.

Art Spector and Virgil Vaughn (r) on eve of Celtics home opening night, 1946, in Boston Arena.
PHOTO COURTESY OF DUTCH GARFINKEL

Virgil Vaughn

I'm one of the original Boston Celtics, from their first season in 1946. I only got to play in 17 games, though, because I was injured and had to have my left kidney removed.

I went to college at Western Kentucky in Bowling Green, and then worked in the trades as a painter, but I continued to play semipro basketball. When I was drafted in the Army in 1945, I was able to play some with pro teams in Batimore and Trenton. It was when I was discharged in '46 that I signed to play with Boston.

The next season I was ready to return to pro ball and was signed as player-coach of the Louisville, Kentucky, team in the American League. But the owners took bankruptcy after only six games, so I went back to the Trenton Tigers. From there I moved up to the Syracuse Nationals in the NBL. After that season I returned to the trade of painting and worked at it until I retired in 1981.

Comparing the builders of the NBA with the teams today is like comparing day and night. In those days, we played for the love of the game, and not the greed of money. We had no wages and no union. We took what we could get, and most of the time it was for short contracts. Salaries were not the greatest, and we didn't have the advantage of commercials to raise our income.

We did not play just one position. I played center and forward, and sometimes I played guard. I'm sure all will agree we played better defense. If you got 25 points in a game, it was really exceptional. Scoring in double figures was very difficult. We played ball together, not as individuals. Today's three-point shot is nothing new. We were good at long shots, but we still got only two points. Two-hand set shots were common then, also left- and right-hand hook shots.

We played most of the time in arenas and stadiums where we had plenty of space and lockers. Our first game in Boston was in the Boston Arena. At first we stayed there at night and slept on cots. We played games with the Globetrotters, with Sweetwater Clifton and Meadowlark Lemon, and with the House of David in

Chicago, Michigan, New York, New Jersey, Toronto and Pennsylvania, traveling by bus, train and plane.

Playing time was from November 1 until March 31. We played 30 home games and 30 away from home. In the American League there were three 15-minute periods, and during the last five minutes of the third we used a center jump after each score. We had a two-minute rest period before the final minutes of play. Coaches were allowed to talk to players from the bench only during timeouts.

We didn't win a lot of games that first season in Boston, but our biggest embarrassment was not a league game. In Boston Garden one night we played a charity event in wheelchairs against some disabled veterans' team, and we lost 18-2.

On the trains going from game to game there was always a lot of card playing, but Chuck Connors was always our best ham entertainer, quoting Shakespeare, reciting *Casey at the Bat* and telling stories. As for me, I was always on the ball and kept my eye out for making hay while the sun was shining. I came up with a good deal at Anderson, Indiana, where it rained all the time we were there for the play-offs. It just kept pouring rain, so I bought a large umbrella and walked the players and their wives in and out for 25 cents a trip. By the way, back then tickets for a World Championship game were $1.00, $2.10, $3.00 and $4.20.

I don't know if you would call the officiating good or bad, but in one game when I was with Syracuse 52 fouls were called and 32 of them were against us – even though the reporters covering the game said that it wasn't a particularly rough game. Another time, in Trenton, at the end of a game decided by one point, the officials charged one player with a foul who wasn't even in the game and sent the wrong player to the line to shoot it.

You can talk all you want about the great shots of the artists playing the game in this day and age, but you should have seen Elmo Morgenthaler make a basket while sitting on the floor. Now that's shooting!

Virgil Vaughn, a painter by trade until his retirement in 1981, performed his basketball artistry throughout the '40s from Bowling Green, Kentucky, to Baltimore, Trenton, Boston, Louisville and Syracuse.

Whitey Von Nieda

I was born and raised in this little town, Ephrata, P A. Football was pretty big here, and baseball even more so. But I was the first from this little area to go into professional sports, and it was in basketball.

I was also the first player from Penn State in the NBA, and there have been only three or four since. Scholarships were few and far between for basketball at that time, but I got a job at Penn State waiting tables for my meals. It was through basketball – the manager arranged it. There were no full scholarships for basketball at Penn State then, in fact only a few for football.

I guess I thought first about pro ball while I was in the service. In 1943 I led the country in scoring, including all service and college teams. I was a gunner, I guess, and got some notoriety. There were a lot of great players in the service. When I got out of the service I was gonna go back to Penn State to finish, but had an offer to play at Lancaster in the Eastern League, now the Continental League. I told the owner I had some eligibility left at Penn State. He thought I was just trying to hold out, and he kept upping the ante and upping the ante to the point where I could hardly refuse to play. So I was going to Penn State and playing weekends in the Eastern League.

I led the Eastern League in scoring and Leo Ferris saw me play in one of the playoff games. He wanted me to come to Tri-Cities in the worst way and he made it very attractive, a two thousand dollar bonus, in one pile of 20s on a table. This was after a playoff game at Wilkes-Barre, and I had to catch a bus back to Penn State. He left the room with this pile of money and said, "I'll come back." And he didn't come back. I had to catch the bus and I'm thinking, how can I do this? If I leave and leave the money there, he can say I took it. I thought, I'll take the money and send it back to him. I fully intended to play for Lancaster the following year and finish my college education. That's what I planned on doing, but as it turned out I took the money and wound up buying a car. And that's why I played for Tri-Cities.

Whitey Von Nieda (left, front row) with the Tri-Cities Blackhawks from a program for an exhibition game in Sioux City. PHOTO COURTESY OF WHITEY VON NIEDA

At Penn State my coach was John Lawther, a very strict disciplinarian. He was great for the zone defense, which didn't help me in the pro ranks. I had to unlearn that, so to speak. And then I had a guy named Nat Hickey, who played for the original Celtics, with Joe Lapchick, Davey Banks and Nat Holman. Nat Hickey knew the game like you wouldn't believe, but he couldn't tell you, he had to show you how to do it.

After the Eastern League playoffs ended in '47, I was invited to play in the *Herald-American* tournament out in Chicago with the Tri-Cities team. They paid my way out there. The least you could make from Wednesday to Sunday out there was 400 dollars plus all your expenses. That was pretty good money. It was 800 if you got to the second round, 1,600 if you won it, 1,200 for the runners-up. These were supposedly the eight best pro teams in the world at that time.

I got out there and we had a practice in the morning for the first game that night. And Nat showed me how, when I was looking to steal the ball, he'd duck in behind me. While I was watching the ball, he'd backdoor me. He was a good guy, a funny man and a rough ref-baiter, too. He taught me by showing me.

We played in different conditions in the old NBL than they do now, I'll tell ya. We had one of the better facilities, the Wharton Field House in Moline, which seated about 6,000 people. We'd fill the place when we played the big teams. Waterloo was decent, too. In Oshkosh and Sheboygan we played in high school gyms. Fort Wayne was like getting down in a little pit. Transportation was mostly by train between the big cities, but sometimes, depending on schedules, you'd have to drive. We'd all take turns driving. We were driving to Syracuse one time from Fort Wayne and got caught in an unbelievable snowstorm. We wound up taking taxis from somewhere near Pittsburgh to Syracuse through the snow, and we got there just in time for the game to start. It was so cold we were cramping up, and they had to delay the start of the game for about an hour.

I wasn't particularly thrilled to go to Oshkosh or Sheboygan, to get off the train and be hit by a blast of cold air off the lake. The facilities and locker rooms left a lot to be desired. Most of the time you got hot showers, most of the time but not always. The janitor might have gone home early. I liked playing in Rochester, and Indianapolis was good. In Syracuse, we played downtown, right across from the old YMCA, and it was not too great. Denver was a good place to play, except you'd get out there on a Tuesday to play on Tuesday night and you'd run the court once and you're dying because of the thin air.

I didn't like the small court in Fort Wayne because I was a running man, that was my best game. I liked the parquet floor in Boston, but the Celtics weren't much then, like the doormats of the league. I really enjoyed the big courts, the Stadium in Chicago, Convention Hall in Philadelphia and Madison Square Garden, where I got a chance to show people I could play the game. Being from Ephrata, P A, doesn't usually get a guy much recognition.

Fred Zollner owned the team in Fort Wayne. The jerseys said Zollner Pistons on the back, and that way he could write off the whole thing as advertising. They did basically the same thing with the Anderson Duffy Packers. We were playing in Anderson one time and the referees were calling it for the home team bias, and Nat Hickey would yell, "That's right, back up your cars after work at the meat packers and they'll fill it up with hams for ya," that kind of thing. You couldn't help but hear it all over the gym. Nat always chewed tobacco and he liked to play. He was a player-coach. He was in his 40s and wouldn't dress all the time, though he did early on until it got a little too fast for him.

But he sure knew the game.

Fort Wayne had Bobby McDermott, another player-coach. He was the only one considered for player of the half-century besides Mikan, had a set shot that wouldn't quit. I caught him at the tail end, when his legs were starting to give on him and he couldn't drive to the basket anymore and all he had was the set, but sometimes that was enough.

In those days we socialized with other teams. I liked to get together with George Mikan when we played in Minneapolis. What a character. He wore a homburg and a long traveling coat. We usually had a few beers after a game. We'd go back to the Nicolet Hotel in Minneapolis and I'd go in there with Don Otten and Mikan, and I'm a foot shorter than either one. It was pretty impressive, eyes would follow. He enjoyed the adulation and excitement. He told me one time he had a regimen of staying up all night and sleeping all day whenever he could. "That way," he said, "I can be rested for the game. And besides, everything that's good and exciting that happens, happens at night. I don't wanna miss any of it." That was his theory. Oh, but he was a competitor. He just wouldn't let anybody outplay him. I appreciated him for that.

Otten and Mikan used to have some tremendous duels. Mikan was by far the superior player, but Otten would get up for a game against George, because Mikan had embarrassed him once in college real bad. He'd match Mikan point for point, 18 to 18. One time in Tri-Cities they held each other to nine each, and the only guy in double figures was old dad here. I had 16, and we won 45-36.

When I had to switch off on Mikan, what was I gonna do? I'd throw up a token hand at the ball, but then take the other hand and put it over his eyes. He'd cuss me out, but his percentage was better shooting against Otten than me because I'd block his vision. He was a nice guy, a class act and a competitor. I loved the guy.

There were regional differences of sorts in basketball back then, but I've always thought that the prime factor in the game was how bad you wanted it. I wanted to play in the worst way. I wanted to find out if I could play in the NBA. I just decided that anybody who wanted to beat me out would just have to beat me. I'm not gonna sit back.

At Penn State there had been all these all-state guys. They whittled it down from over a hundred guys on the freshman team to about 30. And then we had a scrimmage against the varsity. It wasn't announced. I was just there, a gym rat, and

I did extremely well against the varsity. And from then on, I was on the first team of the freshman team. And that's the way it went at every level.

The Tri-Cities team played a series with the Globetrotters in '47. They were a big drawing card, and we played them in Omaha, Nebraska, and three or four other states. We played serious ball, and as a consequence we won most of them. Make no bones about it, they had some great players, like Sweets Clifton and Marques Haynes, classy ballplayers, but they weren't very deep. Goose Tatum was the big man. He could throw the hook, and he was a clown. On the whole they were nice guys, and I enjoyed playing against them.

I met some characters with some unbelievable habits. One guy who played a short time for Tri-Cities, Roy Hurley, his breakfast was a Coca-Cola and a dill pickle every day on the road. That was his unvarying constant standard. You'd eat on the run in some greasy all-night diner. I'd eat a bowl of cereal, you can't go wrong with that.

George Glamack from North Carolina wore glasses as thick as Coke bottles. They called him the "Blind Bomber." He couldn't see the scoreboard if it was right over him, and he'd squint up at it. He couldn't see the basket real well either, but he'd count the floorboards on the court and he'd know just where he was. He had a tough time in Boston with the parquet floor. And he was a character. He'd tear a fifty dollar bill in half and give one half to a girl. He'd tell her, "If you come to my room I'll give you the other half." He'd always keep the bigger half in case he had to turn it in at the bank.

There were some ladies' men, all right. They had their haunts in every city. I wasn't in that circle, I was a little naive. Joe Camic from Duquesne, a good-looking guy, was a ladies' man who always had someone in tow. Blackie Towery was colorful, too, a ladies' man. He used to like to drink a little bit, too. The Tri-Cities doctor had recommended a bottle or two of ale after games, to keep our weight up, but Blackie would drink the hard stuff sometimes. And then he'd get mean, especially the next game, and he would blast guys.

Billy Hassett, whose brother Buddy had been the Yankees first baseman, and I had a restaurant in Moline, The Rendezvous. All the players would come in after a game, the visiting players as well. It did very well till he got traded to Minneapolis and I got traded to Baltimore. Absentee ownership didn't work, but it was a reliable operation for a couple of years. In later years I tended bar at some class watering holes around Ephrata, besides my regular job of selling advertising, but I was never in the restaurant business again. I did all right, put six kids through college, have 10 grandchildren, and I don't need to be sending CARE packages to any of them.

The Tri-Cities owner, Leo Ferris, thought we ought to get involved with local affairs. He had an I-Am-an-American Day banquet out there, about 400 people in this big blue-collar area. And he'd bring in people like Johnny Lujack, and a couple of baseball players from the Chicago teams. Billy Hassett was the master of ceremonies – he could talk for an hour on the sex life of mosquitoes, a great talker. They had the local mayor, the mayor of Chicago, and the governor of Illinois, Adlai Stevenson, coming in.

I was gonna be seated at the head table with all the sports figures, and that's all I had to do. But the night before the event, Billy got laryngitis, and Leo said, "Whitey, you're master of ceremonies."

I'm from Ephrata, P A. If I talked to more than three people at a time it was a big crowd. I said, "Leo, you gotta be kiddin'."

He says, "No, that's it."

I had a chart, with everything written down in order, and I had no problem introducing the sports figures. I handled the names of the mayors all right, and I think I'm getting through all right, and Adlai Stevenson's the last speaker. I get up and I wanna get through it fast, and I say, "Without further ado, I give you the great governor of the great state of Illinois, Alibi Stevenson."

The crowd roared. It was just a slip, a Freudian slip, and I didn't even know what I said. I thought maybe my fly was open or something. He finally got up and said, "I've often been accused of being an alibi artist, but that's the first time it's been publicly announced."

Afterwards, we go over to the bar, I'm apologizing profusely, and he said, "Never mind, that made the night – you mind if I use that some other time?"

I said, "Be my guest." What a good guy. He could have crunched me.

After playing briefly for Red Auerbach in Tri-Cities, I was traded to Baltimore in my third year. Big Ed Sadowski, who had been the only good player for Boston at first, had come over from Philadelphia. Ed was a tank but got his share of rebounds by blocking out. Ed loved me because I would feed him, give him assists. I'll never forget one time down in Baltimore against the Lakers. I would make the pass into him and always go by the left side, so he could take the hook from the right. He'd always fake the ball out to the left, Mikan would switch, and Ed would take his little hook and make it a lot.

Well, Mikan got to realize that Ed never passed off, so he got to the point that he didn't even make an attempt to switch off. So this time I took the ball out of Ed's hand, Mikan was nowhere near, and I went in for a layup. Ed calls timeout, says, "I've been in this league for x-number of years, I know when a man is open, I'll give him the ball when he's open."

I said, "Ed, I was naked, I go by clean and I'm naked."

That whole timeout was so he could chew me out for that play. After the game, he comes over and says, "I'm sorry I chewed you out. You're the only s.o.b. on the team that even throws me the ball." That was Big Ed, a nice guy.

From my three years in the league, the all-star team would be Mikan, Dolph Schayes, Jim Pollard (we were on the all-rookie team together), Al Cervi and Slater Martin. Pollard was exceptional, could do a lot of things but played in Mikan's shadow. Cervi was as tough a backcourt player as there was, better than Bob

Davies, I thought, who was not very well liked, even on his own team. They made a great backcourt in Rochester, though, along with Red Holzman and later Bobby Wanzer.

Slater Martin was tough head to head. I used to enjoy playing against him, and Max Zaslofsky from St. John's, too. Buddy Jeannette, who was my coach in Baltimore, said, "The way you play Max, you have a track meet. He has to play you on defense, you play him on defense." He was a great offensive player, but I used to run. I was in great shape. I'd run and run and run, and Max would have to stay with me or I'd score. I negated Max's efforts almost every time we played them because he'd rest on offense. Bill Sharman was another guy who ran and ran, a class act, and could he shoot fouls!

I loved playing with Buddy Jeannette because he had some smarts. We were the backcourt. Once when we played the Knicks in New York, we got a four- or six-point lead on them late in the game. You didn't have to shoot every 24 seconds, so we'd play pitch and catch with each other. And Carl Braun of the Knicks, I'll never forget it, he'd be watching these passes go, be timing it to intercept, and Buddy would give me the nod. I'd fake the pass, Carl would go for the ball and Buddy would go down the lane – we'd keep the lane open. He got three straight layups on the same play, and he'd say, "I don't believe it, Whitey, I don't believe it, the same play three times."

Usually I'd cover Ernie Vandeweghe on the Knicks, but sometimes Dick McGuire or Sonny Hertzberg. Walt Budko would be on the wing, and I'd give him a lead pass as he came across. Walt was a class act, though I found him a little aloof at first, with that Ivy League air. And then there was Tony Lavelli, from Yale, who played a couple of years with the Celtics and the Knicks. In Baltimore I saw him play the first half and then play the accordion at halftime. I didn't believe it.

Joe Lapchick stands out in my mind among the coaches. I love Joe Lapchick for the simple reason that he was a basketball man from the get-go and I probably learned more basketball from Joe Lapchick just sitting down after a game. In Baltimore we'd go out to an all-night restaurant and drink coffee and he'd smoke cigarettes. He'd even smoke on the bench, go through two packs of cigarettes. And he'd diagram things on the tablecloth there and I'd ask him questions. I asked him one time, "Joe, if you could get one player right now to build a team around, to make a franchise, who would it be?"

"Wilt Chamberlain," he said.

Chamberlain was a sophomore in high school! I had heard of him, but I said, "You're kidding me."

He says, "Whitey, he's seven feet tall, runs the 440, high jumps and has a pretty decent touch for a big man."

I'm a Chamberlain fan. He never fouled out of a game and didn't back away, either.

The officiating then was pretty much like today. There were good ones and bad ones. I'd appreciate the guys who called it the same both ways regardless of where you were. I remember Pat Kennedy, very flamboyant but he was fair. He took the game away from the players a little bit, but he was fair and you appreciate that. Almost all the officials, if it was an either-or play, gave it to the home team wherever you were. That's human nature. Sid Borgia was a good official, Chuck Solodare, too. He threw my dad out of the game one time in Rochester. He was sitting on the bench, because they had a sellout and he drove all the way up there to see the game. And Solodare made some call, my dad went "boo" or something like that, and he pointed out. Chuck was fair.

I didn't make too much of it when a referee became a coach, Charlie Eckman. It was like he said, "These guys know the game – all I gotta do is keep them happy. If I can keep them happy, give them all some playing time, give them the ball and tell them to go win, that would be it." Plus the fact that he had an uncanny ability to get the officials to see it his way. He could go to them and say, "We're gonna play it a little tough under the hoop, is that OK?" And he'd get all the benefits of the doubt on blocking out. That was a great gift, and he could also talk a lot. Besides, he knew he had the players – Larry Foust, Andy Phillip, George Yardley, Mel Hutchins.

I didn't know anything about the gambling until at Tri-Cities I saw Bob Gerber from Toledo looking for the point spread of games. I suspected he bet them; I don't know where or how. I never saw him bet, but he really checked those point spreads – that was the big thing in his life. He was the only one I knew was involved with gambling at that time. He'd win some and lose some but could hardly wait to get the spreads and scores. Among ourselves we'd have friendly bets in the football season, on Penn State or Notre Dame games, five- or 10-dollar bets. Sports was the thing to bet on, but I really wasn't aware of the extent of it.

When the scandal broke I could hardly believe it. I played against Beard and Groza. Beard and I played head to head. There was a guy, I could fake him out but he would catch up. I'd get a half-step on him and he'd catch up, a tough little player who loved the game of basketball. That's all he wanted to do all his life. It broke his heart when he couldn't play or coach because that was his life.

I saw Beard I think it was right after he was grabbed, and he told me the whole story of how it started. And I put myself in the same position and thought, If I'd have gone to John Lawther with money in an envelope, I'd have been blamed. I wouldn't have known what to do. A couple of hundred dollars in those days was a lot of money. Coming out of service I was getting 65 a month from the government and going back to college, and I could almost make it on that.

Then I thought back to the year in college when we went up to New York to play NYU in the Garden on the second or third of January. We gave up our Christmas vacation to practice and practice and practice so we'd be ready. We stayed in the Belvedere Hotel right across from the old Garden, and standing in the lobby some guy asked, "How are you gonna do?"

And I said, "We gave up our Christmas vacation to win and if we don't we're gonna be unhappy."

"Think you're gonna win?" he said.

"Certainly," I said, "but at least we're gonna give it a shot."

"How big?"

Turned out we lost a key player. John Egli, who later coached at Penn State, turned his ankle and couldn't play. We got beat by a couple of points – Jerry Fleishman had a big game against us.

When I quit the NBA it was to be player-coach at Lancaster in the Eastern League. I also coached at Elizabethtown College at the same time, had a dual role. That's the reason I left Baltimore. One of the directors of Elizabethtown College and the owner of the Lancaster team came down to Baltimore and packaged a deal, which turned out to be more than I was making at that time in Baltimore. In those days, you didn't think in terms of making a career because the average life of a pro ballplayer was less than three years, and there was not enough money that you could retire after playing – like now.

I did that for four years in Lancaster, two of them while coaching the college until I started selling advertising for the Yellow Pages. Later I coached Hazleton in '60, and once again in Lancaster in '85, when they were in the Continental League. That was the first year Anchorage was in the league, and that was an experience, too. Some great ballplayers played in that Eastern League, and some thought they could get by on their name but found out that wasn't the case. They had to work at it.

I had Jack Molinas on that club in Hazleton. Eddie Gottlieb was a good friend of mine, and he said, "Get rid of him, he's nothing but bad news and they're gonna grab him." I traded him to Wilkes-Barre for an old basketball and a pair of sneakers. He used to come to practices – and we didn't have that many practices – before the season. He'd have a girl on each arm and a suitcase full of booze. And he wasn't in shape.

I'd say, "You can't play the game not being in shape."

He said, "By the time the season comes around I'll be in shape."

Jack was a piece of work. The guy could play the game. Make no bones about it. But he got caught up in the fast lane and he had to be a little faster. He had disdain for the other players. But he'd be dying after the first quarter, play only five minutes in the second quarter, and I'd have to take him out in the third, with a total of one rebound and two points. "Jack, you're in shape?" I said. That was one reason I got rid of him, but Eddie Gottlieb was the main reason, and Eddie was right – they grabbed him not long after.

I have no regrets. They were good years. I met people I would never have known without it. I was privileged to meet a lot of great guys but then there were a very few who left a bad taste in my mouth. Fans were not as numerous but they were loyal, gung-ho kind of thing. In Tri-Cities they got behind the team real well. We had a few games televised from Chicago and a couple from Baltimore, then radio for the playoffs. We played Minneapolis two straight years, runner-up both times, three games to two with every game won on the home court. That was not by design, but that's the way it was.

It was a fun time. Players in those days cared more about the game than anything else. There was an intensity about the game. We were all there to play. We all loved to play. Our response to the fans was that we appreciated them, and they appreciated us. They appreciated effort. I don't think that's the same today. Players seem to ignore the fans more, thumb their nose at them. We used to think it was a privilege to sign an autograph, not a chore you had to do.

The 24-second clock added something for the fans. But I'll be honest with you, it detracted something from the game, because of some great plays you could get by freezing the ball. Make them come to it. The team behind had to gamble, so some of the finesse is gone. Of course, these kids today shoot much better and the big men run the court like gazelles.

I watch and follow it now but not as intently as I did. I appreciate the class acts, the class players, like Olajuwon with his demeanor, and Julius Erving and Jerry West. The guys that added some class I'd just sit back and applaud. The others – whose attitude is gimme and screw you – I don't like that. That's wrong. I watch college games quite a bit, but even that's to the point where the players are pampered too much. The way they recruit is almost sinful. It's nothing but a money game – money, money, money. I know it's important but I don't think it should be the focal point. It galls me that the guys today don't give anything back.

As for us in the Pioneer Era, we were the ambassadors of the game.

Whitey Von Nieda is retired and tends his garden in Ephrata, Pennsylvania. For his three full seasons in the NBL and NBA (Tri-Cities and Baltimore, 1947-50) plus another decade in service to basketball, he gets no share of the pension fund.

Jack Smiley

The main reason there were so many player-coaches in my day was that management wanted to save money. I don't think that would work now, because the temperament of the players is so different. But a player like Curly Armstrong at Fort Wayne was a good player but really didn't know much about coaching.

I managed without much difficulty to do my playing and coaching and still take care of whatever administrative jobs were required. One thing that made it easier was that my team was overloaded at my position, guard. I had four other guards, so I didn't have to play as much – Buckshot O'Brien, Murray Wier, Johnny Payak and Leo Kubiak.

All personnel decisions were made by management, but in one case I made a personal trip to Bowling Green, Ohio, to sign seven-footer Charlie Share. The Celtics were after him, too, for the other league, but we beat them to him. I laid out 2,500 bucks of my own money to sign him, but of course I was reimbursed. Then, to make sure he was ours, I went to Chicago to get him, met his father, a 6-foot-6-inch teamster organizer, and personally drove Charlie to Waterloo, Iowa.

I grew up in the small town of Waterman, Illinois, 20 miles west of Aurora, south of DeKalb. At that time, I think it gave some prestige to my high school coach for me to go to the University of Illinois, which was actively recruiting all-state players around the state like Gene Vance from Clinton, Ken Menke from Dundee, Andy Phillip from Granite City, Art Matwigen from Dwight, and myself from Waterman. So after high school graduation I went down to Champaign, where I got a summer job and then enrolled at the university.

I was always an aggressive type player, and as I began my sophomore year, when we were first eligible to play, I was the 20th man on a 20-man varsity. One position at a time, I moved up to be a starter. I was a 6-3 forward and Andy Phillip was a guard, but in my junior year Andy and I switched positions.

Jack Smiley. PHOTO COURTESY OF JACK SMILEY

As it happened, I was drafted in the Army midyear, in March of 1943. I served in the artillery, 106th Division, trying to hold off German tanks in the Battle of the Bulge. I brought home a piece of shrapnel, which hit me in my neck in the Bulge battle. After serving three years in the war, I was given special permission to play two more seasons at Illinois, and they were good years for the Whiz Kids. Andy Phillip came back from the Pacific with some kind of ailment that slowed him down that season, and I picked up some of the slack.

I wasn't thinking a whole lot about pro ball, but in my senior year I scored 22 points against Indiana, 15 against Ohio State, and when we went to Ann Arbor to play Michigan I was approached by Carl Bennett, the Fort Wayne Zollner Pistons coach. I was the Illini MVP that year, chosen as a Helms All-American, and played in the College All-Star games in 1943 and 1947.

The offer from the Zollner Pistons was a good one, and my teammate, Ken Menke, and I joined them for the pro tournament in Chicago. The yearly contract was $5,000 for playing basketball and $5,000 more for a job attached to Zollner's company. The amazing thing was that everybody on the team made the same.

Fred Zollner wanted to win and would do whatever it took. That's why his softball team was a world champion and his basketball team was a world champion. It so happened that I played softball during the summers for the Aurora, Illinois, Foxes. There were five teams then in Peoria, Racine, Cleveland, Toledo and South Bend, but that summer before I played basketball in Fort Wayne, my team, the Aurora Foxes, won the Western Division, and then played in the world softball finals at Fort Wayne which the Fort Wayne Zollner Pistons won.

After 2½ years of NBA basketball at Fort Wayne, I was loaned to the Anderson, Indiana, Packers, but after a month was sold by the Fort Wayne Zollners to the Waterloo, Iowa, Hawks of the NBA as player-coach. It was a losing team, troubled with dissension. The next season, in the new NPBL, with Anderson, Sheboygan, Kansas City, Denver and St. Paul, we won 40 games and the league championship.

Waterloo was unusual for that time, a small town but with major businesses like John Deere and Rath Packing. We played in the Hippodrome that seated 11,000, and they'd fill it. Two of my better players were Harry Boykoff and Dick Mehen, but they weren't always good for the team. Once, when we were losing by four points in the final minutes of the game, they left the bench and took off for the dressing room. I didn't see it happen, but when I learned about it I was forced to fine them $500.

Two guys I loved on that team were both 5-8 guards, Buckshot O'Brien and Murray Wier. In one game against St. Paul, a good team with Howie Schultz coaching and Rollie Seltz playing, I told them to press all over the court. We brought up our forwards so they couldn't throw the long pass. Those two little guys pressed St. Paul players bringing the ball down court, repeatedly taking the ball away, and the two players between them scored 10 points in one minute's time. This forced St. Paul to call timeout. Waterloo, and in particular Wier and O'Brien, got a 10-minute standing ovation. Play resumed after the ovation.

Another memorable guy was Paul Cloyd. Ever the opportunist, Paul would put together a little basketball magazine and sell it to NBPL teams to be sold to customers in the stands. And I still remember a hard-nosed player named Wally Osterkorn, not from his pro years, but for the time in practice at Illinois when he cracked my floating rib.

The toughest guys I had to cover personally were Bob Davies and Jim Pollard. Pollard had great jumping ability, and I liked to play deny defense, keep the ball away from my man. Pollard would fake one way, I'd have to go with him, and he'd go the other way and be able to get a high pass near the hoop. He made me change my style of defense, after which I would gamble less on denial and interception.

When I left basketball, I brought my aggressive, no-nonsense style into business in sales and management. I moved up in the ranks of several farm products companies – DeKalb County Grain, Walnut Grove, W.R. Grace – and am now in the water business with one of my sons, Mark Seth Smiley, distributing drinking water systems, conditioners and a product called En-Save Seed Treatment. Claudell Overton, by the way, who played for me in Waterloo, is one of our distributors in Oklahoma.

I still follow the NBA, but I wish they could clean up the center play. That rough stuff under the basket is basketball at its worst. Pushing, shoving, kneeing, holding, have no place in today's finesse basketball. Clean up the center play and the sport has no limits.

A mainstay of the Whiz Kids at Illinois and a Helms All-American, Jack Smiley played in the NBL, the NBA and the NPBL. He led the NBA Pistons in assists in 1948-49 and coached the Waterloo Hawks to a league title in 1950-51. He is now chairman of the board of En-Save, Inc.

Marko (Mike) Todorovich

I started college at Washington University here in St. Louis, playing football and basketball my freshman year, and basketball my sophomore year when we finished second to Creighton in the conference. Then I was transferred by the Marine Corps to Notre Dame in 1943, where, in the V12 program, I played football on a national championship team and basketball on a very good team. After Notre Dame, I was sent to the Philippine Islands where I spent a year – 13 months really – played basketball like four nights a week on a concrete floor. All the floors over there were concrete. That is one reason I have trouble walking well today.

After being discharged from the service, I enrolled at the University of Wyoming and played one year. We won our conference, and I made the all-conference team. I had a year of eligibility left because the year at Notre Dame when I was in the military service didn't count against me. But being married and the father of a son, I decided to go pro.

I was shocked to be selected fourth in a common draft of the two leagues, and drafted by Sheboygan, Wisconsin. I had never heard from Sheboygan prior to the draft. The only one who called or visited me was Ken Loeffler, the coach from the St. Louis Bombers. I assumed then that I would be drafted by his ballclub, but the No. 4 pick came long before the Bombers had a choice.

One of my greatest games in my last year in college was against CCNY. It wasn't a "full game greatness"; it was a "half a game." I scored 23 points against CCNY in Madison Square Garden. Everything I threw up toward the basket went in, from all angles. I was out of my head. And in the second half, they put three guys on me, and I scored one point. I was elated to find out that George Mikan had the halftime record at that point and I had broken his record. It was a great game but CCNY won. My second-half production was one point. My teammates couldn't get the ball to me in the pivot, and they couldn't hit from outside.

Prior to the start of the regular pro season I played in the College All-Star Game in Chicago against the previous year's pro champions. Some of my team-

Mike Todorovich. PHOTO COURTESY OF MIKE TODOROVICH

mates were Andy Phillip, Harry Boykoff and Jimmy Pollard – a great ballclub – and it was the first and only time that the college all-stars beat the professionals. Chicago Stadium had a seating capacity of about 15,000-16,000, and it was filled. It made me feel good to make the team, and even better that I was second to Jimmy Pollard in the voting for the Most Valuable Player award.

One interesting thing about professional basketball then was that we played exhibition games all the time. In my year at Wyoming, we played 28 basketball games, and that was a lot in college. When I reported to Sheboygan, we played 30 exhibition games *prior to starting the league schedule*, and it was unbelievably tough. We played in every town imaginable. The coach would pick up 500 bucks to play in little towns like Mt. Vernon, Illinois; Wilkes-Barre, Pennsylvania; Centralia, Illinois; and Madison, Wisconsin – anywhere at all. We'd be gone for seven days, eight days, 10 days at a time, and we traveled in two new DeSoto Suburbans.

We had a 10-man squad and a coach, and those 11 men, some 6 feet 8 inches, some 6-9, would pile into these two DeSotos and take off, traveling all over the country. We'd go into a town such as Mt. Vernon and play the local All-Americans. They knew for three or four weeks, maybe a couple months, that we were coming, and we as players had no idea where we were going to be the next night until we showed up to play. In my first year I can state that I played 120 basketball games. In fact, we played the Harlem Globetrotters twice one Sunday, at 1 o'clock in the afternoon and again at 7:30 that night. That was when the Globetrotters played pretty good basketball, too. That was a tough day, two games of basketball, and I don't remember sitting out in either game.

I tell you, we earned our money. It was nothing to lose 20 pounds in a season, nothing at all. And when you're 215, 220, and you're losing 20-25 pounds, that makes you look awfully thin. After playing 125-130 games as I did the first two years, I used to come home skin and bones. Some of my friends didn't even recognize me, I was so thin. Today they don't do that sort of thing, and that's such a great advantage to play today with traveling by charter airplane or having your own airplane. That would be a luxury. But we endured, we loved it, worked hard.

Sheboygan was about 65 miles north of Milwaukee, and if the weather was good, that trip would take about an hour or hour and 15 minutes. But most of the time the weather was terrible – snowstorms, ice storms, all sorts of storms. I can remember leaving Milwaukee in a blizzard in the DeSoto Suburbans, and the visibility was so bad that Milt Schoon, a character, 6-10, 250 pounds, said, "Stop the car, stop the car." He went out, got on the hood of the car, chest down, face right over the grille of the car, and his legs sticking up on the windshield. He was directing the driver to go right or left or straight ahead in this blizzard. That trip took us, instead of an hour or hour and 15 minutes, just about five or six hours. We hardly moved at times. That was hilarious.

I can remember one trip that went like this. We played a game in Detroit, got into our DeSoto Suburbans, and spent the night in Blenheim, Canada, getting up the next morning and driving to Rochester, New York, to play that evening. One night in Detroit, the next night in Rochester. To this day, I don't know where in Canada Blenheim is, but I remember the name because it was such a grueling trip. Then from Rochester, you'd drive to Syracuse, from Syracuse to Philadelphia, Philadelphia to Fort Wayne, Fort Wayne to Chicago, then back to Milwaukee, and home to Sheboygan.

I had a rewarding year in Sheboygan. I made the all-star team, and I was chosen Rookie of the Year, beating out Jim Pollard of the Minneapolis Lakers who, I thought, was one of the greatest players of our time. Pollard could jump as high and as far as Michael Jordan does today. In our day, we weren't supposed to dunk the ball. We would dunk the ball during warm-up, that is those who could, the big guys, but we weren't allowed to play over the rim – that is, take offensive rebounds over the rim and jam it down. Against the rules. We weren't allowed to get a defensive board above the rim. Against the rules. Dunking was permissible, but if you dunked and missed, you were in trouble. If you dunked and made the shot, you were showing off, making people look bad. If you missed the dunk, you were going to be pulled out of the game immediately and probably not play the rest of the day or evening, and maybe not the next game.

After my first year at Sheboygan, Magnus Brinkman, the CEO of the ballclub came to visit me at St. Louis to sign a new contract. In my rookie year I got a $7,500 contract and a $500 bonus, quite good at that time, even though I was No. 4 in the draft. Some of my peers were making $2,500, $3,000, $4,000, so $7,500 was a lot of money. But after having a good year, I told him my terms, which shocked him to death. I told him that I wanted $10,000 for my second year, and he couldn't believe that I could ask for such an increase – $2,500. I also asked that I be given a guaranteed contract and that I would be released to the St. Louis Bombers at the end of the year.

I wanted – and my wife wanted – to get back to St. Louis, because our child was about two years old at this time, and housing in Sheboygan was very tough, as it was everywhere. He agreed to everything, and I came to St. Louis for my third year. Then I had to take a $2,500 cut, because they knew they had me. I took it, signed the contract, and inside of two months I was sold, traded to the Tri-Cities Blackhawks.

I had never heard of Ben Kerner, who had taken over the Blackhawks and traded for me. I knew his predecessor, Leo Ferris, who was also from Buffalo. He called me on a Sunday morning at 8 o'clock, identified himself, told me of the deal, told me to get the next plane that left at 11 o'clock, and report to Indianapolis where they were going to play that night at the Butler University Field House.

I said, "Hey, wait a minute, Benny, or Mr. Kerner, I took a $2,500 cut to come to St. Louis."

After a few minutes on the telephone, he made up the difference, gave me my $2,500, and told me their coach, Red Auerbach, would meet me at the airport. So I got a bag, got an airplane, landed, and it was the first time I had ever met Red.

The first thing he said to me was, "Where are your shoes?" And I said, "Oh, my goodness, I forgot my shoes."

So we had to find a sporting goods store, get them to open up, and I got a pair of shoes. We went out that night, I had a big night, and Red and I became close friends. I haven't seen him in many a year, but we're still very close. A good guy. A very good coach, very good. I played at Tri-Cities that year and was second-team all-star.

One thing about playing in a small town such as Sheboygan or Tri-Cities, the fans were unbelievable. In Sheboygan, we had a capacity of about 3,000 people, and the fans were right off the floor. We played in the National Guard Armory. The club was a nonprofit organization modeled after the Green Bay Packers. Stockholders were all local citizens, and they never expected profit from their investment. Sheboygan was one of the original towns to have a professional team. They started in 1939, and they played professional basketball until the big cities voted them out, about 1953, I think.

The fans were fanatical. If you won a game, it took you five or six minutes to get back in the locker room. There were fans all over. If you lost, you could run right into the locker room without any hesitation. They were so involved in their ballclubs. The town was 40,000 people, and the ballplayers were really big fish in a very little pond.

Tri-Cities was similar. They played in a high school gym with a capacity of about 4,500. They were owned by a few citizens in town, but then Kerner came in and bought a controlling share.

Another thing I should talk about was the closeness of the ballplayers. As I said, one year I played 130 games, and many of them were, of course, against the same team. You'd go to Minneapolis and play the Lakers. And after playing them six or seven times in the season, you'd make good friends with your opponents. They'd invite you over to their house for dinner, and of course you'd reciprocate when they came to your town. There was a friendship built up there, which I don't think exists today. I know it doesn't. You got to know each other very, very well, but once we got on the court, it was dog eat dog.

In my four years of basketball, the game progressed quite a bit, not so much in the style of play but in the mode of traveling. In the third year, we took trains on the long trips, and in the fourth year, sometimes we flew in an airplane. But the biggest change was in the size of the ballplayers. When I reported to Sheboygan in my rookie year, I was 6-6, and I was a big man. I was a center, playing the post. There were some guys 6-8, 6-9, but very few seven-footers. Don Otten was a seven-footer, and there was a seven-footer from St. Louis, Bob Kurland, who played for Phillips 66 in the amateur ranks, but very few other than that.

My second year they brought in Noble Jorgensen who was 6-9 or 6-10. He took over the post and I moved to forward. We didn't have strong forwards, power forwards and shooting forwards. We had a front line and a back line. We didn't have point guards, we had guards. Either of the two guards would bring the ball up.

My third year I played the corner again, but in my fourth year, as player-coach, I moved myself to the backcourt. At 6-6 then, I wasn't big enough for the corner. The norm at center was 6-9 or 6-10, and at 6-6 or 6-7 and 240-250 pounds you played the corners. The game did progress in that way.

One of the reasons basketball was so slow in progressing had to do with the 12-foot key. Until the advent of the 20-foot key, and still playing in small gyms, high school gyms and armory gyms, a guy like George Mikan or Don Otten would snuggle in under the basket. It was just a game of throwing the ball to the big guy in the center and having him turn and throw it in. No fun. The big guys had a tremendous advantage. Moving the lane to 20 feet made the big guy get out a little wider and gave the defensive man a better chance of playing some defense.

In my last year of basketball as player-coach, I was making a talk before some Philadelphia sportswriters at a luncheon, and I suggested widening the lane to 20 feet. That was something that I was criticized for, and my friend George Mikan didn't really like it very much. But it did happen a few years later, and then the advent of the 24-second clock opened up the game. That was the No. 2 point that really did it. Twenty-four seconds to shoot. Many times a club would stall the ball for minutes and minutes at a time. That would create no interest from the fans. So I really blame the owners in that era for the slow progress of the game. The ballplayers then and now like to run, like the fast break and they like to score.

We had some great officials in those days. We had Sid Borgia, Arnie Heft, Jimmy Enright. Enright was a sportswriter for the *Chicago Herald-American*, weighed about 235 pounds and was about 5-8. Roly-poly Jimmy. Always had a cigar in his mouth off the court. He always talked to the ballplayers during a game. Prior to calling a foul, he'd have warned you if it was something flagrant you were doing – a little push with the hand here and there, and so forth. He'd say, "Stop this. Don't do that, Mike, don't do that. I'm going to get you on it." And Jim Enright, when he called a foul, he'd shake that little fat body of his all over the place, and he'd scream, and the people loved the guy. He loved it!

Sid Borgia was another. You know, you got to know the officials pretty well because you played so many ballgames, and their schedule was as tough as ours. And they didn't travel together, either. They traveled all alone, so it was a lonesome journey for them. They had a tough route. I don't think they were making that much money. But Sid Borgia was a great, great official. And then Arnie Heft, he was also another great one. He had a lot of character. The townspeople got to know those officials as well as the ballplayers.

Two of the greatest ballplayers I'd like to mention are Bob McDermott and Ralph Beard. People hardly remember McDermott anymore, but he was incredibly good with that fabulous two-hand set shot. As for Beard, he had amazing quickness on defense and was so good on offense that he could wrap the ball around Bob Cousy's ass.

Basketball progressed not so much in the style of play, but in my third year reporters started following the teams, and radio stations started sending out a crew to cover road games. One thing that didn't change was the inconsistency of the courts. You'd still have to play great ballclubs in Anderson, Indiana, in a high school gym. Then you'd go to Indianapolis where you played at Butler University, a regulation-size collegiate court. Then you'd go to a city like Sheboygan where you played in the National Guard Armory where the court wasn't as wide but as long as the regular court. You had different size gyms to play in, so you had to adjust your game to the gymnasium, to the court. Of course, after the merger of the two leagues, playing in Boston, New York and Philadelphia, those were regular-size courts. But even Minneapolis had a narrower court than regulation.

The courts were different surfaces, too. The parquet court in the Boston Garden was very, very tough on your knees and on your legs. Coming in there to play just occasionally, you would really feel it the next morning, even though you were in great shape. You had to play on different kinds of wood, sometimes wood on concrete, and many times, the St. Louis Bombers, for instance, wood courts on ice. That was a tough place to play because you could be heated up, then rest for three or four minutes on the bench, and there was ice for the hockey team right below the court. That made it cold, and you could feel the cold coming right through the wood, and that made it tough on your legs.

I have just a few disappointments to relate. One thing that upsets me is the fact that when I made the all-pro all-star team, my frontline teammates were Jimmy Pollard and George Mikan, the backcourt was Red Holzman and Al Cervi, and they're all in the Hall of Fame along with Bob Davies who was on the second team. Now here I have all these teammates in the Hall of Fame, and I haven't even been considered. It hurts, but I've gotten over it.

To be serious now, it really upsets me that the NBA will not recognize the ballplayers who played in the '46-55 era and give us a pension. The only reason I don't get a pension is that, when I left the service, I wanted to get my degree and I went back to college. Now, if I had gone from the service right into pro ball, which I know I could have done, I would have been eligible for a pension. That doesn't make any sense to me at all.

I also could have played that fifth year and qualified. But Ben Kerner, with Maurice Podoloff's approval, was moving the club to Milwaukee from Tri-Cities, and I was invited to come along, but not as player-coach, and with no specified salary. By that time I had already gotten started in the general insurance business, something that you could build up during the off-season that could continue afterward, so I decided to work at it full-time. When I retired as senior partner, after 35 years with the same company, my two sons took over the business.

I still follow the pro game. When the Hawks moved to St. Louis, I had season tickets. And I also wrote the insurance for Ben Kerner and the whole organization.

Wherever he played, and even as player-coach, Mike Todorovich was among his team's leaders in scoring, free throws, rebounds and assists.

Fred Scolari

I got the nickname "Blubber" when I was about 12. I guess I grew out instead of up. I was broad-chested, looked like I had a 200-pound body on these thin, spindly legs, but I played at about 175 pounds. Later on, of course, they called me "Fat Freddie."

I had only played college ball in my freshman year at USF, and then I had to quit school to go to work. I was playing AAU ball in the Bay Area when I was contacted by Ken Loeffler, who wanted me and Jim Pollard to play for his St. Louis team in the NBL. They were talking about a thousand a month and a thousand bonus, but before I signed any contract I was contacted by the Washington club in the BAA that was just about to get started. Bob Feerick was helping Red Auerbach put the team together, and he got hold of me before Loeffler. We were so poor, we had no phone.

Washington was a great team; we played as a team. We were 49 and 11 during that first year, and I don't know how we ever lost a game. We had taken five of six from Chicago during the season, but for some reason lost to them in the playoffs 4-2. The Stags then lost the title to Philadelphia, who had finished 14 games behind us.

A lot of players on that team, like Feerick and Bones McKinney, knew as much about coaching as Auerbach that first year. He sure learned well, didn't he? I attribute his success to the fact that from the start he had the ability to control a club. He was the boss.

John Mahnken was a good guy, but he had a drinking problem, drank heavily. McKinney was a good friend, a real character, emotional and demonstrative, who acted on the spur of the moment. He was a North Carolinian who had played in front of the knowledgeable fans in New York before, but for some reason he hated New York. Well, the first time the Capitols went to New York we were beating the Knicks badly, and Bones went to the foul line, turned around and shot his free throw backwards. We almost blew the lead after that, but held on to win the game.

At first there was a big regional difference in basketball. The Eastern teams played more of a ball-control game, shot two-hand sets and were more aggressive, smarter, more fundamentally sound. The Western teams ran a lot, shot one-handed, gambled more defensively and were better athletes. They called me a "diver" because of the way I went after the ball, but that meant that I got beat a lot on the give-and-go. I learned not to do that.

The game improved when East and West met. The pro game, where we all played together and mixed both styles, improved the caliber of the game at all levels. In Washington, where basketball was almost unheard of, we would give clinics in the D.C. high schools. And now it's one of the places where the game is played best.

The officiating in those days made it very difficult to win on the road, especially in Minneapolis when they came into the league. We'd go in there to play and have officials we never saw before. They saw things differently. The fans made it hard to make calls against them. I remember one game when the officials were lucky to get out of Syracuse alive. Arnie Heft was working that game and said to me, "Help me get out of here." I liked Sid Borgia, who was probably the most popular ref with the players. There was another guy, a short round Irishman named Boyle, I think. The first time I had him, I got on him pretty good, and he fouled me out really quick. From then on we gained respect for each other.

The second year in Washington, Sonny Hertzberg came in with those long two-hand sets of his. We continued to play well, but were knocked out of the playoffs by Chicago again, in a tie-break game. In '49 we went to the finals and lost to the Lakers in their first year in the league.

Bill Sharman played with us for a while in Washington, and he was my room-mate and a good friend. I was reunited with him in Boston in my last year. When my lease ran out there, it was the Sharmans who took me and my pregnant wife in.

In 1950, when the Washington club folded, I was drafted by Syracuse. One of the owners, Leo Ferris, called to tell me. Then he said that he couldn't pay my salary, that I had to take a salary cut. I said I wouldn't do it. Mr. Podoloff called and told me to come to the league office in New York. So I went and paid my own way, too. He convinced me that I would have to go to Syracuse, but I had one condition. I refused to deal with Leo Ferris, only with Danny Biasone.

Biasone may not be in the Basketball Hall of Fame, despite inventing the 24-second clock, but he's in my personal hall of fame, a good guy who always treated me fairly. Looking back, I think I made a mistake at age 28 to take the player-coach job at Baltimore. I left a good Syracuse team, with Dolph Schayes, that went on to win the title a few years later. Schayes was one of the greatest guys and players I knew.

Baltimore always used to have player-coaches, Buddy Jeannette, Walt Budko, and then me. It was a way to save money. I had Don Barksdale there, one of the greatest athletes I ever saw in sports. But he hadn't played the kind of style or competition we had in the NBA. His biggest problem was that he had dominated in his league on the West Coast, could do everything he wanted on the court out there.

The black players in the league had some problems on the road sometimes, but never with ballplayers. I remember that when Earl Lloyd was with us in Washington, he was denied accommodations at our hotel. So who goes with him to stay at another hotel? Bones McKinney, a Southern boy from Carolina.

I was traded to Fort Wayne and thought I might quit in '53. But Fred Zollner, the owner, and Paul Birch, the coach, talked me into signing for '54. That Pistons team was the best team I ever played on, with Larry Foust, Andy Phillip, Mel Hutchins, Max Zaslofsky, Don Meineke, Leo Barnhorst, George Yardley, Frankie Brian and, at the beginning, Jack Molinas. But we didn't do that well, and I couldn't figure out what was going on.

Andy and I would start, but no matter how well we played, we would come out, and Max and others would play. I once scored 15 points in the first quarter and never got back in the game. I had heard that there were some shenanigans with the team, but I couldn't believe it. All those guys were good guys, I thought, or else I'm blind.

Then Molinas was banned. He was a loner, a single man while I was married so I didn't see a lot of him, but I thought he was a nice guy. Thinking back, I remembered a game against the Knicks in Fort Wayne when Molinas was on Vinnie Boryla, a big man with a good outside shot. We told Molinas to force him to drive, and if he gets around you we'll pick him up. But he kept giving him that outside shot and Boryla had a big game. Maybe something was going on that time, but we could never tell.

It was hard to believe that such good talent like Groza and Beard and Molinas would resort to that. Beard, by the way, was the toughest player I had to guard. Still, I could see how a good talker could say, "Look, for five thousand dollars, you're favored by fifteen points, win by ten, there's nothing wrong with that." That was a lot of money in those days.

I was fortunate enough to play my last year for Red Auerbach again, this time in Boston. Two years later I had something to do with bringing Bill Russell to the Celtics. Red Auerbach asked me to find out if Russell would sign to play with Boston after the Olympics. Despite the USF connection I didn't know him personally, but I contacted Pete Newell to find out, and the answer was yes. I did know K.C. Jones from my Boys Club, and I urged Red to sign him, too.

I was also instrumental in bringing the Lakers to Los Angeles. My Boys Club sponsored a series of three exhibition games with the Lakers, two in San Francisco, one in Los Angeles. On a violent, storming night in L.A., 11,000 people showed up. So when Bob Short asked me whether he should move his franchise to San Francisco or Los Angeles, I said Los Angeles. I'd say it was a good move. Short was so grateful, he once offered me the Lakers coaching job.

It was a good nine years in the league for me. I led the league in free throws my first year and was over 80 percent for my career. I have a theory about why free-throw shooting has gotten worse instead of better over the years. They're shooting a shot foreign to their normal shot. Players today don't learn a set shot. The good ones shoot a familiar shot, while the others are fundamentally off. They're shooting straight, but it's either long or short. A free throw is really a rhythm, anyway, not a shot. You shoot the same way from the same place and the same distance a hundred times, and so it's a rhythm. In clinics I would demonstrate that by shooting free throws blindfolded, and I'd make eight out of 10.

In nine seasons in the league (1946-55), with Washington, Syracuse, Baltimore, Fort Wayne and Boston, Fred Scolari usually led his team in free-throw shooting, averaged scoring in double figures in all but his last two years and was 12-27 as coach of the Bullets. He made the all-league team his first two years and played in the second All-Star Game. From 1957 to 1988 he was executive director of the Salesian Boys Club in San Francisco, the very club of which he was a member as a boy and which he credits for any successes he has had in life.

Fuzzy Levane

In 1945 I was stationed on Ellis Island, playing ball for the base team there, and also playing exhibition games on weekends for 30 or 35 bucks a game. I was able to live off-base at home in Brooklyn, and one night there, at 1:30 in the morning, I get a call from a guy who says, "My name is Les Harrison."

He says he wants me to play for a team in Rochester, to come up for a practice on Saturday, then play against Sheboygan on Sunday. He'll pay me 50 for practice, 100 for the game, and he has a ticket for me to take a Pullman to Rochester on Friday night.

I said, "What's a Pullman?" Then I thought maybe someone was bustin' my chops, and I said, "What's your name again?"

I agreed to come and I was supposed to meet a guy at the station who had the ticket for me. The guy comes up to me and says, "Are you Fuzzy Levine?"

They thought I was Jewish. I was a New York player but I wasn't Jewish. I had won a PSAL championship at the Garden with James Madison High School, the same school that later went undefeated for two years and had five future pros in '46-47. Les wanted Jewish players, and I brought him Dutch Garfinkel who had played with me at St. John's, and Red Holzman from CCNY.

Les Harrison was there to meet me in Rochester at 4:30 in the morning. He was a huckster, had been selling fruits and vegetables, and now was organizing a professional basketball team to play in the NBL. He took me over to meet his center, Big Ed Sadowski. I think Sadowski had seen me feed Harry Boykoff in Madison Square Garden for 40-plus when we were at St. John's, and that's why they wanted me.

Ed said, "You throw me the ball and get lost." That was our strategy against Sheboygan, who was coached by Dutch Dehnert.

Les Harrison knew talent. One example is Billy Calhoun, a 17-year-old high school kid he brought in in '47, who wound up playing eight seasons in the NBL

75

Fuzzy Levane watches teammate Bob Davies drive for Royals against rival Lakers, bespectacled George Mikan at far left. PHOTO COURTESY OF FUZZY LEVANE and NBA. That first year in the NBL, Les put together a great team that won the title. We had old pro Al Cervi, a great athlete named Otto Graham, Bob Davies from Seton Hall, George Glamack from North Carolina, John Mahnken from Georgetown, Red and Dutch. Dutch was great against teams from the Midwest. He would look away and then thread the needle with a blind pass. Against Easterners who were used to the give-and-go and passers hitting the cutters, it wouldn't always work.

Another guy on that team was Chuck Connors. We all knew he was gonna be an actor. He'd come into bars and give eloquent recitals of *Casey at the Bat* and *The Face on the Barroom Floor.* The best thing that ever happened to Chuck was when he was playing baseball for the Cubs organization, they farmed him out to Los Angeles. And the rest is Hollywood history.

Ed Malanowicz, the assistant coach at Rochester, did the real coaching. During timeouts Les would shut up and the players would do the talking. But after games, Les supplied the hot pastrami, corned beef and beers that we loaded on our Pullman cars as we traveled to the next game, with poker games and sometimes craps games going on the train.

I was making a thousand a month and thought I was a millionaire. In Rochester we played at the Edgerton Arena and in Syracuse at an armory, but in Sheboygan and Oshkosh we played in high school gyms. The gym in Fort Wayne we called "Tub of Blood," where the stands came right down over the floor. I remember one time there, coming out after halftime, some lady leaned down and beat Les Harrison over the head with her pocketbook.

The fans were vociferous throughout the league, and it was always rough to win on the opposing floor. I remember some of the officials back then, Pat Kennedy, Chuck Solodare, Lou Eisenstein. We played the same game in the NBL and the BAA. When the four NBL clubs, Rochester, Minneapolis, Fort Wayne and Indianapolis, came over in 1948, it gave the BAA a real shot in the arm and paved the way for the merger the following year into the NBA.

Les cared about a player's talent and not the color of his skin. I give him credit because in '46-47 he hired both Dolly King who had played at LIU and Pop Gates from the Rens. I can't recall any racist attitudes among basketball players, though we had some Southerners in the league. The only racial incident I remember was when we were refused service at a restaurant in Fort Wayne. The whole team walked out and we went back to the hotel to eat.

The scandal shocked the hell out of me. Reading the New York papers in Rochester, I was reading between the lines and putting the whole story together. Of course, you had to be an idiot to play in Madison Square Garden and not know about the betting, with the point spreads in all the papers, and people yelling about scoring and not scoring at the end of games. But I never dreamt that any players were involved.

Left: Fuzzy close to Al Cervi and Buddy Jeannette wrestling for possession. All three were aggressive as players and coaches in the league. PHOTO COURTESY OF FUZZY LEVANE

Right: Integration came naturally to the NBA. Here Fuzzy watches "Blind Bomber" George Glamack of Rochester, World Champions in 1946 and again in 1951, shoot over the Rens, World Champions in 1939, here with stars Dolly King (left) and Puggy Bell.

PHOTO COURTESY OF FUZZY LEVANE

Jack Molinas was a great talent, by the way. But later on, after he was banned and tried to sue, he subpoenaed me. I was named because I had refused to allow a team that had some NBA players on it play an exhibition game against a team of his. Like Podoloff, I was protecting the league and its players, and the court agreed that was the reasonable thing to do.

I had had some health problems in Rochester, and they didn't even know what it was until I had intestinal surgery. But when Syracuse came into the NBA in 1949, I was ready to go over there to play for Al Cervi. Dolph Schayes was our big scorer, and we went to the finals against the Lakers.

The next year I took over as player-coach at Elmira in the Eastern League. We played an exhibition game against the Milwaukee Hawks and beat them. Ben Kerner must have remembered that, because when he fired Doxie Moore as coach, he hired me. So I was back in the NBA for the '52-53 season. Our best two players were Mel Hutchins and Jack Nichols. Kerner proceeded to sell Hutchins to Fort Wayne for $25,000 and Nichols to Boston for $15,000. Then, before the next season ended, he fired me, for my own good, he said. "This team is getting you down," he said. And I was replaced by Red Holzman – once again I had brought Red in to play with my team.

Early in my first season in Milwaukee, I had traded Ed Miller, who was 6 feet 11 inches and had two left feet, to Baltimore for Davage Minor and George Ratkovicz. I had played with George at Syracuse. But I had played against Dave in the '43 NIT finals in Madison Square Garden. He was the Oscar Robertson of his day and had taken Toledo a long way. Joe Lapchick had told me, "You're playing Minor," and I held him to triple goose eggs. Tim Cohane wrote the next day that it was the greatest defense since Carl Hubbell struck out Ruth, Gehrig, Cronin, Foxx and Simmons in a row in the All-Star Game.

We were playing a doubleheader in Fort Wayne, the Knicks against the Hawks and the Celtics against the Pistons. I was sitting with Auerbach and Lapchick when Minor joined the club. He sees me and says, "Nine years ago you stuck to me like glue."

Lapchick said, "He was your boss then and he's your boss now."

Joe Lapchick was a great motivator and the game's best ambassador, the way he could talk about basketball. Among coaches I'd single out Clair Bee as one who was great in the gym and great on the floor.

Obviously I thought highly of Red Holzman as a coach. He succeeded me as coach of the Hawks in Milwaukee and was their first coach in Atlanta. Then I hired him again when I was with the Knicks. When he won the NBA title in 1970, he was blessed with five of the most intelligent offensive players I ever saw – Frazier, Barnett, Bradley, DeBusschere and Reed. So what was Red's contribution? He concentrated on defense.

In 1955, I was officially out of basketball, working for Schlitz, and I'm grateful to them for bringing me back to Brooklyn. But at the same time I was acting as an unofficial scout for Les Harrison at the Garden. At draft time, Les and Bobby Wanzer, who was taking over as coach, were in love with Ed Fleming at Niagara. It wasn't hard to persuade them to take Maurice Stokes on the first round, but on the second round I had to work hard to get them to take Jack Twyman. Fleming was still there for them in the third round, but Twyman would have been long gone.

Now, the next year, Vinnie Boryla is coaching the Knicks and we try to make a deal with Rochester for the No. 1 pick. For Walter Dukes and $15,000 they would draft Bill Russell for us. When Boryla went to Ned Irish to approve the deal that would have brought Russell to the Knicks, he said, "Dukes, OK, but $15,000? Tell them to shove it." The Royals ended up with Sihugo Green, and the Hawks, picking second, dealt Russell to Boston for Ed Macauley and Cliff Hagan.

Two years later, I knew I was going to take over from Boryla. I went to California to see Elgin Baylor and his coach at Seattle, John Castellani. Elgin didn't want to go to Minneapolis, which had the first choice. He wanted to come to New York, and we'd be drafting third. He had another year of eligibility left, and I told him, "Tell the papers you're gonna go back to school." That way, Bob Short, who wanted Baylor, wouldn't take a chance on wasting the draft choice.

Cincinnati, the old Rochester franchise, had the second choice, so hoping the strategy would work with Short, we offered them Guy Sparrow and we'd flip choices. Bobby Wanzer agreed, and at 5:30 the next morning Wanzer calls me to verify that we had that deal. Short, of course, took Baylor anyway. Now, imagine the Knicks with Baylor and Russell during those years when the Celtics were winning all those titles.

At St. Louis, when I coached the Hawks in '61-62, I had Lenny Wilkens, who was in the service and could only play weekends. So I had a front line of Pettit, Hagan and Lovellette, and no one to get them the ball. But imagine if they hadn't made the deal for Russell, imagine the Hawks with Russell and Pettit up front for 10 years. Who would ever get a rebound against them?

Basketball is a reaction game. Today's players don't seem to know how to adjust. How can a Danny Ferry get loose to hit seven threes in a quarter? They're great athletes but they don't know how to play the game. The nuances of getting free without the ball have been lost, and too many of them are fundamentally unsound.

Fuzzy Levane played for Rochester, Syracuse and Milwaukee between 1945 and 1953. As coach of the Hawks and the Knicks he has 106 NBA wins. He remains in the game as a scout for the Knicks.

Red Holzman

I grew up in Brooklyn not too far from the Arcadia Hall, where the New York Jewels played, so I knew all about pro basketball as soon as I started playing. I was familiar with the SPHAs, the Visitations, the Rosenblums and the Rens, and I always wanted to be a professional player.

After finishing up at CCNY I went into the Navy and then got my break when my friend Fuzzy Levane was hired to play for Les Harrison's new NBL franchise in Rochester. Les thought Fuzzy was Jewish, and when he found out he wasn't he asked him to get him a Jewish player. If Fuzzy's name had been Levine instead of Levane, I wouldn't be in the history books.

Les was a shrewd guy who knew horseflesh. He was one of the first to bring black players in when he hired both Dolly King from LIU and Pop Gates from the Rens, and Fuzzy and I roomed and ate with Dolly on the road. Les understood the game of basketball, and he was smart enough to take suggestions, both as a coach and as an owner. For example, when we played Toledo, we always had trouble playing against Frannie Curran, a great defensive player. We told Les to get Curran, and he did.

Right from the start, the Royals rivaled the Minneapolis Lakers as the best team in basketball. Our center was Arnie Risen, who I think was second only to George Mikan. But our strength was the backcourt, where I joined Al Cervi, while Bob Davies, who was taller, was a swingman. All three of us were often on the court, and we played essentially a three-guard offense. Later Bobby Wanzer joined us, taking Cervi's place.

Maurice Podoloff was a very shrewd, smart man, the right man for the job at the time. When he brought the Royals and the Lakers, along with the Fort Wayne Pistons and the Indianapolis Jets, into the BAA for the '48-49 season, he put Minneapolis and Rochester in the same division. That way, only one of the former NBL teams would be in the playoff finals. It wasn't until '57 that the NBA championship

Red Holzman at the center of Rochester's action versus Oshkosh (from left, Bob Feerick, Bob Davies, Ed Riska, Red, Fuzzy Levane, Bob Wager, Fred Carpenter and Otto Graham — before he quarterbacked the Cleveland Browns. PHOTO COURTESY OF FUZZY LEVANE

was won by a team that hadn't started out in the NBL, either the Lakers, the Royals, or, once, the Syracuse Nationals.

The BAA game was a bit more wide open than the NBL game, but otherwise it was pretty much the same. The officiating was good, but it was tough being on the road. At home the familiar surroundings and doing things right to get prepared for a game were part of the advantage. We didn't lose that many games in Rochester. The fans were great there, always behind us, and the arena was always packed. It was also a lot of fun to play in the small towns on the road, like Oshkosh, Waterloo, Moline, Anderson, Sheboygan and Fort Wayne.

We liked to control the ball, especially at the end of a game. Eventually, of course, we had to adjust to the 24-second clock. In 1951 we played in the game that had a lot to do with bringing on that rule. It was the longest NBA game in history, six overtimes. And the reason that it went that long was that whoever got the ball at the start of an overtime period held it for five minutes before taking the last shot. It was usually us, and I held the ball while the fans booed the shit out of us. Finally we lost 75-73. Here's a side note. Those stats weren't kept then, but I played 75 of the 78 minutes, the most minutes ever played in a single NBA game.

Prior to the 1951-52 season, we had been touring with the Indianapolis Olympians, and we kept noticing people in the crowd that didn't seem to belong. We had won the championship, so we were on our way to Chicago to play the college all-stars and the Indianapolis team came along to see the game. And that was where they arrested Beard and Groza. They were both great players. We all felt bad because that hurt a lot of ballplayers.

For the '53-54 season I was reunited with Fuzzy who was coaching the Hawks in Milwaukee and brought me over after I had spent eight seasons with Rochester. Before the season was over, Ben Kerner was ready to fire Fuzzy and he asked me to take his place. I had never thought about coaching, but I guess I was the most expendable member of the squad. Kerner saw that I was reluctant to do it, but he said, "If you don't take it, you won't save Fuzzy's job anyway."

The next year, Bob Pettit came to the Hawks. He had some trouble as a rookie, but he built himself up. By the time we moved to St. Louis the following season, he was already the franchise. I can't say enough about him. Pettit was a great person and a great competitor, one of the great players of all time.

Over the years, the most significant change was that it got to the point that the offensive players were so great that they couldn't be stopped one on one. But the main things were always the same. Long before I coached the Knicks in their championship years, when I was just starting out as a player, we – coaches and players – were always talking about team basketball, about passing the ball, hitting the open man and helping out on defense.

The highlight of my playing career came in the playoffs in '51, when the Royals won the NBA title. In '49 we had finished ahead of Minneapolis in our division, but they beat us in the playoffs. In '50 we had tied in the division and they beat us in the playoffs again. Now in '51 they had finished three games ahead of us though we split our games with them. They had the first two games at home and won the first.

Now for the second game, Les announces that Holzman is gonna start, and he wants me to control the game. The idea was for me to handle the ball and set up the scorers. I was 31 years old, and I was a sensation in that game. Are you kidding? Instead of feeding the others, I got hot and made 10 of 13 shots, plus three-for-three free throws, and then I held the ball at the end of the game and we won by four.

We went on to win two at home and assumed we would win the finals against the Knicks. We swept the first three games, but we must have been overconfident because we lost the next three. The seventh game, at home, was close, too, but we held on and were NBA champs. The only game I started was that second game at Minneapolis, but that was the game that turned it all around.

Red Holzman won titles as a player in the NBL and the NBA, and as a coach with the 1970 and 1973 New York Knickerbockers. With almost 700 wins as an NBA coach, he was enshrined in the Basketball Hall of Fame in 1985. He remains as basketball consultant for the Knicks.

John Ezersky

In the encyclopedias, on the programs, in the press guides, I'd be listed as coming from St. John's or Notre Dame or Rhode Island, but the fact is I never went to college. Everybody knew it. Once, when I was playing in some barnstorming games against the Rens, Pop Gates said to me, "Hey, John, what school you from in Pittsburgh tonight?"

The way it happened was this. I lost my eligibility while I was still in high school at Power Memorial, in '39 or '40. Even as a freshman I was accused of being a ringer. I was the youngest on the team but I always looked older. A couple of my buddies also played on a team called the Americans sponsored by a sporting goods house. The owner, Victor Till, was the coach, and they had these beautiful uniforms. They played their games at the Audubon Ballroom, the same place where Malcolm X was killed. They all wanted me to play, too, but for a long time I wouldn't do it. But I fell in love with that uniform and finally joined them when they were going over to Jersey for some Catholic tournament.

There were three of us from Power on the team and one guy from Fordham, and it happened that I was having a good game. But every time I scored, the announcer said "basket by Dirkey." I went over to the coach and said, "What's going on? Everyone else has his right name," and he said he'd take care of it. But in the paper next day the box score said "Dirkey." Next thing I know, at school, I was called into the Brother's office and told that I was ineligible for amateur competition, that the AAU wouldn't accept any explanation, and that they believed I had been paid to play for the Americans. That was the end of it, and that's the truth.

I grew up poor in Washington Heights. I don't know how my father and mother got the five of us kids through the Depression, but they did. It was Father Forrester, over at Good Shepherd in Inwood, who saw some talent and helped me get a scholarship at Power. We won the first Catholic High School championship in the city, beating St. John's in the final.

Easy John Ezersky. PHOTO COURTESY OF JOHN EZERSKY

Vintage NBA: The Pioneer Era

Brother Loftus was the coach. We played pretty much the way everyone did in those days, lots of pick-and-rolls to free people for set shots. Hank Luisetti changed the game with his one-handed shooting, but we weren't supposed to be doing that. When the coach wasn't around, I'd shoot one-handed, and someone told the coach about it. "I want to see it," he said, and when I showed him, he told me that's the way he wanted me shooting from then on. Some people called me "the Hank Luisetti of the East."

Baseball was the big thing where I grew up. Lou Gehrig lived around the corner, and Buddy Kerr, who took me along on a barnstorming team. I was offered a contract by the Tigers at one time, but when I got to camp I found out how good those guys were. Basketball was the game for me.

I played in the Catskills one summer, at the Morningside, before I was drafted in '42, and then after World War II played for the Laurels. I remember playing against Dolph Schayes in '46. Honey Russell took an interest in me. He was the coach at Manhattan College then, and he tried to get the AAU to reopen my case. He hoped to get me into LaSalle Academy and then come to play for him at Manhattan, but no matter how hard he tried, he couldn't get them to reconsider.

I was just starting out with the New York Gothams in '46 when we played against the Rochester Royals and I had to guard a real character, Chuck Connors. I was actually a little scared, covering Connors, who was a big guy with a bigger reputation. So here he is bouncing the ball at midcourt, just banging it with a high bounce. But he says, "I'm not trying to make a fool of you, not trying to show you up, I just don't want to give this ball up to these guys," meaning his own teammates. He was amazing though, an actor even then, the way he'd sit around bars and recite poems.

One writer I knew and liked was Dick Young. Later on I'd see him at the track a lot, and I'd always remind him of the time in '46 when the Knicks needed to get another player for their roster, and he wrote a column advising them to take Frank Mangiapane from NYU. I was the leading scorer for the Gothams at the time. They took Mangiapane, who never made it, averaged less than a point a game for a few games, but I went on to a pretty good career in what we called the majors, the old National League and the new American, the BAA, that became the NBA.

There wasn't all that much difference between the leagues back then. In '51, when I played for Wilkes-Barre in the Eastern League and led the league in scoring, we played exhibitions with Syracuse and beat them, Rochester and beat them, Philadelphia with Joe Fulks and beat them, too. We all played pretty much the same style, but I really think the toughest players came from the old NBL out West.

I started out in that league with the Tri-City Blackhawks. Training with them in Moline, all we were paid was meal money. We were so broke that all the players had to chip in for one of us to get bus fare to go over to the club office to collect our meal money. Whitey Von Nieda played with us for Tri-Cities. When he opened a restaurant in Moline, players could always get a meal there and put it on the tab, because he knew how little money we all had.

The travel was bad. It was hard to sleep on the road, most of the beds in the hotels were too small for us. I used to be one of the best dressed players. When one of them had a date on the road and needed to wear a tie, they'd always say, "Go see John, John has ties."

From Tri-Cities I went over to Providence and then Boston and Baltimore and back to Boston in the NBA. Doggie Julian had taken over as coach for the great Honey Russell, and he was a very strange man. He would sit on the bench and when he wanted to send in a substitute he'd call him over to sit next to him on the bench. And then he'd forget and call someone else over. One time in 1950 when I was with the Celtics, we were getting our fanny kicked by Rochester, and he called Big Ed Leede over to sit next to him before sending him in. A lot of Leede's friends – he was from Dartmouth – were sitting behind us and cheering for him to go in. Then Doggie forgot and called someone else over, so Leede slid over on the bench. One of his friends yelled, "Ed, what's wrong?" Leede stood up, turned around, and said, "Many are called, but few are chosen."

The coaches controlled everything back then. Buddy Jeannette at Baltimore was a good one. Ken Loeffler at Providence was one of the greatest coaches, but a nasty man. Even on the road, if we all went into the same restaurant, he'd sit by himself and not talk to us. With Boston, Doggie used to yell at us, "If you don't start winning you'll all become truck drivers." I guess I moved up in class when I became a cabdriver.

I started driving in the off-season in 1950, full time when I quit the Eastern League. Drove in New York for 30 years, now in San Francisco for the last 15. Howard Cosell flagged me down once on Central Park West near the ABC studios. He opened the door, looked at me, and without batting an eye, said, "John Ezersky, how have you been?" Another time, I was in Chicago, and there was Sweetwater Clifton driving a cab. He said to me, "John, we're both gonna die behind the wheel of a cab," but he said it smiling.

Some of the characters: Stan Stutz Modzelewski – I played with him in Baltimore – was a wild man from Borneo. His uncle managed some burlesque houses, and he'd wake me up early and say, "Let's go down there," because he could get us in free. Later, when he started reffing, and I yelled about something, he called a tech on me. I couldn't believe it, my old roomie. Of course, we went out after the game, and I asked him how he could do that. He just laughed and said, "I had to do it." Other refs I remember were Chuck Solodare, a good one, and Sid Borgia, a beautiful man and a beautiful referee.

With Boston in 1950 I was rooming with Sonny Hertzberg on the road in Philadelphia. Some people in the next room were having a good time, the usual hotel sounds, and we were playing cards. And we're yelling at each other with every deal, stuff like, "I'll kill you this time" and "I'm gonna kill you now." Then there's a knock on the door, and the hotel manager comes in. The people next door had called him because they were afraid a murder was taking place. Sonny and I both liked the horses. We'd buy the paper and handicap the races and bet a dollar a race, his horse against mine.

Everyone was aware that there was a lot of betting on basketball. But there weren't any fixes. You couldn't fix the pros, because if anyone wasn't playing hard and up to par, the coach would pull him and someone else would be just as good.

One time, I was working in the mountains with my friend Norman Goldman, a ballplayer from Brooklyn who was tending bar – he was engaged to the owner's niece. And he introduced me to his friend Eli Kronowitz, later Eli Kaye. Later, during the winter, I get a call from Normie and Eli. "Hey, we're going to Florida, come on with us, bring your friend, it's on us." I said, "Okay, but I'll pay my own way and my friend's." So they pick us up, and we pile into a Cadillac with Normie, Eli and a guy I only knew as "Mosie the bookmaker." We had a nice vacation, and I had pretty much stopped thinking about it when the scandal broke, and who turns up as one of the master fixers but Eli Kaye. It's always a good idea to pay your own way.

Another time, a friend of a friend in Baltimore wanted to make a connection in New York for some betting action and so I passed along a name of someone I knew, just as a friendly introduction. And that's the last I heard or thought about it. Then one day, I'm sitting on the bench before the start of a game in Baltimore, and here comes a Western Union messenger up to me and hands me a telegram. I thought someone had died, but it was from this bookie in New York asking what I could do about my friend in Baltimore who wasn't paying off his losses. Buddy Jeannette saw me turn all pale and asked me what was wrong. I mumbled some excuse and stuffed the telegram down into my shorts until I got a chance to burn it.

Some of the college dumpers later played in the Eastern League, but I was out of it by then. One was Sherman White from LIU, one of the greatest players I saw. He was never convicted but I wouldn't have gotten on the same court with him. He was so arrogant, he said, "If the opportunity came, I'd have done it again."

I didn't try to keep up my basketball contacts, but once in a while I'd bump into someone or other. One time I parked the cab and came into the Garden for a Knicks game and got a seat in the mezzanine behind the announcers. John (Bud) Palmer was doing the radio broadcast and he saw me and tried to get me to come down for an interview. I wouldn't, and when he asked why not, I told him I wasn't dressed for a radio interview.

I don't remember whether Dick McGuire was still playing then, but Dick was a great guy, a great player and then coach – unlike his brother. I got him a couple of times after I had retired from the game. Once was at Roosevelt Raceway – we all loved the ponies – when I came up behind him and shouted, "Get your feet off the seat!" He wheeled around and then broke up when he saw who it was.

The other time was even better. I got married for the first time when I was 35 – not that I didn't like the ladies. I married Princess Yasmin, a great belly-dancer from Algeria. It lasted three years – she had a drinking problem – but it was a pretty wild three years. Anyway, she was performing in Detroit and I traveled with her and decided to go to see a Pistons game when Dick was coaching them. I asked for a seat right behind the Detroit bench, and I started getting on Dick right away. I yelled McGuire this and McGuire that. Why don't you... and why the hell didn't you... and I was getting worse and worse. Finally he turned around, looking like he was gonna come after someone in the crowd, but broke up when he saw who it was.

I defend the players of today. We had no option, no free agency. They sent you a contract and it was take it or leave it. My second year in Boston they sent me the same contract as the first year. I sent it back unsigned, and I didn't hear a word from them. When I called, I was told they assumed I didn't want to play.

The game hasn't changed that much. For a long time I didn't follow it much, but I got back into it with this year's playoffs, a great show. As far as playing above the rim is concerned, you'd never dream of doing that. You'd do it once, dunk over someone, and if you tried to do it again they'd let you have it. They get three points now but the shooters were just as good then, like George Yardley and Paul Arizin. Marty Glickman used to call me one of the best three-point shooters, but that was the hard way, scoring while being fouled, and I got banged up a lot doing it.

John Ezersky, a three-year NBA veteran (1940) but not covered under the pension plan, continues at 74 to drive a cab full-time in San Francisco. He played with Baltimore, Boston and Providence. In '48, after switching leagues from the NBL Blackhawks, he nearly matched Ernie Calverley and Kenny Sailors point for point for the Steamrollers.

John Payak Jr.

I played ball in Toledo with Paul Seymour and Bob Harrison – three high school teammates who played in the pros. Bob went to Michigan, played in Minneapolis, and ended up in Syracuse. Paul never did go to college, got started early with Sid Goldberg's pro team in Toledo. He went through the so-called chairs, got hooked up pretty good with Syracuse and got to be player-coach when Bob was there. And I went to Bowling Green, played there and in the service, back to Bowling Green, and then the Philadelphia Warriors, the Waterloo Hawks, the Toledo Mercuries and the Milwaukee Hawks.

Back in those days, and it's still true even now, it's a question of getting hooked up with a club where you have good chemistry, not only with the coach but the other players. Paul and I have talked about taking all the rejects from the NBA and you could probably have a near-championship team with them, a question of being at the right place at the right time with the right chemistry.

The game was easier in those days. I look at films and focus on the post play, and there's space between players. There was more of a finesse aspect to the game. It's gone now, and they'll never get it back. It's a muscle game, players are recruited for strength, and it's the same way in college.

When I was in college, even going back to high school, we never thought about officials. They didn't often enter into the game then the way they do now, probably because of the kind of activity involved. It wasn't body to body, pressure defense as such. It was fairly clean-cut then. Now there are many gray areas because so much is going on.

I really don't remember officials, except for one funny incident. Another Toledo connection was Chuck Chuckovits. He was originally from Akron, but was an All-American at the University of Toledo back in the '30s, lived in Toledo, and was working as an official in the NBA. When I was playing at Milwaukee, Chuck had a game there, and of course I knew him well, so I thought I would have a free ride, a gravy train. That son of a gun fouled me out in the first half. I think he overreacted because he didn't want to show any partiality.

At 6 feet 4 inches at that stage of the basketball game, I was a big guard, which was what I played in college. Coach Harold Anderson made me a guard at Bowling Green. We had Don Otten to begin with, our seven-footer, and then after I came back from the service, we had Charlie Share, another seven-footer, Stan Weber at 6-7 and Mack Otten at 6-7. I was 6-4, and then Leo Kubiak who was 5-11 or 6-0. We had a big club. Anderson was a great recruiter. He'd get 200 guys so no one else would get them. Vern Gardner from Utah, who played with me in Philadelphia, asked me once, "How did you guys ever lose with the talent you had?"

We ran a lot and played a power game, which was the Midwestern style. Eastern ball was always more of a finesse game. They'd give-and-go and set screens. I don't think I even knew what a screen was until I played with Philadelphia. I was drafted by Eddie Gottlieb, the Philadelphia owner and coach. Joe Fulks was still there; he was on his way out but could still shoot the ball. Mike Novak had come over from Rochester. He was near the end, too, and so was Big Ed Sadowski. Gottlieb didn't really have much to do with the players, but one time he asked Sadowski what was wrong with the team. Big Ed didn't pull any punches. He said, "You're the goddamn coach; figure it out for yourself."

We usually took trains in those days, and it was generally uneventful, but sometimes we flew. I remember once we were flying with the Lakers into Minneapolis to play them. I was sitting with Mike Novak, playing gin, when the plane hit an air pocket and dropped 500 feet. Everything flew away and everyone was thrown – I thought it would kill George Mikan.

After half a year, I was traded to Waterloo, Iowa, where I played that year plus the next year. I was probably disappointed because I didn't succeed as far as I was concerned at Philadelphia, but then I was happy to get a reprieve, so to speak, at Waterloo, where I played well, got to play more, started and scored well, along with Dick Mehen, Harry Boykoff and Leo Kubiak from Bowling Green. It was a good setup, a town of about 110,000, with Rath Packing and John Deere. We had a nice place to play, called the Hippodrome, that seated seven to eight thousand people. It was all the people had to do, and we probably drew as well as any team in the NBA at that time. We had it made at that time. People loved us in Waterloo.

But it was hard to get to. You had to fly to Cedar Rapids, about 80 miles away, then come the rest of the way by car. I found out I had a sinus problem there and had to wear a hat all the time. It would get to 30 below. My new Buick wouldn't start when I had to drive to practice in Cedar Falls. I remember driving through snowdrifts from Waterloo to a game at Tri-Cities. We almost didn't make it.

In those days, in most places, like Sheboygan and Anderson, you played in high school gyms. The Brannum twins played at Sheboygan. One time I was dribbling up the court in that high school gym and I went ass over elbows. I looked up and some woman, had to be 80 years old, had tripped me with her umbrella. Stuck the damn umbrella between my legs.

Jack Smiley was our coach and Blackie Towery played with us in Waterloo. He was a guy who would say what he felt like and when he felt like it. Once we were playing Boston in Hartford, Connecticut, and there must have been 200 people in the stands and everything reverberated. Now Smiley had been one of the Whiz Kids at Illinois but I didn't think he was much of a player any more. But toward the end of the game he'd put himself in. He had the two-hand set and he'd throw it up 50 feet in the air.

That night he throws one up and Blackie jumps up and yells, "Fore!" Everybody laughed. Well, that night a lot of us went out after the game and had a couple of drinks. We had a curfew, midnight, but we were only about five minutes late. Smiley was waiting for us and he suspended Towery for a week, not the rest of us. It was not about curfew but about yelling "Fore!" on his shot.

We were shocked by the scandal. Of course we were well aware that there was a lot of betting on basketball games in college. Bowling Green would play during the season at Madison Square Garden and Boston Garden, against LIU with Sherman White and Holy Cross with Cousy and that bunch. We broke the Garden record, even for the pros, Bowling Green did. Scored 98 points and thought we were God's gift to whatever and came back to Bowling Green to be greeted by a crowd of students. Two years later we found out they had thrown the game.

In the NIT we played Bradley, with Unruh and Melchiorre. We were favored to win, which we did, but learned later that the fix was in and a substitute for them had screwed up by beating the point spread. I'm reasonably certain none of our players was involved. After early upsets we were favored to win that tournament. In the semis we played San Francisco with Don Lofgran. Coach Anderson was worried, and that day, instead of giving us free rein to play cards or go to a movie, he made us stay in our rooms, had our trainer give everyone a rubdown. (We never had trainers on the road in the pros, you know.)

We had been averaging around 80 points a game. We ran pretty good. Well, San Francisco beat us by 10 and I don't think we scored 40 points. Charlie Share had 20, I had seven or eight, and that was the ballgame. We couldn't throw it in the ocean. Now, in retrospect, if any game was suspicious, that was it, but to my knowledge nobody on Bowling Green was even approached.

There was only one time I know of that we came in direct contact with the gambling. We always stayed at the Paramount Hotel in New York, on 44th or 45th between 7th and Broadway — the teams would just walk over to the Garden. One time we were waiting to play, waiting for Anderson to come down, sitting in front of the elevator. There was a fellow talking to us — I didn't even pay attention to who it was. Anderson gets off the elevator and sees this guy and he turns beet red and tears into him and — obviously swearing at him — tells him to get out. Apparently he was a gambler, would come in, nicey-nicey, find out if anyone was hurt. I'll never forget Anderson's face when he saw him.

After Waterloo folded, I played for a year for Sid Goldberg, a great mind who had a team, the Toledo Mercuries, that traveled with the Harlem Globetrotters. I ran the club for Sid. I made more money that year with the driving plus the per game plus the per diem than I made any of my three years in the NBA. In fact I wanted to do it again, but my wife said no because we left in October, came home for Christmas Eve, left Christmas Day, and got home in April. My mother cried when she saw me, 6-4 and I think I weighed 140 pounds.

The Globetrotters helped the NBA. We used to play doubleheaders with them. People would come to see the Globetrotters; they wouldn't come out to see us. The crowds thought they were the world's greatest and were filled with enthusiasm. They didn't have much enthusiasm or involvement with the pros, though Milwaukee wasn't too bad and Waterloo, the exception, was good. The Globetrotters couldn't really compete with the NBA teams; at best they'd be respectable. They were a show team, but they could draw 13-14,000 people.

That year I played with Toledo against the Globetrotters we had a pretty good ballclub. We had Stan Weber and myself from Bowling Green, Ed Dollar who had been All-American at Duquesne, and Cal Christensen, George Lindemann and George Bush from Toledo. We always went along with the show, like someone would chase Marques Haynes while he did his dribbling act. Then one night in Pittsburgh we damn near beat them – in fact, they didn't put the show on, but were all out to beat us.

Now Abe Saperstein never came to the small towns. We played 180 games in six months. He'd come to L.A. where we'd play for a week and New York for a week of games. Abe's brother Maury would be in charge. After the game I went to Maury and said, "I heard if we beat 'em, you were gonna send us home." He didn't care much for them. He just said, "Go ahead and beat the niggers."

Two weeks later we were up in Minneapolis, and that night everything we did was right. And we did beat them. People in the stands, late in the game, were yelling, "If you let them beat you now, we're gonna tar and feather you and run you out of town." Yet I never heard any racial remarks among the players, either on that tour or in the NBA. In Milwaukee, Dave Minor was my teammate – he was funnier than hell, and we had no racial problem on that team.

Abe Saperstein thought he had the best team in the world. They were good players but they weren't that good. They were nice guys. We didn't exactly live with them, but nearly did. After all, we played two games a day with them. Goose Tatum was not too congenial, a loner who didn't hang out with his teammates. Once, before a game, I got to the arena early and was about to walk past him because I didn't want to be snubbed. Instead I was taken aback when he stopped me and drew me into a friendly conversation for about 10 minutes. I had never seen that side of him before.

The next year I was back in the NBA. I was signed by Ben Kerner for the Milwaukee Hawks, the Atlanta franchise now after passing through St. Louis. Fuzzy Levane was our coach. Playing for Ben Kerner in Milwaukee was like passing through swinging doors. He'd bring a guy in for one or two games and then release him. We had Jack Nichols and Mel Hutchins, but the team didn't do well. I always liked Jack Nichols, though he didn't mix too much; later became a dentist I heard.

Mel Hutchins used to drive Mikan nuts. He was about 6-6 but could jump. He would watch Mikan, would wait and time his jump. Mikan didn't have that good of a hook shot. He would kind of turn and shoot but not high in the air. Mel would time it and just knock the ball away, and Mikan would get so damn mad at him he would want to kill him. I enjoyed Mel. There was a little bar in Milwaukee we'd go to, not for any aggressive drinking, but to sit around and b.s. On the road he was my roommate sometimes, but roommates were not regular, were catch as catch can.

I used to watch Bob Davies, but the most difficult for me to watch, the one that stands out in my mind, was Bill Sharman. He never stopped running, that's why he was such a good player. He was perpetual motion. I used to tell him, "I'm getting tired, stop running."

That year was my best year but it was my last. It was something you wanted to do your whole life, you know, play pro ball, and then it kind of wore thin. When I came home from Milwaukee I said that was it. There wasn't much money, you were gone half a year, worked menial jobs the other half, and never got anything established. My best year was 6,000 bucks. I think Mikan made 12 and he was voted the best player of the half century. Pro basketball was still in its infancy, a crawling-before-you-walk type syndrome. I don't know how anybody made any money, don't know whether they did in fact. So it got to the point where I thought, "I don't need it anymore." For 40 years now, we've had a general agency insurance business.

I'm still a fan, but I don't much care for the pro game. My allegiance as a spectator is for the college game. I refereed in colleges for 15, 16 years – Mid-America Conference, Big Ten, some NCAA Tournaments – and after I quit officiating was Basketball Supervisor for the Mid-America Conference. Of course I'm amazed at the talent in the NBA today, but I think something's been taken away from the game, from true basketball, by the emphasis on muscle, brute force, the physical aspect.

John Payak played with Philadelphia, Waterloo and Milwaukee between 1949 and 1953, passing off to the likes of Joe Fulks, Dick Mehen, Harry Boykoff and Jack Nichols. He has been an official and supervisor in college basketball over the years while maintaining a general insurance agency in Toledo for 40 years.

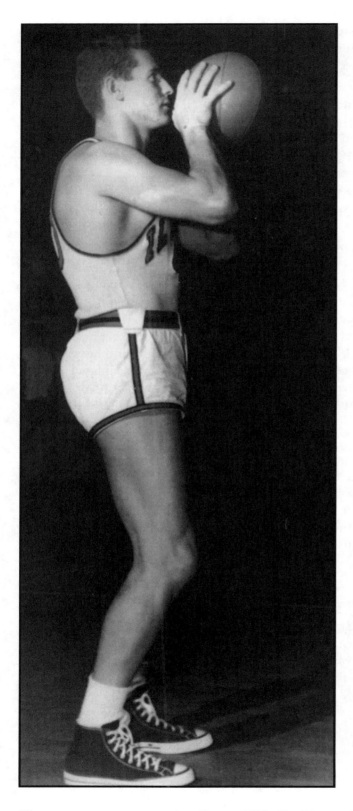

Dike Eddleman with his famous "kiss shot." PHOTO COURTESY OF DIKE EDDLEMAN

Vintage NBA: The Pioneer Era

Dike Eddleman

I grew up in basketball country, Centralia, Illinois, about 60 miles due east of St. Louis. One year in high school, we played 48 games.

I enjoyed my career in pro ball, but I retired after just four years. I was about 30 years old at the time, after 3½ years in the service and college. I had a family, and I felt like I was into the rope. Besides, I had been dealt to Baltimore and I didn't want to go way out east to play.

Service ball was rougher than college ball; there were more picks. In college, though, I also played football. I'd only have a week after the football season to practice for basketball, but football helped me in pro basketball. I learned to withstand contact.

In Miami, Chuck Taylor was the coach of that service team. He claimed to be one of original Celtics. We had a great team, with Bruce Hale (Rick Barry's father-in-law) and Big Ed Sadowski. What a character he was. Jimmy Doolittle's wife was involved. It was all for fund-raising for the Army Air Corps. We flew all over and played anyone, anywhere. We played the Globetrotters, we played in Fargo, North Dakota – the coldest place I've ever been – and we played a 20th Century-Fox team in Hollywood. Lucille Ball was on the second team. I had never met a movie star before, and it was all a lot of fun.

Back at Illinois, Harry Combes had taken over as coach from Doug Mills. Then in the pros we ran through a lot of coaches. In my two years at Tri-Cities, there was Roger Potter, who had retired from Moline High School, and then Red Auerbach finished the season on his stopover between Washington and Boston. The next year we started with Dave McMillan, who had retired from the University of Minnesota, and finished the season with a couple of player-coaches, John Logan and Marko Todorovich. The next year, when the franchise moved to Milwaukee, Doxie Moore was my coach until I was dealt over to Fort Wayne where Murray Mendenhall was the coach. My last year there, it was Paul Birch.

There was a bunch of great players in the league when I started, like Red Holzman and Al Cervi. Bob Cousy was the toughest I had to guard. He could handle the ball, he had the great peripheral vision and could see everyone on the floor. He was pretty doggone tough, and Bob Davies was, too.

We had a good team at Tri-Cities in '49-50 and got off to a great start, eight or nine in row. We had Gene Vance, Johnny Logan, Andy Phillip and Jack Nichols. Then Vance, Logan and Nichols, who were all in the reserves, got called back into service. It was the time of the Korean War. It was a struggle after that, but we made the playoffs. Anderson had a good team and beat us two out of three.

You know, the playoffs didn't have much hoopla back then. They didn't get much publicity. Anyway, Anderson lost to the Lakers. I don't think I was ever on a team that beat the Lakers. George Mikan controlled the whole game. They seemed to let him do things they never let other players do.

The Warren Field House in Moline was a nice place to play, but it didn't hold enough people, and I think that's why the franchise moved to Milwaukee. In Fort Wayne at first we played at the Northside High School, then in the Coliseum. One good thing in Fort Wayne was that the Zollner Pistons were the first club to fly in their own plane. That was a great relief from the trains, where big guys had to sit up all night in smoking cars because they were too big to fit in the sleepers.

We had a good club there with Mel Hutchins and George Yardley. Freddie Schaus was my roommate, a great guy and a great asset to pro ball. He was a good ballplayer, a tough guy to guard, and I think he doesn't get enough credit for being as good as he really was.

It was always exciting to go into New York, a thrill to play out there. In college there was also big alumni backing in New York, no matter who was playing. I had high-jumped there in the Melrose Games, and in '49 Illinois lost there to Kentucky in the NCAA semifinals. You know, I had played in the Olympics in '48 with Beard, Groza and those guys. Personally, I would have thought they'd be the last to throw games, Ralph Beard especially, because when I was with him he wouldn't drink anything but Coke and wouldn't even cuss.

I still love the game. The players now are taller and faster, they jump better and they're more agile. I thought the 24-second clock was a great addition, but I liked that fast, running style anyway, and I hated it when guys like Wanzer and Davies would hold and handle the ball and there was no action. And they've made it more exciting with the three-point shot. We often shot from beyond that point, you know, but we only got two and you couldn't make a big comeback that way.

The only official I remember well was Charlie Eckman, and that's because he later became a coach. You didn't get too close to officials back then. They seemed to have more control over the game then, but I'm not sure whether that was better or not.

Red Auerbach was a good coach, no doubt about it. But he loved to try to play us one-on-one in practice, and that may have been fun but it wasn't much practice.

I'll tell you one story about Red. We were having a bad game, especially me. I was shooting from outside as usual, but nothing was going in. At halftime, Red was chewing us out pretty good, and finally he turns to me and says, "Dike, you would shoot from the dressing room."

"Yeah," I said, "I would, if the door was open." Needless to say, I didn't play much in the second half.

After 17 years in the personnel department of Central Soya, Dike Eddleman returned to the University of Illinois as a fund-raiser for athletic department scholarships. In the NBA with Tri-Cities, Milwaukee and Fort Wayne (1949-53) he averaged double figures in scoring and played in the first two NBA All-Star Games after earning 11 varsity letters for the Illini in football, basketball and track.

Walt Budko

I'm a New York boy, from East New York-Brownsville, and went to Franklin K. Lane High School. I always loved Columbia and used to listen on Saturday afternoons to their football games. Those were the days of Sid Luckman. I was young in school because I had been accelerated. The public school system had it so that you could graduate in the middle of the year, February. I was a 16-year-old senior, playing for the high school team, and I was a fair ballplayer.

I remember very vividly it was the last game of the season, and I asked the coach, "How do I go about getting into college?" He said I should go to one of the tryout leagues they used to have at Coney Island and Sheepshead Bay, where all of the schools like NYU, LIU, City College and St. John's used to recruit players. It just so happened that a referee was passing by when I asked, "Who do you know at Columbia?" He stopped and said, "Are you interested in going to Columbia?" I said yes, and he said, "What kind of grades do you carry?"

My coach interceded, talked about the honor roll and all this jazz, and he said, "Let me get back to you. Give me your address. I'll have someone call and talk to you about it." I got a call next day at the candy store – we had no phones, I was a poor kid. The coach from Columbia said he'd like to have lunch with me at the University Club. After telling me all the nice things he had heard about me, he asked if I would I be interested. Sure, it was a dream.

It ended up that Columbia couldn't take me because I was going to graduate in February. But they asked me if I was interested in going to this private school in New York, Trinity School. They had fellows like the son of President Conant of Harvard, and Truman Capote was a couple of classes in back of me. They took a couple of scholarship kids a year, so I left high school and commuted an hour and a half each way from Brooklyn to this private school. I played ball there and it just so happened that I sort of blossomed there, and then all the schools from the New York area came after me. But I wanted to go to Columbia.

When I started there in '42, World War II had broken out and they allowed freshmen to play. Our interim coach was there under a Navy program, a fella named Cliff Battles. What a ballplayer! That man was so deceptive looking. In street clothes you just didn't see the athleticism. He was a great basketball player, and I could understand how he was a great runner.

I went into a Navy program at Columbia for one year, and Elmer Ripley was the coach. Then I spent three years in the Navy. When I came back I was on Gordon Ridings' first team there. He was Jack Molinas' first coach at Columbia, and when he died Lou Rossini, who was assistant coach , took over.

The absence of big-time college ball at Columbia didn't hurt me because when I went into service after my second year I went to boot camp at Great Lakes and we had a tremendous schedule. We played DePaul with Mikan, Notre Dame, Illinois, Minnesota with Whitey Skoog, and Bowling Green when they had Don Otten and a couple of other guys around seven feet. It was a good baptism of fire and I learned a lot there.

Because of my specialty as an electronics technician, I didn't get to go to other places to play like most of the guys who were physical instructors. I had to go through the schools and I ended up in the Pacific. But right at the time the war ended I spent a year — the last season before I went back to Columbia — in Hawaii. We had a league with pros and big-time college ballplayers there. Joe Fulks, or as I always called him, Joe Folks, played for the Marines' team.

When I went back to Columbia I was ready for bear. In the Ivy League, Tony Lavelli at Yale was the big gun. He was easy for me, played a shooting kind of game that took him out of the play, though he could make those shots. His arm would be out of bounds when he made hook shots from the corner. But you'd get him under- neath and you'd pound. Tony was a nice man, played a good accordion, too. I can just see him playing "Granada" at halftime.

I never had any thoughts of pro basketball. In the New York area it was almost nonexistent at that particular time. The Knicks originated after the war when the BAA started as a rival to the NBL in Sheboygan, Oshkosh and Tri-Cities. I had a degree in civil engineering from Columbia, but money was money and I didn't know what I really wanted to do. I could handle myself with all the other fellas, and I got drafted by the Bullets as their first choice and also by Tri-Cities.

I think both leagues had a kind of salary cap where the most they could offer a rookie was $500. And when the fella from Moline met me at the Hotel Edison, he said, "We'll give you a contract for $4,000 and I'll give you a thousand dollars up front." And he threw this wad on the bed in a rubber band. The rubber band broke and all these twenties and tens spread out. I never saw that kind of money, and I almost went, but I wanted to stay in the East so I went to Baltimore.

Buddy Jeannette was the coach and still playing, but he was hurting. If Buddy Jeannette had kept playing I think I could have lasted in the league for 10 years. He was a brilliant backcourt guard and a tremendous tactician who knew where everyone was on the court. We had some good ballplayers but when we lost Buddy we didn't have a smart point guard. He had the experience and he was a go-to guy. When things got tough, you gave the ball to Buddy and he'd drive – a great, smart, tough ballplayer. I have a tremendous amount of admiration for him.

I ended up replacing him as player-coach when they fired him. It was the worst thing I ever did; killed my career. But, of course, I was so full of myself that I thought I could do it. I lasted just half a season, and I was replaced by Freddie Scolari. He was as dumb as I was to do it, a fine ballplayer who shot off the wrong foot. That's how he got away with it. If you know basketball, you go by fundamentals. A right-hander shoots off the left foot, and he shot off the right foot. That's how he got it off, you just didn't expect that.

I ended up in Philadelphia where I played for Eddie Gottlieb. He knew how to gather talent but as far as being a coach per se he didn't show me much. We had Paul Arizin and Joe Fulks, and I roomed with one or the other on the road. We also had George Senesky and Andy Phillip. They were the old-time guys who had everything wrapped up. At that time you had five guys and that was it, you stayed with those five guys.

As a former coach, I tend to think that it's the players that count. Red Auerbach, for example, won with good talent in Washington with Bones McKinney and Sharman – a totally unrecognized guard. He could shoot the eyes out of the basket and he was strong, too, a great ballplayer. When Red went to Boston he had Easy Ed Macauley and Cousy, a fine ballplayer and everything, but until Bill Russell came along he didn't win. Russell allowed all the other fellas to take chances, because they knew he was going to cover up mistakes. He made Red's reputation and I think he made Cousy's, too.

I used to love playing against Bones McKinney, and we had a great time playing against each other. Bones was tough and smart, always active, go in, go out, do a lot of things. But the thing about Bones that made him so much fun was that he never stopped talking, always preaching or something. Not like some guys now, and I think it's a sad thing to see it happen, who try to use intimidation, and this in-your-face kind of stuff and taunting has gotten to all the kids. Bones was tough, but as a conversationalist he was fun.

Another guy like that was old Goose Tatum, who always had a big smile on his face. My Great Lakes Naval team played a team from Grand Island, Nebraska, when he was there. Goose would get into the pivot and he had the longest arms in the world. He'd make those hook shots and then say, "How'd you like that, young white boy?" "Oh, yeah?" I'd say, "Watch those rebounds." And then I'd take one off the boards and he'd say, "You sure did get that rebound, young white boy."

Goose and Bones, you had to talk when you played them, because they invited conversation.

When I was in Baltimore I'd end up having to take George Mikan all the time when we played Minneapolis. My chest was pummeled with black and blue marks.

He got away with that in the pros – the name guys always got away with something – but he deserved it. George was awful tough. I played against him when I was at Great Lakes and we played DePaul. We whipped them pretty good in the Stadium there one time. He learned when he got into the pros. He was a bright guy, and he had a hell of a supporting cast, Jim Pollard and Vern Mikkelsen, because if you could check out George then Mikkelsen, a big strong guy, would beat the hell out of you under the boards.

I didn't take any kidding about being an Ivy Leaguer because I was from Brooklyn. My heritage was Brownsville-East New York, not Choate or Andover. Let's face it, basketball in those days was really a Jewish game, and where I grew up it was a Jewish neighborhood. Until the West Coast guys started coming in and shooting the one-hander, the game that we all knew in New York was pick-and-roll, set up a little this and that, and it wasn't a pounding kind of a game. A lot of the guys I played with and against in the pros, I had played with and against somewhere else – in the school yards, in college, in the mountains, at Great Lakes, in Hawaii. So there was no stigma attached to me being an Ivy Leaguer, like there might have been for Tony Lavelli, who was a delicate kind of guy.

Joe Fulks and I burned our uniforms in the Onendaga Hotel after we lost in the playoffs to Syracuse in 1952, and I had decided to quit playing. (Joe went back for two more seasons.) I'm not much of a drinker, and I was a little shaky by the time Joe and I got on the plane for Philadelphia. I had to change planes for Baltimore, and by chance Charlie Eckman was on the same flight. He did me a real service, a real generous act, looked out for me, took me off the plane at Baltimore, took me home with him and called my wife to pick me up. I'll never forget him for that; I wish I had had a chance to tell him how much I appreciated it.

Charlie was a class act, though I was dismayed later on at the salty language he started using to spice up his after-dinner speaking engagements. It was a bit of a shock for a referee to become a coach, but by the same token, from my experience, a player makes a bad coach, and the better the player, the worse he is as a coach. Al Cervi at Syracuse, a good player but not a great player, and Buddy Jeannette, of somewhat the same ilk, as player-coaches just put all the wheels together. But Charlie was an observer. He got the horses together – Foust, Phillip, Yardley, Hutchins, Meineke – he had no particular axe to grind about getting famous himself, and he just gave them the ball.

Being a tall fellow, I always had the impression that anyone who was small and had a whistle had a Napoleonic complex. That was the great evener, you know, and you needed some guys like that to be officials. Big guys have a tougher time, whether college or pro, because they are assumed to do some damage just because they're big. Anyway, some other officials I remember were Matty Begovich, Sid Borgia and Norm Drucker. Pat Kennedy was a little bit of a showman who in his prime made all the moves. And there was Lou Eisenstein. I had introduced him to the coach up there at Columbia, to try to get him in to do the college games, because we came from the same section of Brooklyn.

It was while I was coaching Baltimore that Groza and Beard were arrested. As important as that event should have been I don't remember details. I know I was shocked because of the way those two fellas comported themselves. I always thought Beard had more class than that. I just didn't believe that he was susceptible to that sort of situation. Groza was a good ballplayer, not a great one, and I always thought that Wah Wah Jones was the key man on that team, like Bobby Jones much later, who did everything – played big, played little.

Oh, sure, I was aware there was a lot of betting on basketball. I knew it went on in the Catskills, and whenever you went to shoot pool you'd hear stories about who was taking money, who had an apartment house, who was driving around in a new Cadillac. You never heard it from any players, it was all rumors and innuendo. At that time, with the war over, the pool hall was like a recreation place. You'd go in and see the board with the odds, the point spread. People would ask me, "How do you like the points on so-and-so?" – everybody looking for inside information.

My best buddy when I was in college liked to gamble and I knew that. We were playing Penn one Saturday night, and Willie called me up that morning. We had maid service at Columbia in those days, little Irish women, not young, who came around and made our beds. Bridey came in to tell me I had a phone call, and I said, "Tell him I'm too sick to talk." Then I told her to call the coach to tell him I was sick. Well, wouldn't you know, the line went from 10 points to pick 'em. Willie probably had a coterie of guys and in New York, you know, you can't keep a secret. I played that night but not well, and we won but only by a point, I think. Gamblers are almost like actuaries. It's almost a science, and now it's an industry.

For some reason I was immune to it. In New York they were always accusing people. That was one of the great tragedies of Madison Square Garden, that the gamblers got involved and everybody thought everyone else was involved in gambling, which wasn't necessarily true. Still, I could see how it could happen. Most of us lived in tenements and didn't have a pot to pee in. It wasn't that we didn't know any better, but I can see the attraction for Sherman White and guys like that. I was shocked about CCNY, guys like Roth and Dambrot, and it bothered me because I thought there was money in the family. I was shocked about Kentucky and then Bradley, yet it didn't totally surprise me. But all for a piddling sum of money, to sell your soul for a pittance. Well, you can't legislate morals.

I would like to say some more about Buddy Jeannette. He was a new kind of character for me. I was raised in New York and on the streets, so I thought I knew what tough meant. But here was a totally different kind of tough and intense individual. He knew what he wanted and basically he got what he wanted. I remember one particular thing which I thought was a brilliant maneuver.

We had lost six or seven straight games, and it seemed everything we did went wrong. To this day, I remember we were playing in Indianapolis or Fort Wayne. We got there the night before and Buddy said, "Everybody up in my room," and there he had all these canapes and the bathtub full of beer. "Let's relax and have a good time." It was amazing. We killed whoever we played next day. When I think back, I marvel at the wisdom of it. When you're losing, your mind gets into it. You start thinking too much, trying too hard, you pull up, and if something can go wrong you know it will go against you. Buddy ended up totally relaxing us and to this day I think it was a brilliant stroke. I wish to heck I could have coached long enough to use it. Buddy was my first exposure to this kind of individual, and I thought that Al Cervi was another of the same school.

Dutch Garfinkel was out of the league by then, but I used to play with him up in the mountains. I played up there on the Brooklyn Jewish Community Center team. I was the only goy or shagetz on the team, the only guy not in the garment industry. Dutch had a couple of passions, his first being Al Jolson. When *The Jolson Story* came out, with Larry Parks, he'd go see that picture any time he could. His other passion was betting on baseball games, three-team parlays on the three New York teams. Dutch would arrange our games, and he'd bring a radio along. We'd be playing a game, Dutch would call timeout and he'd call us all over while he got the baseball scores.

The first time around the league with the pros was exciting – the adulation, the autographs. Each town was different, but by the same token they were all the same. You're only in there for a day at the most, you have to find some place to eat, you might have a couple hours to kill, you read or go to the movies, and you're always around the hotel or the gym where you played. I was straight, didn't play around too much, got married after my first year in the league, and so I don't have a lot of colorful stories to tell.

We didn't have any practical jokers per se, but there were characters with odd habits. Chick Reiser, who played with us in Baltimore, had a passion, and I picked up the habit from him. He drank a squeezed lemon in warm water for breakfast, it kept him regular, and it worked for me, too. I always liked to eat five or six hours before a game and nothing heavy, but for Big Ed Sadowski, the regular pregame meal was Coney Islands. Ed would load up on hot dogs with pickles, relish and sauerkraut. You didn't want to get close to Ed.

Big Ed was a real presence in the league. When he got in the hole, you couldn't go through there, he was so big. One time in Philadelphia, before we were teammates in Baltimore, when he was with the Warriors and I was feeling my oats with the Bullets, I had to take him and he had to take me. You'd learn things in the course of a ballgame, and I found out that if I moved out a little bit when rebounding Ed would turn around to block me out. And every time he turned around to keep me out, the official would blow a foul on him. So I took to going straight for the basket, he'd turn, and I'd get the whistle. I thought I had it made.

Ed's glowering at me, one tough old Polack, crew cut, looked like a thug, though he was really as gentle as could be offcourt. I saw him glowering at me, but I got carried away with myself and I tried it again. Instead of turning around and standing straight up, he bent over, ducked under, and I went right over him. I saw stars, and I drew the foul all right, but he looked at me and gave a wry smile, and I thought twice about going straight to the basket again.

In Philadelphia, Paul Arizin always was a gentleman, tremendous to me. Joe Fulks was a good old boy, a great guy to be around and a great guy to go out with – except when he started drinking the hard stuff. Then he became a belligerent bastard who would fight anybody. When Jumpin' Joe started to lose it, he knew it, because he couldn't get off his feet anymore.

The first black player I remember was Earl Lloyd for Syracuse. There was no racial tension in pro basketball. The difference from baseball was both the ethnic and the geographical makeup. New York wasn't the be-all and end-all of basketball, but that's where much of its fame emanated from. And in that area the blacks started coming in right before the war. So most of us played on teams with blacks and thought nothing of it. A lot of the fellas were in the service with blacks and played with them there. I never heard anyone cussing anyone out with racial stuff. You know, most ballplayers become ballplayers because it's the easiest avenue to success.

Maybe we had a lot more experiences than the fellas do today because the travel was a little tougher. We didn't fly everywhere. For example, with Philadelphia, there was a nasty road trip where we played in Chicago, took a train to play the next night in Indianapolis, a bus to Fort Wayne for the next night, and still had to get home to Philadelphia for a game the next night. So we'd charter a bus from Fort Wayne to Columbus, Ohio, pick up some sort of milk flight at 3 in the morning, fly into Pittsburgh, and reach Philadelphia at seven o'clock that morning.

Another thing that made it a little rough was that they'd sell a game to an outside town. For example, when Johnstown, Pennsylvania, opened up the War Memorial Center, the Baltimore Bullets sold them a game to commemorate the opening. We were to play Minneapolis, but I don't know how they got there. We chartered a flight from old Capitol Airlines to go to Johnstown, and it was just us on the plane. We were pretty open and quite informal with the pilot and crew, and the pilot told us they used these charter flights to train new pilots. He also told us that the hop from Baltimore to Johnstown was a little rough because of the air currents and the mountains and that a lot of accidents had happened there.

We were a little dismayed by that, but landed all right on the top of a mountain where they had a little shack by the runway for an airport. We had a bus waiting for us and we took this scary drive down to Johnstown. Now after the game in Johnstown it's raining, but at the airport it's snowing. There's maybe a thousand, two thousand-foot difference in elevation. Then at the airport we had to shovel the runway off before we could take off. You did those things. It was part of the game.

One character that everybody used to try to avoid on the plane was John Mandic. As soon as he got on that plane he had that whoopie cup out. The worst sound anywhere is the sound of the guy in back of you retching, and he just couldn't make a flight without doing it. We'd make a wide berth around this fella.

I was done as a coach in '52, as a player in '53. I lost interest in playing basketball. I couldn't handle opposing players like I used to, and I lost enthusiasm. I wanted to have a family, and I thought I needed to work on a regular basis, to develop discipline. I was 28. In 1953 fellas got out of sports and owning bars was the height of success for them. People have short memories, there's always a next hero coming down the line. I always thought it was sad to see people hanging on, not realizing that you put your pants on the same as everyone else, one leg at a time. I had built a house in Baltimore so that's where we settled. I put my engineering education to work for a time with a construction firm, worked in commercial real estate for three years, and for over 35 years I've been my own boss in the insurance business.

I love the college game now, but I don't like the pro game too much. The sense of drama that I enjoy in college games is missing for me in the pros. This year, though, I liked the playoffs and especially the finals. Houston and Orlando comported themselves well. There was not all this taunting and trash talk. I'm tremendously impressed with Olajuwon, a tremendous class act. He has his feet on the ground and the whole team, Drexler and the rest, seems to reflect that. And to give Orlando credit, this O'Neal man is a delight. He doesn't take himself too seriously, and the team itself knew what they wanted to do without all this in-your-face crapola. I take a lot of offense at all these guys hitting heads and butting each other. It proves nothing to me.

People ask me about the good old days, but we didn't compare to these guys. What we did have, and it's a reflection of the 24-second clock, we had maybe one, two, three or four plays a quarter. And this lent some drama to the game. It took some time to develop a play, and if it worked it was great. But now these guys are so good there's no time to develop anything like that. The 24-second clock saved the game, no doubt, lifted it above the college game, where it had started in imitation of the college game.

I wouldn't want them to go back to a no-dunk rule. Don't penalize a guy who's big or can jump. But some of the most valuable guys can't dunk. Good point guards are worth their weight in gold because they know how to play and get a team to play. There's nothing so bad when you're a big ballplayer as getting the ball off the boards and never seeing it again. That wounds you. The athleticism of a lot of the big men today is fabulous, though they get away with a lot of traveling and carrying the ball. But something has been lost with the gains, some science has been lost. Then again, pro basketball is no longer a game, it's big business.

In the three seasons Walt Budko played in Baltimore (1948-51), no one scored more points, got more rebounds or played in more games for the Bullets. As player-coach, his record was 10-19. In his last season, as a reserve for Philadelphia, his shooting percentage ranked third behind Paul Arizin and Neil Johnston.

Marty Glickman

It was all fun, sensational fun. Those were the days when we felt that everything we did was great. Basketball was not broadcast until December of 1945 when I persuaded WHN to broadcast the college basketball doubleheaders from Madison Square Garden. Those were major events, tickets always in demand, and now the broadcasts became an instant success.

During World War II, as a lieutenant in the Marines based on the Marshall Islands, I used to spend time thinking about how to broadcast basketball. Baseball and football, I reasoned, were good to broadcast because they are sports that have set geographies. To set the scene in baseball, you give a pitch count, the number of outs, what runners are on which bases, and everyone can visualize the scene of the action. In football, you give down and yardage, set the line of scrimmage and the formation, and the stage is set for the audience to see.

Basketball, however, is a fluid game, without the pauses between pitches or plays, so I had to set up a geography of the court, using the vernacular of the game, to set the scene. Then I could describe dribbling to the top of the circle, cutting from the sideline through the lane, passing to the baseline, right-hand hook off the glass and the listeners could visualize the action just as it happened.

In 1946, before the first season of the BAA, there was a meeting at Toots Shor's, with Ned Irish of the Garden, his assistant Fred Podesta, Burt Lee, who was my program director at WHN, and me. The question on the table was, what about broadcasting Knicks games? Ned Irish asked, "How much would it cost me?" and Burt said, "Not only will it cost you nothing, but we'll pay you $250 per game." That's how it came to pass that we did Knicks games even in that first season. It was very successful, too, and the price went up in time to $1,750 per game.

There were 11 teams that first season, the westernmost being the St. Louis Bombers and the Chicago Stags. We didn't do all the games, because if there was a conflict with the college doubleheaders we'd do all those games in the Garden. We didn't do the first BAA game, either, the Knicks at Toronto, because there was a conflict with a hockey broadcast. But we did the second Knicks game, from St. Louis.

It was Irish's idea to form the Knicks team from New York City players. So he put together a team that had Bob Mullins from Fordham, Dick Murphy from Manhattan, Ossie Schechtman from LIU, Ralph Kaplowitz and Frank Mangiapane from NYU, Sonny Hertzberg from CCNY, Tommy Byrnes from Seton Hall and Leo Gottlieb from DeWitt Clinton High School. They didn't have any size at all, so later they got Bob Cluggish, 6 feet 10 inches from Kentucky. He was awful. We used to call him Sluggish Cluggish.

There were other pro leagues and there were AAU leagues, and teams in places like Buffalo and Scranton were often part of loosely organized leagues that kept shifting members and franchises. But everybody loved it because the players all loved to play. There was a kind of joy almost always present.

Talk about fun. I remember broadcasting a Knicks game against the Washington Caps in Uline Arena, the Caps up nine or 10 in the final minute of play, and Bones McKinney at the free-throw line. We're broadcasting from the baseline, looking under the basket. Bones has this big grin on his face, turns around and shoots backwards through the hoop. Still grinning, he does it again and then runs back on defense waving side to side to the crowd like a politician in a parade.

The game was rough and the officiating very loose, though there were some good ones, like Pat Kennedy, Sid Borgia and later Stan Stutz when he quit playing. One of the league's goals from the start was to clean up the pro game, make it more like the popular college game. In the final minute or two, games turned into a parade from foul line to foul line. It was the primary role of players like Al McGuire to come in and commit fouls in the last minutes. Fouling was the only way for a trailing team to get the ball back, give up one point for a chance at two. The leading team would do the same. As a result, there was a parade from baseline to baseline, and the final minute of play was almost interminable in the final minutes. I put a clock on it and timed it as long as 25 or 30 minutes. I'd say, "Ball put in play − foul, ball put in play − foul."

Danny Biasone, a nice, bright guy who had the Syracuse franchise, came up with the idea of the 24-second clock. Along with the idea of a limit of team fouls, that changed the game and saved it. My personal point of view was that it should have been 30 or 35 seconds, so there could be more than one play and one shot per possession, but the clock idea was absolutely necessary.

The game was played in a number of remarkable arenas. I broadcast a Knicks game against the Waterloo Hawks from Waterloo, Iowa. Waterloo in midwinter gets pretty damn cold, and the armory was heated by hot air blowers at one end. They would turn up the blowers when the Knicks were shooting fouls at that end, and it would give a knuckleball effect to the shots.

At the Edgerton Park Arena in Rochester, the seats were only on the sides. Not far behind the endline of the court there were doors to the outside, so that if a driving player got pushed he could run right out the door into the snow. In Syracuse, if a visiting player got pushed on a drive and went into the crowd, the fans would hold on to him and not let him get back onto the court. Playing at the

County Fairgrounds there, Red Auerbach would get jabbed by a woman wielding a hat pin as the Celtics walked up the runway from the locker room to the floor. Red lost his cool once and went into the stands after her. That was the building where the backboards were suspended by cables from the ceiling with four corners of the boards anchored by cable to the balcony. When the Knicks shot fouls, fans would reach over and shake the cables to try to shake the shots out of the basket.

When the Knicks went to Philadelphia, at first they played in the Philadelphia Arena, which seated maybe 5 or 6,000. An elevated ran right by the building and smoking was allowed at the time. The smoke would get so heavy during the broadcast that I'd have to look behind me to see the scoreboard for the time and the score, because I couldn't see the scoreboard in front of me across the floor. And the Knicks would have to bring their own towels and soap with them, because to save a few bucks Eddie Gottlieb wouldn't provide them.

When the NBA landed its first television contract with the DuMont Network, the first *Game of the Week* was going to be played in Rochester's Edgerton Arena. Maurice Podoloff called Les Harrison and told him in no uncertain terms that he didn't want to see any local ads on the walls of the arena where the camera would pick them up. When he arrived, there was a big ad for a local haberdashery strategically placed. Podoloff was furious, and he personally climbed up to tear down the paper signs while a livid Les Harrison watched.

The competition was terrific, despite the difficulties of travel and playing conditions. I remember sitting in the Garden a few years ago with Carl Braun. I said to him, "As captain of the Knicks, perennial all-star and holder of the then single-game NBA scoring record of 47 points, what did you make in your best year?"

"I made $19,000," he said, "and I would have played for nothing."

That was the kind of joyful attitude that made the game so attractive. I remember Ernie Vandeweghe, who was in medical school when he played for the Knicks. He could make most games at home and some on the road. Once he dressed in the toilet on a DC-3 on his way to Indianapolis to play the Olympians. Lapchick saw him coming into the arena and waved him right into the game. He reported onto the floor and immediately called timeout so he could tie his shoes. That's the kind of warm-up he had.

When the scandals broke, they knocked college basketball out, and the pro game was there to take up the slack. It's almost unbelievable now, but from 1946 to 1951 there were no blacks in the NBA. I have strong feelings about racial integration in the league. I believe that Red Auerbach was the Branch Rickey of basketball. He signed Chuck Cooper for the best of reasons, because he was a hell of a basketball player, and that opened the door for Earl Lloyd, Sweetwater Clifton, Don Barksdale and the others who followed. Red and I, by the way, played against each other in high school. We didn't realize it until we compared notes years later, but my James Madison team played against Red's Eastern District team.

Back in the first couple of years, the Knicks had Lee Knorek and Stan Stutz, who were able to speak Polish with one another. There was one trip to Washington, when the players were wearing derby hats, just for fun. Their hotel was walking

Ned Irish assembled a group of greater New Yorkers for the first Knicks squad, but he had to look westward for some size. Bob Cluggish (right), a reserve center from Kentucky, was not the answer. Leo Knorek (left) helped some until Harry "the Horse" Gallatin arrived from Northeast Missouri. PHOTO COURTESY OF TOM KING distance from Union Station, and on their way over, Knorek and Stutz were fooling around and traded raincoats and derbies. So here was Knorek, a big 6-foot-7, with a little derby perched on top of his head and his arms sticking out of his coat up to his elbows, and 5-11 Stutz with his hat down over his eyes and his coat dragging on the ground. Then they storm into the hotel, claiming to be the Polish ambassador and his assistant, and in Polish and broken English making a scene with the desk clerk who cannot find any reservations for them. Everyone else, of course, is breaking up.

The most famous travel story of the early years in the league is shared by many. It concerns a peculiarity of scheduling that had teams playing on Saturday in Rochester and then in Fort Wayne on Sunday. They would leave Rochester late Saturday evening, catching the *20th Century Limited* headed toward Chicago. Then at 5 a.m. they'd be awakened in their sleepers for a nonscheduled stop in a prairie in the middle of Indiana. The only thing there was an uncovered wooden platform.

Traveling with the Knicks, I knew that our instructions were to walk on a two-lane blacktop road toward a blinking yellow light a half-mile away. That turned out to be the only light at a crossroads where there were 10 or 12 buildings, nothing taller than two stories. Then we were to look for the plate glass window with the sign of the Green Parrot Cafe. Carl Braun was our designated shooter of the pebbles up to the second-floor window, because he had the softest touch. After two or three pebbles hit the window, a frowsy-haired woman would look out and say, "Oh, the Knicks."

She'd get on the phone, and in a little while four or five cars would gather and drive us the 40 miles into Fort Wayne. We'd go right to bed and get up for the game that day or night. That was the only way to get to Fort Wayne from Rochester. Sometimes, there'd be a writer or two along, but usually it was just me and the team. We'd pick up a local engineer for the broadcast wherever we played. Leonard Koppett heard that story and didn't believe it, so he came along once.

I remember very vividly the fourth NBA All-Star Game, which I broadcast from Madison Square Garden with a standing-room-only crowd. That was the game that the East won in overtime, with Bob Cousy scoring 10 of the East's 14 overtime points to win the game. They had to revote to give Cousy the MVP, because they had voted for Jim Pollard before the end of regulation. But what I remember best was what sent it into overtime. The West was down two points with seconds remaining when Mikan was fouled. The East called timeout and there was Big George walking around smiling. He never stopped grinning during the timeout and made the first free throw. The East called another timeout, and George was still smiling when he made the second to tie the game. I'll never forget him jumping up and down like a little kid.

Another vivid memory is the basket that didn't count in the Knicks' championship series against the Lakers. They were playing the game in St. Paul, and in the second quarter Al McGuire shot from the head of the circle. Sid Borgia was underneath the basket looking for fouls on the rebound and didn't see the ball go in. Stan Stutz was the other official and he saw McGuire fouled, whistled it, but didn't watch the shot go through and called a two-shot foul.

Lapchick goes out of his mind, and Johnny Most, who was my associate broadcaster at the time, is screaming at them. There's a 10-minute delay, while the officials tried to decide what to do. They even asked Podoloff, who was watching from the stands, but he said, "It's not my business to make a call." They stuck with the decision, because, no matter what anyone else said, they hadn't seen the basket made. McGuire made one of two, the game eventually went into overtime, the Lakers won, and they went on to win the title in a seven-game series.

Boston was just a hockey town through the early years of the NBA. I can remember a Celtics game with the Knicks when the attendance was so sparse that there were more people involved in the running of the game – ushers, vendors and so on – than fans in the stands. I remember sitting with Red Auerbach and Walter Brown before a game in Boston, when we started talking about the broadcasting rights fees. I asked Walter what he was getting, and he didn't want to tell me. "It's embarrassing," he said. Finally I got him to tell me that it was $5,000. "That's pretty good," I said, and he said, "For the season?" I was getting paid $100 a game at the start, by the way.

I was asked by an ad agency to come up with a phrase like Mel Allen's "Ballantine blast" or Russ Hodges' "there it goes, into Chester-field." I was already using "Good!" to announce a shot that went in, so it was a natural thing to say, "Good – like Nedick's." The broadcast booth was as much of a joy for me as the court was for the players. And often I wasn't alone.

Johnny Most was my associate, Connie Desmond worked with me until spring training started in February and Curt Gowdy was my associate. When they weren't coaching a game in the Garden, Joe Lapchick, Clair Bee and Nat Holman would often be in the booth with me. Bud Palmer, when he was playing with the Knicks, thought he wanted to be a broadcaster, so I would have him do one quarter of a game if there was a doubleheader at the Garden. If he was playing in the second game, he'd do one quarter of the first. If he was in the first game, he'd stay to do one quarter of the second. That's how he learned, and in time was hired to do the Knicks games on television.

Then there was Marv Albert, whom I remember as a ballboy, one of the shyest, most reserved kids I've known. But he was serious about wanting to learn the business and would ask if he could sit in the booth. He followed in my footsteps by going to Syracuse University, and when someone was needed to broadcast the Knicks games in the '68-69 season, I strongly recommended him. They said no at first, because they wanted someone with a name, but when things didn't work out they came back to him and gave him a shot. Good – like Nedick's! Yes! And it counts.

The voice of Marty Glickman doing basketball play-by-play from Madison Square Garden is emblematic of the rhythm, pace, keen intensity and excitement that led millions of fans to say, "I love this game."

Arnie Ferrin

In college at Utah, I was on a team that won the NCAA Tournament in 1944 and the NIT in 1947, both of those championships in Madison Square Garden. That's how I had became acquainted with Ned Irish. He called me in the summer of 1948 and asked me if I intended to play professional basketball. He told me if I did, they would draft me. I told him that I didn't think that I would play and thanked him for being interested in me.

I was selected to play in the *Chicago Tribune* All-Star Game that fall against the champion Lakers. It so happened that the Lakers had drafted me, but I had told them that I didn't think I would play pro ball. I had also been drafted by the other league but had told them the same. I got to the all-star game, and every one of the college players but me had signed a pro contract. The Lakers won the game handily, but I was selected the Most Valuable Player of the game.

After the game, representatives of the two teams that had my draft rights from the different leagues contacted me about signing with them. Because I was the only player on the all-star team that hadn't signed a contract, it became a little bidding war. The initial salary the Lakers offered me escalated a thousand dollars, but it wasn't as much as I could have made playing in the other league. I elected to stay and play for Minneapolis, not because of the money but because of the stimulation of continuing to play basketball at the championship level that the Lakers and the NBA afforded me.

There were no agents. The contract was a standard contract. The minimum salary in the league was between $3,500 and $4,000, but because the Lakers had the potential to win the championship, they made it sound better by guaranteeing you $1,500 to $2,000 in playoff money. Of course you earned that yourself but it made the contract look a little better.

The contract specified that you would play exhibition games and regular scheduled games and the playoff games. I didn't get there for the preseason games, but I believe the team played over 130 games that year. After we won the championship, they took us as part of our signed contracts on a postseason tour, where we played 32 games in 30 days. I don't remember whether they paid us additionally for those games or not.

I would guess that the total payroll wouldn't exceed $80,000. When I was general manager of the Utah Stars, I used to muse that I had one player that was making four times as much money as our whole team did in Minneapolis.

There were no trainers. My first year we were the farthest team west. It was an overnight train ride to the next city. Meal money was seven dollars per day. We traveled mostly by train, occasionally by airplane during the playoffs, but some of the teams traveled by car. It was great winter driving coming to Minnesota.

Endorsements were a lot different from what they are like now. If General Mills mentioned your name, you got a case of Wheaties. There were no rings for NBA championships. Occasionally, there was local TV. One of the biggest games each year was our game with the Harlem Globetrotters. I believe we played them five times, losing only once, and that was when two of our starters were hurt.

Sometimes we'd be gone for three weeks, traveling by train at night, so black shirts were a must. The traveling was the hardest part, but the one good thing I remember about those overnight train rides was the magnificent baked apples we'd get, hot from the oven, as the first ones in the dining car in the morning. Some people suggest the value of the dollar would make our pay scale somewhat commensurate with today's high salaries. My highest salary was $10,000. I bought a new Cadillac for $2,250. I guess you could compare today's salaries with the cost of the Cadillac and find how much they've changed.

I enjoyed playing with the Lakers very much. The players were close-knit and supportive of each other. Coach John Kundla led by example. Four of the Lakers that played during that time have been enshrined in the Hall of Fame. There were three Minnesotans on the team, including the coach, and the other guys lived in a hotel across the street from the arena. Some were bachelors, some others married but living like bachelors during the season. It made no sense to move wives and families to Minneapolis for the winter, when we spent so much time on the road. I guess the Ferrins and the Pollards were the exceptions.

As great as that Lakers team was, people tend to forget that we were not that big a team. On our first NBA champion team, 6-foot, 4-inch Don (Swede) Carlson started at one forward and 6-4 Jim Pollard at the other, with 6-8 George Mikan at center. The next season, when 6-7 Vern Mikkelsen replaced Swede as a starting forward, it was still a small front line. At 6-4 I started at guard, but I was also the first substitute at forward and the first substitute at center.

But we played bigger than we were, especially Pollard, who was a great leaper, and 5-10 Slater Martin, who played just as hard on and off the court. We always played well against the good teams, but we had a tendency to let up against the others, perhaps just coasting or saving our strength. George Mikan didn't accept that. He was an intense competitor who wanted to win every game and never accepted responsibility for a loss or a mistake. Once at Tri-Cities, in a game that was closer than it should have been, George threw a crosscourt pass toward Billy Hassett that was intercepted for an easy layup at the other end.

In the locker room at halftime, coach Kundla said, "Well, Mr. Basketball, we don't throw crosscourt passes."

George was not happy and said, "I wouldn't have thrown it if Billy hadn't called for the ball."

That same season there was a game at Baltimore when Jim Pollard was playing against veteran Blackie Towery, and he was going around and over him so easily that he was making him look old. Towery was so frustrated he doubled up his fist and sent Jim four rows into the stands. At halftime, Jim said to us, "Don't worry, I was a boxing instructor in the Coast Guard, so I know how to roll with the punches." And we looked at him and could see the big red welts on his face.

Memories continue for me. In New York City at that time college basketball was a bigger attraction, so we played many of our games against the Knicks at the 69th Regiment Armory. The last two arenas that we played in 1949 that they were still playing in were Chicago Stadium and the Boston Garden. As these were replaced this year, it means that all the facilities of that time are gone, except in my memories.

It's fun to be part of statistics, and one statistic that I'll always be part of is that we played in the lowest-scoring game in the history of the NBA. That was before the 24-second clock, so it will never be broken. The most exhilarating feeling I remember, though, was winning the 1944 NCAA finals over Dartmouth in overtime.

A week or two before the start of my fourth pro season, the president of the company my father worked for came to see me. "What are you going to do?" he said. "If you're going to go into coaching, stay and play. But if you come to work for me, in three years you'll be making more than you can make playing basketball."

There was really no financial incentive to stay and play, and we had won two championships in my three years. Playing the games was fun, but the traveling was difficult and we had two children by then. I went to work for him at the Schenley Distilling Company, and he was right. In three years we were much better off financially and had a better family life. The subsequent moves I made in business were always to better and better positions.

But I wasn't through with basketball. For three years I was general manager of the Utah Stars, an enjoyable experience because our owner, Bill Daniels, always wanted everything to be first class. And then, when I went back to the University of Utah as athletic director, I served six years on the NCAA basketball committee. The most rewarding experience of all was serving as chairman of that committee, choosing and seeding the best 32 teams in the country. I still follow basketball very closely, both the pros and the college game.

Arnie Ferrin has often been an integral part of winning basketball teams: star of NCAA and NIT champions at Utah, starter on two NBA championship teams at Minneapolis and general manager of the ABA champion Utah Stars.

Kevin O'Shea

It was World War II that took me from San Francisco to Notre Dame. I got out of high school in '43 and contemplated going to Stanford or St. Mary's but I was leaning toward going to Santa Clara. Then they abandoned their athletic program, so I started looking into V5 and V7 programs, and there was a priest here in San Francisco that was pushing Notre Dame. My father thought it was a nice idea, so I went for a visit.

I wanted to be able to play ball, continue playing in the service and go back to continue my education. It was the middle of June and I was 17 when I went to see Notre Dame, and would turn 18 July 10. Leahy had all his football players working out and I lived in the dorm with Johnny Yonaker, Big Jim White, Pat Filley and Syzmanski from Detroit. So we all went up to take a physical in Chicago for the V7 program. We had punctured eardrums, chronic knees and all kinds of injuries, but it was all taken care of by the coaches; it would be overlooked.

We went up on the South Shore train, and I'm thinking, I'm glad there's nothing wrong with me, a 17-year-old kid. Well, they flunked me out for having an overbite in my teeth. These guys come out and they'd all been accepted and were going home happy, except me, and I went to Krause who had just become basketball coach at the time, and he talked to Commander Barry who said, "Don't worry about it, we'll take care of that."

"How are you going to do that?" I asked Coach.

"We'll take care of the dental part of that," he said. "It's not a big problem."

"So what happens then; how long do I get to stay here?"

"Six months, then another six months at Northwestern, and then you go to Great Lakes."

That didn't sound so good, and I said, "I'm not so sure I want to do this." And I didn't.

I came back home and enlisted in the Coast Guard and spent three years, playing with Jim Pollard on a team that won a California championship. But afterwards I went back to Notre Dame, and the reason was that coach Krause had told me, "You could come back with one leg and one arm and the scholarship is yours. They'll never take it away from you." And I know guys who never played a game for Notre Dame who went through on scholarship after the war.

It was something I really appreciated at the time. I liked the place and I'm glad I did it. I still go back from time to time. We have a Monogram Club back there, 350 old jocks, have a golf tournament and a lot of fun.

I wasn't thinking much about professional basketball – there wasn't any money in it. I was a baseball nut. I went to school with Charlie Silvera, Gerry Coleman and Billy Martin, played semipro with Jackie Jensen. I was gonna be a Yankee, that was all there was to it. Basketball came easier, it was easier to get 10 guys to play basketball than 18 for baseball. But I went back to Notre Dame to play baseball, then had a knee operation that first year so I never played baseball for Notre Dame. Meantime I got married and had children. My wife graduated from Berkeley in '48, at the end of my sophomore year, and we got married then, went back to Notre Dame, and she got a taste of the Golden Dome.

I wasn't gung-ho about the pros because, when you live in San Francisco, air travel is expensive. I was the No. 1 draft choice for the Lakers and offered $15,000, but flying back and forth took $1,500 of that. You couldn't put away any money that way, and by the same token I had two bad knees to start with, so I was faking it from the day I started. But I made enough money to make a down payment on a home at the right time.

The pro game didn't excite me. Had the 24-second clock come around a little sooner I might have stayed longer. I think that made a lot of guys hang around. We played a very deliberate style in those days. You had to have a lot of physical size to cope. We had it on our team, with Mikan and Pollard and Mikkelsen, but I didn't. George carried the ball. With Pollard, Mikkelsen, Slater Martin and me, your job was to get the ball to George.

I forgot how to shoot. I was a running player, liked the transition game. I just thought the Lakers style wasn't for me. With the Bullets it was different, when I played with Freddie Scolari. I grew up in town with him – we had a lot of San Francisco guys on that Baltimore team, by the way. We were in last place, too, though. Freddie would get mad at me. I was a point guard before there was a point guard.

He said, "You gotta start shooting."

I said, "How can I? Someone's open in there, I gotta hit him with a pass."

He said, "If you don't start scoring, they're not gonna keep you."

I said, "I can't do that. I gotta play to win the game." He's averaging 12-14 points a game and telling me to do it, and I just couldn't bring myself to play that way.

In those days, if you won a couple of games away from home, you won your division. It was the officiating. The home team got all the breaks so it was tough to win away from home. One official, Pat Kennedy, was a good friend of mine. Another, Sid Borgia, when I'd moan to him about the walking, he'd say, "This is what's making the game" – he as much as told you they were told to do it. Without saying it. The premier players were allowed to walk, double dribble, and do things because they were premier players. And the crowd wanted to see the scorers and what they did. Mikan was allowed to use his elbow to clear out, he'd cream the guy, and make the shot – he'd get away with murder, but there was no way they'd foul him out. George knew it.

Mikan, you got to give him credit, he put out all the time. Jim Pollard, who was a good friend of mine, wouldn't put out on the road. He would save himself for the home games, which would frost the hell out of George. He'd get mad as hell at that. That was George's style, he wanted to win every place. By the same token, some of the players didn't play that hard on the road. It wasn't worth it – you weren't going to win on the road. You could win some, but you'd have to beat the hell out of that team to do it.

My first year in the league, 1950-51, we played for the Western Division championship against Rochester. And George played on two broken ankles. They sprayed him with ethyl chloride and shot him up with Novocain. Rochester's Wanzer and Davies were the toughest pair of guards for us. Davies got me once and I ended up in the fifth row. I said, "I'm gonna get you." And he said he was sorry, and I said, "No, you're not sorry," and I got him back when I had the chance.

To give an example of what it was like, one night in Syracuse, we're down one point with 10 seconds left. I've got the ball out of bounds on the baseline, trying to get it in to George. Al Cervi was on me, and he takes his two fingers and jabs me in both eyes. I'm blinded, lose the ball, no whistle, game over. Cervi ran off the court and locked himself into his own locker room. Much later he comes out and finds me and says, "Kev, you still mad at me?"

Bud Grant and I roomed together in Minneapolis. He and Slater Martin were opposites. We used to have great card games, but Bud was his conservative self even in those days. He wasn't happy with the Lakers because he was a football player, basically. He was a very well-known figure in Minneapolis, well thought of, and he kept getting an offer to play with the Philadelphia Eagles. But he didn't think he was big enough to play in the NFL and he weighed 225. This was when they first came out with tight ends – tight end wasn't even the name yet – but he finally went.

He wrote back to me and said, "Kev, this is the greatest racket in the world. You gotta come and play this football. You work out in August, you make the club, you don't even put the pads on again until the Sunday that you play. All you do is run around during the week, run through some drills in shorts. And on Sunday, if you actually play more than 10 or 12 minutes, that's a long time. The greatest thing is, you fly to the game the night before and you fly home right after. You're not even away from home but one night a week."

That was the kicker. Here in basketball we were traveling four, five days or even 10 days, two weeks at a crack. The travel was unbelievable. Exhibitions were the thing — they made you play exhibitions coming out your ears, and you got no extra pay. Minnesota was a red-hot basketball place. People would drive miles and miles to see the Lakers play a game. For the league our travel was by train, and some of that was unbelievable. The roomettes were so small you couldn't get in 'em, and I was a little guy. You got seven dollars a day for meal money and you couldn't get a hamburger on the train for seven dollars in those days.

But then we got into the air with Northwest Airlines. The Lakers had a DC-3 chartered. It made about 90 mph ground speed. But Northwest then had Martin 202s and Martin 204s. They had some DC-3s and DC-6s and some Boeing Stratocruisers. And they lost, in a year and a half, five of those Martins. They were told by the FAA they were servicing too many different kinds of planes, so they got rid of the two DC-3s they had and they wanted us to fly in the Martin 202s. We took a vote and said, "See ya later, we're not flying in any Martin 202s." Then they tried to put us on the commercial flights.

The DC-3s were terrible. The doors would fly open in flight. We were flying to Tri-Cities one time and it was socked in. We were running out of gas and had to land in Chicago. They had fire engines waiting and everything, and it turned out that the reason we couldn't make an instrument landing at Tri-Cities was that the Tri-Cities page was missing from the manual.

One time we were waiting for a plane at LaGuardia. We had to leave the DC-3 in Johnstown or Hershey where we had played an exhibition and bused to New York to get another plane. We had to wait a couple of hours and were getting antsy. Finally, we took off for Boston and as soon as we were airborne we turned around and landed right away. The pilot landed, popped out the door, saying "I'm not flying this god damn airplane — you can have it." He walks off the airplane, the pilot's gone, the copilot behind him, and we had to wait another four to five hours for another plane to come in from Northwest to get us to Boston. Turns out that this guy got grounded in the air, because on his checklist he missed removing the pins from the wheels and couldn't retract the wheels in the air. An automatic grounding.

Another time we were flying over Niagara Falls and someone said he didn't see it, so the pilot banked around and took us right down over the falls. Another time we were in Minneapolis playing in the playoffs, and we're all in the airport waiting to go to Syracuse in a snowstorm. The whole Midwest had been socked in for days and there were no planes in the air. When you take off you have to have an alternate site besides Syracuse. Well, Cleveland opened up for the first time in three days, and if Syracuse was open we could fly. We were arguing about whether to take the train, but we couldn't make it in time, and the team would forfeit the money to the league. Like cattle we boarded that rotten plane, and of course as soon as we were up Cleveland was closed and we ended up landing in Syracuse in a snowbank, the airplane on its wing, and we had to jump out into the snow to get out of the stupid thing. We had landed all right but got caught in a crosswind that blew us onto the one wing.

Another time we were playing an exhibition in northern Michigan, way up above Green Bay, and had to play the following night in Tri-Cities. We were traveling by bus, and there was a hill, two miles down and two miles up, covered with sleet and ice. We finished the game at like midnight and at the top of the hill they stopped everybody. There were cars all over on both sides of the road. You couldn't make it until they got them all off and put cinders down. We waited an hour, an hour and a half, the bus is freezing, and finally they said we could take a shot at it, just the bus, they wouldn't let any cars go. There were two teams on the bus; I think Milwaukee was the other.

Well, we didn't make it either, got halfway up the other side of the hill and the bus started going sideways, and we all had to get off before the bus tipped over. It was scary. The thing was getting ready to tip, and when you jumped out you jumped into mud and slush up to your knees. It was a mess. Well, we got to Tri-Cities that following night half an hour before game time. People who paid to see that thing – I felt sorry for them. We weren't about to put out. We went through the motions but were just awful. You had to do it, but thinking, "What am I doing here? Stupid!"

I enjoyed some of the flying, in that it was a new experience and I had once thought about becoming a pilot. In these charter flights, they let me sit in the seat between the pilot and copilot. One night at Midway, on our way back to Indianapolis, we were in line and I could hear on the radio one flight after another canceling out, these big four-engine jobs, and we're a two-engine plane.

I said to the pilot, "We're not going either, right?"

And he said, "Oh no, we'll go, we're a charter and not subject to the same restrictions as regular commercial flights."

The weather was so bad there were no commercial flights in the air at all, but as a charter we could take off with just one alternate destination. So we're taking off and I'm sitting between the two of them and they're sweating bullets, the wind so bad you felt like you could reach out and touch the hangar as you went over it. The pilot's saying, "Son of a bitch, this damn airplane, if we had a Martin we'd be up and out of here," and I'm thinking how glad I was we had a DC-3.

We got stuck in traffic at 5,000 feet, and he kept begging air traffic control to let us go to 7,500 feet. The deicers weren't working, we were icing up, and he's reaching around outside, in flight, to wipe off the windshield. Airplanes all over the place, the guys in back all getting sick, and I'm not because fortunately I'm up front – interesting but scary, too.

Going into Pittsburgh, there was always all kinds of turbulence. We didn't play there, but Capitol Airlines often stopped there. When I played for Baltimore, Scolari and I refused to fly when we went to Syracuse and Rochester. We'd play a game on Saturday night and then either Rochester or Syracuse on Sunday after-noon. They used to put us on a flight that left Baltimore at about 11 in the morning, and it made three stops, Wilkes-Barre/Scranton, Binghamton and Elmira, before Syracuse or Rochester. It was a puddle-jumper, Colonial Airlines. They had an-other flight that left at 12:45, a DC-6, that was nonstop, but we were on that cattle-run job because they got a much better rate. Freddie and I would take the train to New York instead, leave the night before, sit on a railroad siding at the station, get up and go to church, and then take the train to meet the team in Syracuse or Roch-ester.

So if you wonder why you quit early, the travel was one of the reasons. The season's much longer now, but it's not harder because the travel's so much easier. In '52 I played in Baltimore with Dave Minor, a gregarious, funny guy who had been a classmate of Don Barksdale at UCLA. He lives back home in Gary, Indiana, now and wouldn't come out here for a promotion because he didn't want to fly. I think it goes back to those days in the league.

There were no racial animosities then. The players didn't care. We had only a few blacks – Cooper, Clifton, Lloyd, Minor and Barksdale – the rest of them went to the Globetrotters. There were no racial problems, but every club had problems with regard to the fact that there was only one ball. Barksdale had a tendency to let the ball fly quicker than most, so some of the other players didn't care for him, but it wasn't an ethnic thing. It was his style of play. You know what they say about Dominique Wilkins – he could be in a phone booth and tell you he's open. Certain players are just that way, and it's something you have to live with.

You got up for the games in the big towns back then. I know I did. Even in college, when you went into Madison Square Garden you were pumped up and you put out more. Eastern fans were different from Midwestern fans, more schooled in basketball. There was more contact in the Midwest, the East Coast more give-and-go. By the time the league started we were pretty much interchange-able, but earlier the Eastern guys shot two hands from the chest, the Westerners one hand from the shoulder – we were from Luisetti country, and then there was Freddie who used to shoot from his ankle. I don't know how he did it, but he did – and he's got one bum eye besides.

You had to be aware of all the betting when you went to New York, and in the pro game, too. With Notre Dame we beat that great Kentucky team with Beard and Jones and Groza. I had a great night, and now I'm not so sure that wasn't a fix. Another time we were in the Commodore Hotel with Notre Dame to play NYU in the Garden. They had won 19 straight, with Lumpp and Forman and Dolph Schayes, and we beat them.

The day of the game we worked out in the Garden, 10 or 11 o'clock. My roommate was Leo Barnhorst, and he sprained his ankle at the end of the floor where there was a two- or three-inch drop-off. He went down and was helped off the court, got it iced down and we got him back to the hotel. But when he went down there were guys running all over the place – it was a sight to see – and when we got back to the hotel, 15 or 20 minutes at the most, the phone was ringing in the room. It was a guy from South Bend who owned a restaurant, and he's saying, "How's Barny, how's Barny?"

"How did you know?" I said.

"How is he?" he kept asking.

Turns out all the phones were bugged. This was when Hogan was the D.A., and thank God I didn't say any more than I did.

Physically, I got too small for NBA basketball. They started getting bigger and bigger. So I was figuring how I was gonna get out of there. I was 25 when I started, and I had played three years in the service, and that was like playing another three years in the NBA, playing out here on the West Coast against Dick McGuire and Jim Pollard and a lot of good college players.

I don't watch much now, though I'll watch some of the playoffs. I think they're tremendous talents. Their physical ability is awesome and I acknowledge that. But I can't stand the double dribble and carrying the ball and the walking and all that crap. I could play yet if I could get away with that. It's disgusting.

Even in our day, with all due respect – and I hope this doesn't sound like sour grapes, I hate to sound that way – but it's a fact that certain players were always given an extra step. Cousy and Sharman got two steps. It burns your ass when you made them walk and they don't blow the whistle. That may sound like I'm talking jealousy, but it's not, it's just frustration and irritation. It used to bother us that certain guys got away with stuff and I mentioned Cousy and Sharman because I was exposed to that most often. Slater Martin and I used to take them, and Bones McKinney used to knock both of us down if we weren't quick enough to get around his picks. But when you made the guy walk and never got the call it was frustrating.

Some of these guys now – I'm still amazed at some of the things Jordan can do, even though he does some of that walking and carrying the ball. Elgin Baylor – I thought he was fantastic, some of the things he could do. These kids today, they move. I just don't enjoy watching. I do watch the NCAA finals; I think that's the best thing going. But now they're doing as much walking and double dribbling as the pros. You start working with your grandkids and then it really upsets you to see it. You don't know what to do. It must be tough coaching today.

I want to tell about one game in February of '52 after I had come over to Baltimore from Milwaukee. It was played in that old cracker box in Fort Wayne. Don Barksdale, Frank Kudelka, Dave Minor, Stan Miasek and I were the five guys that started and the same five guys finished, without substitution. It had never happened in the NBA before and it has never happened since. We won it, too. Now, why isn't that in the official Encyclopedia, the guide or the record book?

We tried to get David Stern and the league to rectify that, but at the same time we were talking about the pension. Frank, for example, had played four years but was excluded from the pension, even though he spent three years in the service before he went to college. Barksdale also had four years – he lived across the Bay here – the first black to play in the NBA All-Star Game. Don was one fine guy, and he and Frank were pushing the pension situation. Both of them died within six months of each other, both with cancer. I was very close to Frank, grew up with him, went to kindergarten together in San Francisco – I had to take the ball, had to follow through on Frank's behalf. He made me promise I would.

Bill Tosheff and I have put in a lot of work on it, but we haven't accomplished it yet. We were led to believe that we were going to be taken care of in the new collective bargaining agreement. We felt like we were making headway and that we'd be included one way or another. There aren't that many of us left who have been excluded from the pension plan, and some of them are the guys who need it more than anyone else. We paved the way for the easy road they have today.

This mishmash they're going through now has got us flipping our lids a little bit. Hopefully, it's temporary, but if these guys don't understand what baseball is going through and what hockey went through they're crazy. I can't believe they're going to the extent that they are. I can't believe they're letting it happen. The players are naive, and the owners are, too. You'd think they ought to be able to sit down and take a look around.

Basketball is in a tremendous situation. They're making a lot of money right now. Granted the owners are making more – that's a fact and we all know that – but they ought to be able to sit down and figure out how to spread it around a little better. I think the kicker is that there's so much money in that NBA Properties. I don't think the players are getting their fair shake on that end, though you don't hear much about that part of it in the press.

I didn't like anyone in administration back in my playing days. You were a horse and they were horse traders. I thought they were taking advantage of us, and Ben Kerner, who had me in Milwaukee, was one of the worst. What was bad was the home clubs didn't share the gate, and they always thought they could get another patsy to play. Are they any better now? The way they treat us veterans from the Pioneer Era says maybe not.

Kevin O'Shea played for the Lakers, Hawks and Bullets in his three years in the NBA (1950-53). He has recently retired after almost 40 years in the fire and casualty insurance business.

Whitey Macknowsky

When I graduated from Seton Hall, I was notified by Les Harrison, the owner of the Rochester Royals, that he wanted me to sign a contract to play with two other Setonians then on the team, Bobby "Hooks" Wanzer and Bob "Li'l Abner" Davies. I remember thinking, "Wow! This is the ultimate in life – to play with two of my college buddies in professional basketball."

I was to meet Les at the Paramount Hotel in New York City to make it official but he never showed up. I was saddened, disappointed, frustrated and even angered at being stood up, so without contacting Les about the circumstances, I signed with the Syracuse Nationals.

It wasn't until later, during the season, that I realized the truth. Les hadn't met me in New York because Syracuse had secretly and deceptively warded him away with a story that I was their property because I had played with the Scranton Miners. Syracuse claimed it had some kind of affiliation with Scranton, but I had signed nothing and played on a per-game pay basis, as did Bobby Wanzer for Scranton and a few others who later came into the NBA via similar routes with prior experience on teams like the Philadelphia SPHAs and the Wilkes-Barre Barons.

I didn't know anything about sports contracts or an agent. I took my contract to a lawyer who looked it over, said it looked OK to him, so I took the contract to Syracuse for an official signing. I talked with Leo Ferris, a shrewd negotiator hired by owner Danny Biasone, and needless to say, I lost. Oh, I got a contract all right, "A standard contract for *all* rookies coming into the league," according to Leo Ferris. After some haggling, I was promised a $1,000 bonus, "if the club made a reasonable profit," so I signed.

Every time I walked into the coliseum, I'd look up at the stands and was delighted with the packed house. They were hanging on the rafters and some had to be turned away. We drew fans because we had seven rookies, most of whom were All-Americans, and Bill Gabor was Syracuse's own All-American boy. Also Al

Whitey Macknowsky. PHOTO COURTESY OF JOHN MACKNOWSKY

Cervi, who had played for the Rochester Royals in a severe rivalry against Syracuse, was now player-coach of Syracuse. Best of all, we had Dolph Schayes.

At 6 feet 8 inches, Dolph, who became my roommate and good friend, was the finest example during my time of a player who advanced his game to the highest level by learning the "little man's" game of cutting, driving and outside two-handed set shooting. He was absolutely murderous and the scourge of the league. He was a little too big for the little man to stop his set shot and too cute with his drive for anyone his size to brave his outside game. I wonder even now if there will ever be a rebirth of the old-fashioned two-handed outside shot that served Carl Braun of the Knicks and Dolph Schayes so well during my time.

Anyway, in anticipation of getting that $1,000 bonus, I bought a spanking new Buick Special with all the trimmings, my first car, but when the season ended and I came to collect the bonus money Leo Ferris promised, he said: "We didn't make a reasonable profit – we're still in arrears from the two previous seasons of poor attendance." I was aghast at the news!

Well, now this green kid just out of college learned two things in a hurry: First, always get a lawyer or agent who is familiar with the lingo and terms of professional sports contracts. They are different. Second, be alert and aware of possible legal deals done in secrecy behind closed doors with respect to playing time, bonuses, playoff money, etcetera.

I remember specifically the team was promised a certain sum of money if we got to the playoff finals. We did, and at the banquet after the season, each basketball player received a basketball ring instead. Certainly a mere pittance to the cash promised each member. The complaints were heavy from team members and some threw the rings at the speaker's table in protest, but to no avail.

I was still to learn another grave lesson about professional sports – the politics of the game. I have always maintained that there is little difference between the last guy on the bench and the starter on this professional level of competition. The five who start generally seem to gel better together but may not individually be better overall players than some on the bench. In other words, given the opportunity to play, a player who normally rides the pines, for whatever the coach's reason, can become a star if allowed adequate playing time. My contention is if you are good enough to make the pros, you are good enough to play, but politics come into play.

I discovered that the favorite sons of the owner or coach can do no wrong, get preferential treatment and greater playing time regardless of performance. I have seen good scorers intentionally used sparingly when the game was not in jeopardy but used more readily of necessity when the game required point production. If later circumstances in the game changed in our favor and it was no longer urgent to have the point producers play, they were eased out of the game, sometimes with the flimsiest of excuses.

This unwritten law by the owners and/or coaches was to control point productions by individuals, certainly not to imperil the outcome of the game and most definitely not to shave points in any gambling venture. It was practiced to control the minutes played so that individual ballplayers wouldn't experience exceptional scoring nights.

The reason for this is that a ballplayer's repeated effectiveness and favorable performances, such as increased scoring average per game, fortify his argument for a more lucrative contract next year. A lawyer in town who was a particular fan of mine helped me get an increase in salary by computing the minutes played and points scored, rather than games played and points scored, as a measure of point production. On this basis I was the second highest point producer, second only to our leading scorer, Dolph Schayes.

Defensive records, rebounds and assists were not accurately, systematically or scientifically maintained in those days. Therefore, this kind of intangible data was not a very significant argument for a better contract. Every time a player came into the game, even for a minute, it was tabulated as a game played and went against his total production average. Naturally, those with more playing time had greater opportunity for scoring, which served as persuasive evidence for a salary increase.

I recall we were playing against the Sheboygan Redskins away from home and we led by 20 or more points the entire game. Everyone expected to play a goodly share of time, but it wasn't until the final two minutes or so that I heard Al Cervi call my name to report to the scoring table. I decided not to report and didn't as the game ended. His fury in the locker room afterwards was only overshadowed by my own as I heard him say, "I'm the coach and when I say report, you report."

His lack of respect for me infuriated me even more and fisticuffs would have been the outcome were it not for the team's interference. I said, "If you don't have enough faith in me to maintain a 20-point lead, when will you ever think I should play to get one?" With that incident, I knew I wanted to be traded, released or sold. Cervi's action to keep a player from participating in those circumstances would never have been tolerated by the fans at home. This debilitating tactic was always done to the players on the road.

My problem with Al Cervi actually began when I was a well-meaning, hard-working, naive rookie – perhaps some might say "dumb" would be a better word for my behavior. In a jocular plan, my teammates told me if I wanted to make an impression on the player-coach, I would need to have him take notice of my variety of shots and ability to score against him, because he prided himself as a great defender; on the other hand, if I were to display an effective defensive stance against him, he'd surely take notice.

During the next scrimmage game, my teammates made sure I lined up with Cervi and suggested I take him in the hole (deep pivot) where I was freely fed the ball. Now I know how big men feel when they are the concentration of passes from above and I realized then that big men are effective because of the "oilers," back-court men who feed their ravenous appetites for the ball.

Well, I had a picnic! I scored at will – hook shots with either hand, fadeaways, drives with scoop shots, little jumpers – and I threw feints at him that had him turning around toward the basket while the ball was clasped between my knees, to reap an easy layup. In complete humiliation, Cervi abruptly called an end to the practice session, as all the players guffawed in sheer delight at how well their joke worked. I looked "mahvelous" but the realization of what I had done instantly struck me and I threw the ball at the guys in disgust.

Even after Cervi realized he was set up, it made no difference. I was on his "shit list" thereafter, so eventually I requested to be traded, released or sold, but to no avail. The lesson about the politics of the game was clear: never make the coach look bad, rather always make him look great. If you know the technique of "browning up" the coach or boss, it can be a great talent if the coach's personality is amenable to that kind of subterfuge. There were a few on the team who were truly skillful in this regard and I marveled at the target's lack of perception.

I also realized that certain powerful ballplayers rule the roost and often suggest club policy and even dictate who plays. Certain ballplayers are frozen out of the activity in the game while others are favored in play. Players form cliques and they look for each other for their own aggrandizement. This is never done at the expense of winning; however, this self-indulgence cannot always be controlled and its negative ramifications reverberate throughout the team.

Ever since that awful scene when I looked "mahvelous" against the coach, I knew mine was a wasted talent but they refused to peddle me off to another ballclub. I was Syracuse's property to do with as it pleased for the life of my playing days. The right to my athletic life was possible merely with signing an ordinary playing contract. How I wish now that I had an agent or lawyer then who was familiar with the way it worked.

My naivete in sports was fostered by relationships of the highest order with my high school coach and especially with my great, beloved Seton Hall coach, Honey Russell, now in the Basketball Hall of Fame. He always stressed defense and we worked hard at it half of every practice session, so my work ethic for defensive play was honed fine and we always took pride in it. He always said, "Rest on offense, never on defense. You can be off offensively but you can't be off defensively."

One day during a scrimmage at Seton Hall, I drove for the basket at top speed and crashed into the back supports of the basket with such force that I bruised my ribs, lost my breath and was somewhat dazed by the impact. In this condition, I suddenly jumped up, ran the full length of the court, stopped at the distant foul line and faced my basket in a slumped position. I tried to regain my breath without fully realizing where I was.

It was an instant reaction to excruciating pain, as one might jump up and down or run in circles after having slammed his finger with a hammer or dropped an anvil on his toe. My abrupt behavior cracked the other ballplayers up and they guffawed wildly as I tried to get my breath. At this point, Honey ran out on the court toward me and bellowed, "What the hell are you guys laughing at? Here's a kid who almost killed himself, and what did he think about – defense!" I truly loved this guy and my being awarded Seton Hall's Honey Russell Plaque for "Outstanding Achievement in Athletics as well as Life" is one of my proudest trophies.

Syracuse's "Bullet" Billy Gabor was the fastest starter from a standing point I'd ever seen. He was an electrifying performer as he darted out and stole lazy passes for easy layups. On one such occasion, Billy shot out for an interception and missed. Now I'm caught between two guys driving for the basket while Billy continued down court to become a "hanger." As my man scored an easy layup, Cervi yelled, "Whose man is that?" I raised my hand, and with that gesture I was benched with the terse remark, "Sit down." Although my switch to prevent the score was the right play to make, I rode the pines.

This rookie learned still another lesson in a hurry. Although the team's won-lost record is paramount, there are times when a player needs to look out for his own play, for his own point production, for his own survival in the league. Some, I venture to say, play in that mode every game. Pro ball is a business, big business, and many of the ethics I learned in college sports aren't applicable in pro ball.

One ballplayer who came to Syracuse as a rookie was Don Lofgran from San Francisco. He had great credentials as MVP in the Dons' NIT championship and was full of dreams and high hopes as he began his professional workouts. This 6-foot 6-inch gazelle-type ballplayer in a short period of time was so shaken by the behavior of the coach and the politics of pro ball that he just vanished one day and never showed up for any future practice or game. None of us had a clue as to his whereabouts. As I understand it, he was terribly distraught and depressed about his future in the pro game. He was later found near Chicago in an amnesiac state. Don apparently was having trouble handling the transformation to pro ball. He played parts of three more seasons, but not for Syracuse, and never fulfilled his dreams or potential. It's a dog-eat-dog confrontation of survival, and survival in the game of basketball often hinges on how well you play the game of politics.

Some teammates to gain a more favorable status with the owner or coach would collaborate with them and reveal teammates' activities, nightclub whereabouts and social excursions. The private and social life was monitored, very deceitfully sometimes by the very ballplayers in your company. The very nature of pro ball is survival and sometimes scruples fall by the wayside by owners, coach, and/or players.

A rather humorous incident comes to mind which reflects the control that the hierarchy tries to exert on its "property." On one of our road trips out west, we had not played as well as expected, so the coach curtailed our usual jaunts to the city after the game by restricting the team to the hotel. There was really nothing to do in a small hotel in Oshkosh, so we pooled our funds and gave the bartender and waitress a very generous tip to serve us vodka and soda secretly all night. As the evening wore on, a rather somber and morose group of guys began to feel the "spirit of life" and expressed their ardor with jokes and laughter that rose in a crescendo of hilarity.

During the entire proceedings, the Syracuse leadership, seated some distance from our tables, began to look askance at our frivolous behavior and couldn't understand it. The more they looked our way with questioning, stupid looks, the more hysterical we became. Our boisterous laughter soon became contagious and we all laughed at anything and everyone. It became more farcical when Cervi questioned the waitress and bartender and even smelled a drink going to our table. He continued to scrutinize us all night until he realized he was now the brunt of our giddy laughter. They all left the dining room without ever sniffing out the cause of our rambunctious behavior. Cervi later tried to befriend some of us to tell him what was going on, but we all remained solid on this one.

This reminds me of another very innocent experience with liquor. Truthfully, some of us did not drink at all, a few of us enjoyed a few beers after a ballgame, and a few might indulge in a highball or two. That was the extent of it, so our reaction time to alcoholic beverages of any sort was pretty quick.

Whenever we took a trip west to play the Denver Nuggets, we'd play one night, rest the next day, and play again the third night, for it was too distant to travel for just one game. After having thoroughly thrashed Denver the first game, five or six of us rented a Hertz car and decided to tour the countryside. We stopped at a resort area in the mountains of Colorado Springs for lunch, and as soon as we walked in, the people recognized us and made us their guests for food and drink.

A suggestion was made that we enjoy a cocktail before lunch. Some of us tried a Manhattan, and others, including myself, decided on a non-sweet drink, a martini with an onion. These were served in elegant glasses and everything looked harmless enough and quite tasty. None of us I'm sure had ever indulged in this kind of delicacy, and before long we were all bombed. I still don't know how we ever got back to the hotel that night.

Certainly we were not in a position to play the next night, especially in the Mile High City where the air was too light to play in normal circumstances let alone with a pounding headache. I'm sure many of those people who wined and dined us the previous night made a pretty good buck on the following game.

Now I'm 72 years old, and as I watched the exciting '95 NBA playoffs, I couldn't help but reflect on the opportunity Syracuse had to be league champions in 1950 when we played the Minneapolis Lakers in the finals. This was a great team, with Big George Mikan, Vern Mikkelsen, Slater Martin, Arnie Ferrin and the "Kangaroo Kid," Jim Pollard. I recall how desperately they had scouted for outside shooters to relieve the collapsing and double-teaming pressure that Big George felt in his deep pivot position. The acquisition of outside threats in the persons of Ferrin, Martin and Pep Saul permitted Mikan to go on a rampage, and the results of his accomplishments are in the basketball record books.

Nevertheless, we had the best won-lost record that season, so we had the home-court advantage. We played 10-minute quarters in those days, dunking was not allowed and there was no 24-second clock so a team could freeze the ball at will. The very first game at home was nip and tuck all the way, and with a minute and a half to go, we had the ball and the score was tied. The home crowd was going bananas and we could hardly hear each other when we called timeout to organize ourselves for the climactic play and win.

Our plan now was a simple, standard play. We froze the ball (they didn't dare foul) and called timeout again with about 15 seconds left. Now the strategy had to be more definite. We decided to freeze the ball in a wide circle until about eight seconds were left on the clock, then give the ball to Dolph where he said he wanted it and get out of the way and become spectators. As we were milling the ball around, Cervi suddenly began driving down the center lane for the basket, completely disregarding the game plan. Everybody was shocked and out of synch with this unexpected move. Somebody slapped the ball away from him, a Laker retrieved it and passed to Bob Harrison near midcourt, and he fired a "hail Mary" at the basket. Game was over – Minneapolis wins.

Even before the Syracuse fans could get over their shock, Al Cervi ran out of the gym, gathered up his clothes from the locker room, and, in uniform without taking a shower, was gone. The silence in that coliseum was unbearable, but it was over. We always felt that had we won that first game we would have been champions, for the series went six games and the rest were won by the home team. Oh, what could have been.

I just marvel at the different scene the NBA presents today. Oh, they wear the same uniforms we did, hear the same crowds, are written about in the paper the same way, enjoy the idolatrous fans as we did, and have the same title I had as an NBA player. But where they make big, big bucks, we were just helping the NBA out of its doldrums state during its infancy. My contract was $5,000 per season. We got $4.50 for meals per day. More often than not, we dug into our own pockets to tip the waitress.

Some of the courts where we played were glorified high school gymnasiums with the stands almost jutting out on court. I will always have some very noticeable scars on my shins from having been knocked into the steel frames of the seats. And you're fortunate if you can get back to the court without some fan's trademark left on your body.

Some of the places reeked of popcorn and other goodies which also attracted insects. The roaches in the Anderson, Indiana, locker room were literally the size of humming birds that flew in swarms from one end of the locker room to the other as we dressed. If one flew within the strike zone, we'd take a vicious cut with a sneaker for a home run. I hit about five into oblivion.

Buses and trains were our principal means of transportation, but occasionally the pressure of a tight schedule necessitated our traveling on the fearsome DC-3, an Army derelict with a defective heating system, that bounced around so dangerously some of the ballplayers, like Jerry Rizzo, would not board one. He'd take a Pullman a day ahead of time, ride it all night, and hope to get to the game on time the next day or pay a fine.

Today's endorsements, I understand, bring in millions to the players. My royalties for granting permission to the Kallfelz Baking Company to use my picture on their loaf of bread with the caption, "Johnny always calls for Kallfelz," was two shirts, two sweaters and two britches — but, of course, they all matched. I remember George Mikan sitting behind a Singer sewing machine to demonstrate its comfort. I can't believe we played in the same league as the guys do today.

If there are any regrets at all about having played in the NBA, it is that I did not accumulate or keep safe over time more mementos of my glory days. When my ex-teammate, Alex Hannum, heard I had not saved some memorabilia or souvenirs of my playing days, of his own volition he mailed me from his home in California a box of newspaper clippings, programs and pictures. These are irreplaceable items which he sent for my grandchildren to appreciate, only requesting that I duplicate those I wanted and mail them back. I'm flattered that Alex risked priceless memorabilia for my sake, but this epitomizes the bond of friendship that the NBA Pioneers have established.

We loved the game and in the depth of our souls we all knew we must give of ourselves if the NBA was to succeed. The old Pioneers played basketball with a determination and resolve because we all knew that the NBA's survival hinged on what we did. And old owners like Danny Biasone of the Syracuse Nationals contributed to the NBA's present abounding success by inventing the 24-second clock.

Every time I hear of the passing of guys like Chuck Cooper, Sweetwater Clifton, Alex Groza, Jim Pollard and the rest, I feel like a family member has passed. When you get old and you reflect on the knockdown, drag-out battles of yore with these guys in our youth, you develop a bond, a fraternal organization of "special people" who look at the NBA as an enterprise we built so that the guys today can make their millions.

I do not begrudge them their due. But in all likelihood they will never be in need of a pension, while some tribute should be paid the Pioneers. The three- or four-year vets must not be discriminated against or discarded. How can anyone associated with the game discount the old-timers' contributions to the NBA's well-being? Today's NBA "Fat Cats" eat well because of the persistence and endurance of past players and owners to have the league succeed, at times with great sacrifices monetarily and physically. We must not lose sight of them, as if they were nothing in the affairs of the NBA, for surely they are only too quickly passing into oblivion.

Although I meet the responsibilities of my non-extravagant lifestyle without great concern, I am nevertheless without a life insurance policy. I care for a 1987 Chrysler gingerly to maintain transportation and, according to my mechanic, my wife's 1981 Honda Civic "still runs good." These facts, however, are not complaints. Basketball has been good to me. I received an education, worked on a job with youngsters I love, and I have established and maintained permanent friendships with some very fine people indeed.

Now is the time for the NBA to ascend to the heavenly gesture of acknowledgment, of offering the Pioneers a "thank-you" pension in their waning years for the historical contributions they made to the welfare of the National Basketball Association. I hope that this project to highlight the Pioneer Era will bring it to the forefront of the sports world's conscience with its anecdotal account of our experiences. Maybe these human interest stories will be the instrument for all to appreciate the downtrodden three- and four-year veterans who are denied pension rights. We helped keep the league alive in its infancy and allowed it to flourish for the current NBA players to become millionaires and reap the harvest we planted.

Whitey Macknowsky played three winning seasons for the Syracuse Nationals (1948-51) before a broken wrist ended his playing career. As coach in New Jersey at Parsippany High School and Drew University he continued his winning ways. A member of the Seton Hall Hall of Fame, he lives in retirement in Dandridge, Tennessee, and is the author of Dynamics of Basketball *(1993).*

Bob Wanzer

Two years in a row, my Benjamin Franklin High School team won the New York City championship. We didn't even have a gym, would practice every day at a different school and Madison Square Garden was our home court. My coach, Bill Spiegel, thought I should go away to college, because if I stayed home in the City I'd play basketball somewhere every night and never do any schoolwork. He knew Honey Russell would take care of me, and so I went to Seton Hall. I was in the Marine Corps for three years, '43-46, when they sent me to Colgate and then out to the West Coast, but I came back to finish up at Seton Hall.

Honey was a strong defensive coach. He tried to teach us never to turn our heads on defense. One day in practice I was really hot, and he decided to teach his lesson. "Tomorrow," Honey said, "I'll play you, and you're not gonna score." I decided I was gonna get him, and I cooked up a plan with the team.

So the next day, we carried it off. With Honey on me, I tossed up a long set shot, deliberately short. But I acted as if it had gone in and started back down court to set up on defense. Honey, of course, hadn't turned his head and started to move down court himself. Then I turned quickly and ran by him toward the basket, where someone tossed me the ball and I made a layup. I didn't stop, ran straight off the court into the locker room, saying, "Honey, you turned your head, you turned your head." He kept yelling at me, "Come on out, come on out," but I wouldn't, I was through for the day. He never held it against me.

We still tell stories about Whitey Macknowsky, who was my teammate at the Hall. He was the kind of guy who always took a lot of teasing. He was a hell of a ballplayer, a great shooter and a heck of a defensive player. His pro career was cut short when he broke his wrist and lost flexibility there. I remember one time at school, when I went by his room and saw him at his desk studying under a lamp. His head is over the book, between it and the lamp. I said, "Whitey, what are you doing?"

"Studying," he said.

Bob Wanzer (right) trails the play as Fuzzy Levane drives against Ed Dancher of the Redskins.

PHOTO COURTESY OF FUZZY LEVANE

"But you can't see the book."

"OK, then," he said, "I'm drying my hair."

The connection between Seton Hall and the Rochester Royals was well established. They'd come down in the fall and work out for two weeks with us. It was legal then to do that. Bob Davies was with the Royals, and Bob Fitzgerald had also gone on to the pros. Whitey and Pep Saul and I all followed, and later Richie Regan and Walter Dukes.

Les held out for the rights to me and Saul as part of his deal with the league. Lazar, as I called him, was ahead of his time. There were a lot of similarities between Honey and Les as coaches. Both were strong individuals, with a keen sense of what players could and couldn't do. They both were good motivators, and they had no set offense, with a lot of free movement away from the ball. Honey spent much more time teaching defense, though.

With Les we always went first class. We always were on the Pullman cars on the trains, and when planes were available we'd fly. He treated us well. There was just one time I remember, after a bad loss in St. Louis when we played a very bad game, he got mad and made us ride in day coaches all the way home. The best story about travel in those years is the one about the Green Parrot Cafe on the way to Fort Wayne from Rochester. I'm sure someone like Marty Glickman will do a better job of telling that one.

It was an unfortunate thing that the NBA put both Minneapolis and Rochester in the same division. We were the two best teams in basketball, but we never could play each other in the finals. When we did play it was always a dogfight. We both wanted to win, and we knew each other very well. Mikan was the dominant player in the game and their whole front line dominated. We were a backcourt team, that's where we had to beat them, and Bob Davies and I suited one another very well.

When we won the title in '51, they had a better record during the season. When we had the better record, they managed to beat us in the Western Division finals.

When I first came into the league, Pat Kennedy was the only flamboyant official, but he was an excellent one. Then there was Sid Borgia, who'd always say, "I got the call, I got the call," when both officials blew the whistle. Later on, I liked Mendy Rudolph, Jim Duffy and Jim Gaffney.

I was probably pretty obnoxious to officials, both as a player and as a coach. But I always found that the good clubs got the breaks and the bad clubs didn't. So in that sense you made your own breaks. I remember a game against Boston, when we had a new young ref, and in the first half I was thinking, "We got a ref, we got a ref," because he was calling it straight, even calling Cousy for walking. At halftime, Red Auerbach went after this young ref, and that was the last time he called a walk on Cousy.

Yes, I know I am the answer to a sports trivia question. Who was the first player to foul out of an NBA All-Star Game? Here's how it happened. That was the game that Mikan sent into overtime with two free throws in the final seconds. The East scored first in overtime, so we had to foul. Cousy had the ball and I had Cousy, so I had to keep fouling him or they'd freeze away the game. He kept making free throws and I fouled out. I made him the MVP. They had voted for Pollard until the overtime, but they had to vote again to give it to Cousy. He owed it all to me.

I was deeply shocked when the scandals hit. We had won the World Championship, and we were on a preseason tour with the Kentucky team playing as the Indianapolis Olympians. We ended up in Chicago to play the college all-stars, and the Kentucky team came with us, to see the game, and then go on for its season opener at Tri-Cities. In the second half of that all-star game, we noticed that they weren't there, and we didn't know why. Later we found out that that's when they had been arrested.

What was so shocking was that they were just like us, they loved basketball so much. The only other incident that brought me close to the gambling happened when we came into Madison Square Garden for a game, and a friend of mine who was on the vice squad told me, "Don't make any calls out of the Garden, the phones are all tapped." They were about to crack down. And as for Jack Molinas, you know he was a great player, because he was starting ahead of George Yardley for Fort Wayne. He would have been my teammate on the West in that overtime All-Star Game if he hadn't been kicked out.

I really didn't pay much attention to the racial integration when it happened in the NBA. I had played with four black starters in high school at Franklin, so my experience was that basketball was always integrated.

After five consecutive years as a player in the All-Star Game, the next year I was the coach of the West. It was my first year coaching, and the Royals led the division at the break. That's how the coaches were chosen at that time. That was the night that, just before the half, Sharman threw a pass to Cousy the length of the court, too high for Cousy, but it went in the basket. That's when you knew it wasn't going to be your night.

We had a good young team, but it was a transition year and we didn't stay up there long into the season. Richie Regan had joined us from Seton Hall. He had excellent credentials from college, and it was good to see him. We had Jack Twyman, a fine offensive player. And we had the rookie of the year.

I always thought Maurice Stokes was the forerunner of the modern NBA player. At 6-foot-7 and 250 pounds, he could run the floor and lead the break. In the three years he played, only Bob Pettit had more rebounds (by 25 and Stokes missed nine games the third season). His only flaw was his shooting, but he was tough as nails, coachable, loved the game and wanted to win. If he hadn't got sick, he and Oscar would have been a hard combination to beat in Cincinnati.

The move to Cincinnati was tough. We had settled in Rochester. It was truly home. But Les had to do it, because he had been losing money with the club. And as usual he did it on his own terms. They included territorial rights to Oscar Robertson and, when Jerry Lucas came out, whatever else had taken place we would have the draft rights to him.

We got off to a terrible start in '58, and I was let go. Back in Rochester, I sold securities for Bache & Co. for a year or so and then got the chance to coach at St. John Fisher, a local Division III school. They offered me the athletic directorship as well after a couple of seasons, and it was really an ideal situation, without scholarships or pressure.

Being elected to the Basketball Hall of Fame was a great joy to me, a feeling of deep satisfaction to get the recognition by my peers, especially after being buried in a small town throughout my career away from the media centers.

Looking back, I think that the 24-second clock took something out of the game. It had been a very competitive game, with a premium on working hard for a real good shot. Then it became a shooter's game, where you had to run, and it took away the virtues of ball control. I still follow it, college and pro. It makes no difference. It's basketball.

Five consecutive years an NBA all-star guard (1952-56), three straight years on the all-NBA team (1952-54), first NBA player to shoot better than 90 percent from the free-throw line for a full season (1951-52), Bobby Wanzer retired from St. John Fisher College in 1987, the year after being enshrined in the Basketball Hall of Fame.

Nelson Bobb

I grew up in West Philly, a hotbed of basketball. My high school, West Philadelphia, sent several players to the pros, and our rivals at Overbrook produced Wilt Chamberlain and others.

After my freshman year at Temple, I went into the Army Air Force for 3½ years. I was a bombardier. When World War II ended, I didn't have enough points to come home and was based on Tinian Island. We had a team that played in some tournaments in Hawaii, and I remember playing against Chili Eddlestein. Later, stationed in Tucson, I played against a team from Phoenix that had Gene Mauch before he resumed his major-league baseball career. When I got out, I returned to Temple, where I played three more years, graduating in '49. Josh Cody was my coach, Harry Litwack was the assistant.

The Philadelphia Warriors made me their territorial draft choice. The pros played the same style of basketball I knew from college and the service, but the difference was that the competition was so much better that it was much more difficult. The game was in a transitional era, from the set shot to the jump shot, and I never learned to shoot the jumper. We'd run the weave a lot, to set picks for set shots. Now, of course, the players are bigger and faster and play above the rim.

Eddie Gottlieb was the coach and the owner. He also made the schedules for the league and arranged the transportation for our team. A benevolent dictator, he was affectionately known as "The Mogul." He was quite a character and a very honorable fellow. If we ever had to pay cab fare, he'd reimburse us to the penny. When we traveled by car, he'd sit in the front seat and give directions to whoever was driving. If you were waiting at a red light and could only turn left, he'd have to say, "Wait at the red light, then turn left." But he had a great memory. For years after he quit coaching, he'd make the schedules for the league. He knew the train schedules by heart, and he'd work out the game schedules without using a computer.

Eddie loved to win, even in exhibition games. If we saw we were going to lose a game and had traveled by car, some of us would run to a car without showering just to avoid riding with Eddie after a loss. He always seemed very comfortable with me, maybe because we were both Jewish, but he must have felt he could yell and scream at me and not the other players. If we were getting beat in the first half, he'd send me in for the last minute or two. Then, at halftime, he'd direct all his yelling and screaming at me. We all knew it was meant for the whole team, but I was the designated scapegoat.

When I came to the team, Jumpin' Joe Fulks was the star. He was a colorful character who doesn't get the acknowledgment he deserves. He kept the league together and revolutionized the game with that jump shot. He was the kind of guy who would ride on a fast elevator up to the 30th floor and he'd have to say "God damn" to you in that big Southern drawl of his. When I was a rookie, he used to send me out for Alka-Seltzer all the time. I didn't know what for, at first, but he was a big drinker and it was for his hangovers. I think the drinking cut short his career, but he later gave up alcohol and became a deacon of his church. In my opinion, he doesn't get the credit he deserves for being the great player he was.

The other star on the team my first year was George Senesky, a great, honorable guy. He had a rapport with Gottlieb that allowed him to say things that no one else could. In a way he was too honest, because he'd always speak his mind. He was a team player. In college he had been a great scorer, but he became an assists and defensive player for the Warriors because that's what we needed.

Andy Phillip was a great passer. He was leading the league in assists, and when he was going for a single-game record for assists, Gottlieb instructed us to get him that record. We had a big lead at the time, but it made it hard to play the rest of the game because we could only shoot if Andy had passed us the ball.

It was Paul Arizin, though, who turned the team around. A fabulous player and a nice guy, Arizin made the Warriors winners, and when he went into the Marines the team bombed.

Neil Johnston joined us first on a tryout basis. He had some natural ability, but we didn't really think he would make it in the pro game. Through perseverance, though, he made himself a great player, a Hall of Famer.

My last year with the Warriors, we were joined by another Temple graduate, Bill Mlkvy, who was known as "the Owl without a vowel." Bill was a great college player, had been outstanding as a freshman during my senior year. He played briefly in the pros, and then decided to go to dental school.

When I started, there was a $55,000 salary cap for the whole team. I made $3,500 a year and was glad to get it. In the off-season I went on unemployment insurance at $35 a week. Road trips were grueling. We'd travel in automobiles if the distance was short enough or by train to keep expenses down. Only for the longest trips would we fly, on DC-6s I think. We played an awful lot of exhibition games, and throughout my years our meal money allowance was five dollars a day.

In Philadelphia we played in The Arena and then Convention Hall. In places like Fort Wayne we would play in a high school gym. I remember the Rochester Arena because it was a lopsided building, very short on one side, and that always threw us off to play there. I loved going to Madison Square Garden because my cousin, Feets Broudy, was the timekeeper for the Knicks games, and I got a kick out of seeing him go in and out of the Garden like he owned it – some people thought he did.

I always knew there was a lot of betting on basketball, especially in New York. When I was in college, I used to get 10 dollars plus a free weekend to play games at Grossinger's, which I thought was a great deal. Of course, there was betting on the games there, too. I met Eddie Gard and Sol Levy there, both of whom were implicated in a betting scandal. Tom Gola once joined us for one of those weekends at Grossinger's. He was still in high school but could already play at a higher level.

By the way, while I was at Temple we beat Kentucky 60-59 in Philadelphia, but I don't know whether that game was thrown or not. We never won in Kentucky. It was difficult to win there, because most of the referees, I thought, were homers. I remember that coach Rupp used to come over before the games, and I didn't think very much of the way he would patronize coach Cody, a fellow Southerner, from Florida.

All our players for the Warriors in those years were white, but I never heard of any racial problems in the league. I remember that when we were about to play the Knicks after Sweetwater Clifton joined them, Eddie Gottlieb called Joe Fulks aside, our one Southern boy, and asked him how he felt about playing against him. Joe gave him a big smile and said, "He's just another nigra to me," but he said it totally without malice or prejudice. In fact, Fulks and Clifton later became very friendly. You would see them get into confrontations with each other whenever they played in televised games, but Joe was sure to tell us, "Aw, we're just doing that for TV."

I was a marginal player for four years in the NBA, with the Philadelphia Warriors, and I've been in the insurance business ever since. I've done well, but those were four of the best years of my life.

Nelson Bobb is president of the American Creditors Life Insurance Co., which moved its headquarters from Philadelphia to Newport Beach, California, in 1992.

Kenny Rollins

Frankly, there is very little I want to remember about the Pioneer Era of the NBA. Moving the wife, then later a child and wife, two or three times a year, the poor traveling accommodations (train, bus, auto, some planes) left me completely exhausted by the end of the season. Add to that, very low pay, small, dirty, dressing rooms all over the league, plus typical Chicago and Boston winters that left me longing for the warm South.

When I signed on with the Chicago Stags, I had no agent, and therefore with my poor negotiating skills was taken advantage of by a slick attorney for the Stags. I signed for the minimum. They did not have a place for my wife and me to live, nor did they offer to help find a place. We had to pick up and move three times in Chicago that first year and twice the second year, searching for accommodations in a large city we knew nothing about.

The transition from Kentucky to pro ball was not that difficult. The difficult part was being recognized as a good player, and accepted by the "cliques" – and there were several, especially in Boston. It was common to be "frozen out" both on and off the floor by a few players. Speaking of "frozen," another aspect was playing on that Chicago Stadium floor that was sometimes hazardous to one's health. The floor in most of our games was laid on top of the hockey ice, which caused the wood floor to sweat and become very slick. In addition it was cold for those on the bench.

And speaking of cold, I can't remember ever getting off the train in Minneapolis when it was above 5 degrees below zero. The attitude back then was to save money by any means possible, so we walked in that weather two blocks to the old Nicolet Hotel where we stayed.

The level of play was good, lots of effort, still a lot of two-hand set shots back then. The chief differences I see in today's pro player from those of our era are: (a) the jump shot, (b) larger players, (c) better shooters and (d) greater athleticism.

There was very little media coverage, and what we did get was with the under-lying feeling that "This won't last long." Most of the trades of players took place in the off-season, very little during the season.

After my first year in the league, my old teammates at Kentucky were coming in as a new franchise in Indianapolis. They tried to buy my contract from Chicago, but the Stags' price was much too high for a fledgling team. Later, when Ralph Beard and Alex Groza were arrested, no one was more utterly shocked than I was. All the time that I had played with them at Kentucky, I had seen nothing but total effort and commitment. Coach Rupp may have had friends in Lexington who were big-time gamblers, but I don't believe they had any contact with our players.

In the spring of 1950 I was so disillusioned by the attitude of the Stags, the NBA, the travel, the weather, that I agreed to switch to a new league, and played one year with a team in Louisville sponsored by Reynolds Aluminum Co. It didn't last even one full year, but I was offered a job with Reynolds and took it.

In the summer of 1952, Red Auerbach called me at Reynolds in Louisville, and asked if I would be interested in playing for the Celtics. I said yes, but not if I had to give up that job. The Celtics worked behind the scenes somehow and got me a six-month leave of absence without pay, and I played the '52-53 season for the Celtics.

The only memorable thing there that year for me was toward the end of the season, maybe 10 or 12 home games left, when Walter Brown decided to televise a game, a "first" in the NBA as I recall. Club officials tried to discourage him by saying, "Once people see it on TV, they will never come to the games." At the time we were averaging around 7,500-8,000 fans at the games. After that first televised game, people called the Celtics office wanting to know where Bob Cousy went to college (Holy Cross is only a few miles away), why Ed McCauley was called "Easy Ed," where Bill Sharman went to college, and the like. From then on attendance was always in five figures at the games.

I left there knowing I would not play another pro season even though I knew I could. The travel for me was a killer. "Easy Ed" was my roomie on the road, and he was appropriately named. He could sleep anywhere, at any time. I've seen him asleep in a plane, on a runway, before we would even taxi for takeoff. In the pre-season, playing exhibition games traveling in my car all through Maine and Massa-chusetts, I drove while he slept. I could never do that, could never relax and sleep like that, and as a result I was tense all the time, and again exhausted by the end of the season.

I went back to Louisville, went to work again for Reynolds Aluminum, stayed with them for seven years. The last location was Grand Rapids, Michigan, where I was line salesman. The weather again got to us, but Reynolds would not transfer me south so I resigned. Then I got lined up with a shipping container firm called Container Corp. of America and stayed with them for 25 years as an account manager selling boxes to industry all over central Kentucky, and I retired in 1987.

We lived in Lexington 13 years, then Lawrenceburg, Kentucky, for 15 years, and moved permanently to Florida in July 1994.

Captain for two seasons of the "Fabulous Five," Kenny Rollins held Bob Cousy without a field goal en route to Kentucky's 1948 NCAA championship and won a gold medal in the Olympics that year. His professional success came in commerce rather than basketball.

Wallace (Wah Wah) Jones

As an all-state high school player from Harlan, Kentucky, I was heavily recruited by colleges, but it came down to a choice between Kentucky and Tennessee. There was a lot of support for the Vols in my part of the state and the pressure to go to Knoxville was very strong, but I held out for Kentucky and went to Lexington to play for two coaching legends, Adolph Rupp in basketball and Bear Bryant in football.

This was at the end of World War II, but I never had to serve. When I was called up they said I was ineligible because they found some bone chips from a basketball injury. So I got to go straight to college and arrived in time for the football season my freshman year. I played four years of football and three of baseball for Kentucky, besides my four years of basketball.

A lot of others had problems with coach Rupp, but I always had a good relationship with him. Our only difference of opinion was that he didn't like me playing football. He actually held me out of a basketball game once because he said I wasn't ready to play – it was right after football season. That was one of the few games we lost during my years at Kentucky.

We had a great team all four years, won 130 out of 140 games. We won the NIT my freshman year, 1946, and went to the finals in 1947. In 1948, we won the NCAA and then won the gold medal at the Olympics, and in my senior year we won the NCAA Tournament again. Ralph Beard, Alex Groza and I all played in the College All-Star Game in 1949 against the world champion pro team, the Minneapolis Lakers. During most of those years, I played in the shadow of Beard and Groza, so it was an honor to be selected to that team along with them. And then I was MVP for the collegians in that game, scoring 22 points. We had a good thing going. I'd fake to Beard, they'd jump out to stop him, and I'd turn to shoot from the top of circle.

They gave us, the Kentucky team, a pro franchise as the Indianapolis Olympians team, because they wanted to take advantage of our popularity. Wherever we played on the road, the people came out to see us. It was as if everyone wanted to get in on our glory deal.

I really enjoyed the first two years in the NBA in Indianapolis. One of those years my wife moved up there with me, and we lived across the hall from Joe Holland and his wife. It was a real good experience and a fun time.

They really treated us fine in Indianapolis and attendance at our home games in Butler Field House was always good. I remember that when we'd leave for an all-night train trip to Syracuse and Rochester, our friend Bernie would fix food for us. We'd leave Butler Field House, pick up our prepared meals at Bernie's diner, and be on our way.

Dolph Schayes, Vince Boryla and Leo Barnhorst were my toughest opponents to guard. Of course, against the Lakers, I'd sometimes have to help Groza out on George Mikan. Mikan would get the ball, fake to get defenders in the air, and then go up with his shot and draw a foul for a three-point play. One night in Butler, he made his fake, and I went up in the air. Before I came down I decided that he wasn't going to get three points. I came down, grabbed him by the neck, and put him on the ground. Big George didn't take kindly to that, and there was some pushing and shoving when he got up, but he got only two free throws on the play.

At the start of the third season, I was having trouble with my knee, hadn't quite recovered from surgery, so I didn't go on the usual exhibition tour. They didn't want me risking the knee by playing in those small gyms and armories all over Wisconsin. So I wasn't with the team at the College All-Star Game in Chicago when Beard and Groza were arrested. I heard the news on the radio the next morning. I got some calls at my mother-in-law's house in Lexington, but I couldn't tell anyone anything about it, because I simply didn't know anything. It all came as a total surprise to me.

At the end of that season I just didn't want to pursue pro basketball. My knee hadn't really recovered after the first operation and I would need another operation if I wanted to continue playing. Instead I got into the game of politics. I was the first – and last – Republican sheriff in Fayette County, Kentucky.

For 30 years I've been publishing *Around the Town*, a magazine for hotels, motels and the chamber of commerce in Lexington. Now I also distribute a 16-page book called *Leonard's Losers* with predictions about football, both pro and college. I've been in the travel business, too, but now my son owns and runs Blue Grass Tours and Charters with all its excursion buses.

I still follow basketball quite a lot, but the pro game has gotten pretty tiresome. It isn't real basketball; there's too much pushing and shoving. I follow the college game closely; I go to all the Kentucky games – basketball and football, and though my knee doesn't allow me to drive the ball very far any more, I still hit it straight down the middle when I play in a lot of charity golf tournaments.

Among his many athletic honors, Wah Wah Jones has one unique distinction: He is the only Kentucky player to have his jerseys, with his retired number 27, hanging both in Rupp Arena and Commonwealth Stadium.

Joe B. Holland Sr.

I went to high school in Benton, Kentucky, in Marshall County, at a time when they had eight high schools. Now there's one. During World War II, 1943 was the only year that Kentucky gave up its "Sweet Sixteen" arrangement for the high school tournament and had regional and sectional play. We got through those and made it to the final four.

As an all-state player, I was heavily recruited. Coach Diddle wanted me at Western Kentucky and Murray State had their greatest graduate, Joe Fulks, try to get me there, but I was headed for the University of Kentucky all along. I went up to Lexington and started summer school, but I was only there a couple or three weeks when I was accepted into the V12 program, which I had forgotten I'd even applied for. And they promptly sent me down the road to Berea College.

There I was transferred into the V5 program of the Naval Air Corps, and that's where I played my first season of college ball. We had a successful season for a small college, actually came within five or six points of beating Kentucky, with Bob Brannum. My second year of college basketball came with the Iowa Pre-Flight team. I was the leading scorer and rebounder on a team that beat Wisconsin and Kansas, and lost to Notre Dame, with Vince Boryla, by one point. I had my primary training in Norman, Oklahoma, then advanced flight training in Corpus Christi, Texas.

As soon as the war ended and I knew I was getting out, I got a call from coach Rupp. "Get on back here," he said, "we're getting ready to have a basketball team."

That was an understatement. With Ralph Beard, Wah Wah Jones, Jack Tingle, Jack Parkinson and Wilbur Schu, we won the NIT in '46. For the next season, Brannum was back but later transferred to Michigan State. We also had Alex Groza, Kenny Rollins and Cliff Barker, plus freshmen Dale Barnstable and Jim Line, who contributed heavily that year and for the next three years. In the SEC tournament that year we won by pretty easy margins and the first five of both the all-SEC team and the all-tournament team were Kentucky boys – Beard, Jones,

155

Rollins, Tingle and Holland. But then we got beat in the '47 NIT finals by Utah when Wat Misaka held Beard to one point.

Coach Rupp and I had a disagreement at midseason the following year, and I was benched for several games, which led to my losing my starting slot on the NCAA championship team to Barker and consequently my place on the Olympic team. However, I did make up with Rupp and went to London that summer anyway, with Barnstable and Line, mainly as alternates to the Olympic team.

My introduction to professional basketball began with a barnstorming tour through Kentucky and parts of West Virginia. I had graduated in 1948 and, although I had a year of eligibility left, I chose to go to work instead of returning to school. Four of my teammates, Groza, Beard, Jones and Barker, all graduated in 1949 after winning the NCAA Tournament. They immediately organized a barnstorming tour headed up by Babe Kimbrough, a sportswriter for a Lexington newspaper. They called me to ask if I would join them and I immediately said yes. I had found that I really missed basketball and wanted to play some more.

We had a very successful tour, and during the tour we got a call from Leo Ferris, who ran the old NBL. The NBL offered us a franchise in Indianapolis. In the meantime, the NBA president, Maurice Podoloff, was talking to coach Rupp to try to get him to influence Groza, Beard and Jones to join the teams from the NBA which had their draft rights. I had been drafted the previous year by the Chicago Stags, but after a visit was not interested. Now we were being recruited like kids out of high school.

The NBL offered us, Kimbrough and five players, the entire franchise, to own all the common stock. Ike Duffy, owner of the Anderson Packers and head of the NBL, offered to put up the necessary money and take preferred stock in the club. After Groza and Beard made their decision to go as a unit, we accepted the offer of the NBL and signed up to enter the league in the fall of 1949.

That was a coup for the NBL, but instead of renewing the strength of the old league that had lost Minneapolis, Rochester and Fort Wayne to the BAA the year before, it led directly to a merger in a 17-team league now renamed NBA. The Eastern Division consisted of the New York Knicks, Philadelphia Warriors, Syracuse Nationals, Washington Capitols, Baltimore Bullets and Boston Celtics. In the Central Division were the Rochester Royals, Fort Wayne Pistons, Minneapolis Lakers, Chicago Stags and St. Louis Bombers. The Western Division had the Sheboygan Redskins, Waterloo Hawks, Anderson Packers, Tri-Cities Blackhawks (Moline, Davenport and Rock Island), Denver Nuggets, and us, the Indianapolis Olympians.

Each team had one or two great players and the rest good solid players in some phase of the game. Joe Fulks was still a factor in Philadelphia and in successive years they added Paul Arizin, a rising star, and then a center named Neil Johnston. Syracuse had Al Cervi and Dolph Schayes. Rochester had Arnie Risen and Bobby Davies. The Knicks had Vince Boryla and Dick McGuire, then

Sweetwater Clifton. Boston would soon have Bill Sharman, Ed Macauley and Bob Cousy. Washington still had Bob Feerick and Bones McKinney.

Minneapolis had the greatest team of that time in George Mikan, Jim Pollard, Vern Mikkelsen, Herm Schaefer, Slater Martin and Bob Harrison. The Chicago Stags had our ex-teammate Kenny Rollins and Max Zaslofsky. Ft. Wayne had Fred Schaus. Tri-Cities had Dike Eddleman and Gene Vance. The Anderson Packers had a good competitive team, led by Frankie Brian.

We had a great first year in the league, winning our division, though Anderson beat us in the playoffs. By the end of the next season, there were only 10 teams left in the league, and this time it was Minneapolis that knocked us out of the playoffs. We were a young, improving team and we took some lumps, but we also gave some.

We traveled north by train, and believe me it was no picnic! Our pay was low – between $6,000 and $12,000 per year with a small per diem for travel. Attendance was very good for that era, but the gyms were mostly small, especially where some of the old NBL franchises played, and not well-suited for the pro games. We played in Butler Field House which seated 10,000 plus, and we filled it every night. But we only had radio to carry it to the public and no revenue from that. However, we had a nice profit in both the first and the second year in the NBA.

It appeared that we would be a strong threat in the league well into the future. Groza and Beard had both made the All-NBA Team both years and were surely headed for lasting stardom. We had acquired several other good players. Joining the five from Kentucky and ready for our third season were Bill Tosheff from Indiana, Leo Barnhorst from Notre Dame, Marshall Hawkins and Paul Walther from Tennessee, Bob Lavoy from Western Kentucky, and big Joe Graboski, who had played two seasons for the Stags. We had also hired Herm Schaefer of Minneapolis to coach, replacing the player-coach arrangement we had used with Barker and Jones.

We were doing well in the exhibition season and now knew we could compete at this level. So we were approaching the third year with a lot of optimism. The optimism ended in Chicago right after the College All-Star Game. As Beard, Groza, Barker and I came out of Chicago Stadium, walking to get a cab, we were approached by a group of men who showed their badges, took us by the arm and put us in the back of squad cars.

They were detectives from the District Attorney's office in New York along with Chicago police, and they were taking us down to the Cook County Courthouse. Beard and I were in the back of one car, and on the way he said to me, with that little stutter of his, "Th-th-they want to ask us some questions about those fixes of a few years ago. B-b-but don't worry, we're OK."

Well, I was worried, because I had sensed that something was going on. They separated us, putting Barker and me in one room, Beard and Groza in another. They kept us all night, until six in the morning, but Cliff and I had very little to say.

Then, around 6 a.m. they brought us all together in a large courtroom and announced that they had confessed to accepting money from gamblers. Our old teammate, Dale Barnstable, had also been picked up in Louisville.

Beard and Groza both looked beat up. They had been under the lights all night. Alex asked me to call his brother in Martins Ferry, Ohio, which I did, but of course it had been on the news all night and John already knew. Barker and I called Babe Kimbrough, our manager, and we got together and bailed Beard and Groza out of jail, and then we headed for Indianapolis.

This ended any dreams of owning a team in the NBA. Jones was out for the season with a bad knee. Barker and I were all that remained. I lost my interest in basketball and Barker must have too, because he wasn't competitive any more. Herm Schaefer didn't see fit to play me much, even though I had developed a jump shot. We played out the year but the handwriting was on the wall.

I tried to maintain my interest in the team, going so far as to hire a lawyer to attend meetings but nothing came of it. The league made sure we gave up the franchise. I feel that they overreacted, and a lot of innocent people suffered. Bill Spivey, for example, would have been one of the greats of all time, as Groza would have been. There was no doubt about Beard. He had already shown that he could dominate players like Slater Martin, Al Cervi, Bob Cousy and Bob Davies.

Other things were happening in the NBA, other franchises folding and moving. The NBA was still struggling, but TV was just around the corner. And with TV came the long-awaited prosperity, but the Olympians were not to share in it. A group of Indianapolis businessmen took over the franchise after my last year, and they called it quits after one last season, a losing one on the court and financially.

I didn't go to a basketball game for five years. But it's a great sport — my son played — and I became a fan again, of pro and college basketball. Kentucky has one of the best coaches now, Rick Pitino, and the athletic director, C.M. Newton, has been a good friend of mine for a long time.

No one should ever doubt that the present day was set up by pioneer owners, players, officials and fans. Basketball is a great game with a wonderful past and a bright future.

Joe Holland's Chevrolet dealership has been a fixture in Charleston, West Virginia, since 1956. Now run by his son, it also has Volkswagen, Isuzu and Hyundai. Bachman Chevrolet in Louisville, which they've had for 11 years, is run by his son-in-law, Steve Bachman, while a manager holds the fort at Joe Holland Chevrolet in Lexington, site of many of Joe's triumphs as a Wildcat mainstay of the deep Kentucky squad misnamed "The Fabulous Five."

Bob Lavoy

In 1946, which was a very interesting year for me, I was discharged from the Army. Prior to entering the service I had made a commitment to the University of Illinois for what would have been the fourth year of the Whiz Kids. Now, having just been discharged in July and with school starting in September, I was just not ready to go back to college.

I had several options open to me. One was I could sit on a street corner. Two was to sit on a street corner and draw my "52/20" – twenty dollars a week for fifty-two weeks. And the third option was to go back to school. So I decided to go back to school and went to the University of Illinois, played one semester there, was unhappy about it, was not ready to go to school, dropped out and came back home to Aurora.

I then went to work for Stevenson-Adamson, known for its softball teams, and that's why I went to work for them. They gave me a job as a bearing grinder, and I played softball for them. I wasn't their best pitcher, but I was one of them. That was the first year of the BAA, but of course, since I had only been a high school player and then went into service and briefly to college, I wasn't contacted by any pro teams.

During the summer of '47, I received a long-distance phone call. My mother called me to the phone, saying it was Bowling Green calling. So I answered the phone and the gentleman I spoke to was coach E.A. Diddle of Western Kentucky. Anyone who knows about coach Diddle knows that it was impossible to understand what he was saying. But I did understand him to say that someone would be getting in touch with me the following week.

When the call came, it was the coach's assistant, Mr. Ted Hornback. He explained to me a little bit about Western Kentucky. However, we never used the words "Western Kentucky," we kept talking about "Bowling Green." In the interim between Coach's call the previous week and Mr. Hornback's call this week I went to the dictionary and found that Bowling Green was a small college in Ohio, and

Bob Lavoy. PHOTO COURTESY OF BOB LAVOY

Vintage NBA: The Pioneer Era

that was it as far as I was concerned. Well, it was explained to me that I would be able to catch a train out of Chicago and go to Louisville, Kentucky, where I could catch a bus out of Louisville and it would take me to Bowling Green. To me that was a long way to get to Bowling Green, Ohio. It wasn't until a later conversation that we figured out it was Bowling Green, Kentucky.

So I did that very same thing. I took the train from Chicago and rode all night. Then I took the bus from Louisville and rode most of the day, 125 miles from Louisville to Bowling Green. I got off the bus at the depot, took a cab and rode up the hill. At the top of the hill was Western Kentucky. I got out of the cab and went down to the gymnasium where I was introduced to coach Diddle and coach Hornback. Fifteen minutes later I was out on the court practicing my wherewithal. I guess they were going to see if they would keep me or what would happen. But to make a long story short, I became very happy at the University of Western Kentucky.

I stayed there from '47 through '50. '49 was a pretty good year for me. I had been known for a guy that spoke his own mind, but Coach didn't appreciate a lot of the things that I had learned in service. I don't mean shooting people, but other things I had learned to do, such as drinking and smoking. Coach was very adamant about those two subjects, especially the smoking part of it. Well, by 1949 I had found a lovely coed. Coach got her off to one side and tried to get her to change some of my habits with her wiles. At least some of them changed, the drinking part of it, and so I became a valued part of the Western Kentucky Hilltoppers.

During my last year, '49-50, I was contacted by the people up in Rochester, New York, as I had made a pretty good record. I also got a telegram from the Indianapolis Olympians, advising me that I was their No. 1 draft choice and would be getting in touch with me that summer to discuss a contract. It was a team made up at that time of five players from Kentucky – Ralph Beard, Alex Groza, Joe Holland, Cliff Barker and Wah Wah Jones – who had been on the Olympic team in 1948.

So we started our first year with Indianapolis in 1950. I got a $2,000 bonus and a $6,000 contract. We were thrilled to death but we were sorry to lose out on the offer of a new Dodge that would have been part of the Rochester deal. In August of 1949, I had married that lovely girl from Cave City, Kentucky, and the following August we had our first child. We arrived in Indianapolis in a '46 Ford, pulling all our possessions on a flatbed trailer hooked onto the bumper. It was slow going because the car went one way and the trailer the other. We checked into a motel with $10 left in our pocket and I proceeded to go down to the offices of the Olympians, told them of our plight, and they advanced me some money to get a house or apartment, and that's how my pro career started.

After we had found a place to live and settled in, then practice started. I had never met any of the players, had never even played against them, although Kentucky and Western Kentucky had both been quarterfinalists in the 1950 NIT. But this was a new era, a new climate, a new set of circumstances. Some of the players got along very well. I knew what my duty was. I was there to relieve Alex Groza in the center position and accepted that role, and we got along just fine.

The team did not seem to progress in any great manner. We didn't win a whole lot of games, simply because we were not a team. The team was owned by the Kentucky players, and they had chosen one of their own, Cliff Barker, I think he was the oldest, to be the coach of the team. They brought in several other players during the preseason. Even though we had a contract, we had to make the team. I recall going on the road to an exhibition game one time and at the halftime of that game the coach, Cliff Barker, made the comment to everyone in the room that if they didn't pick up their ability to play the game by the end of the game that there were going to be some ballplayers no longer with the team. And after the game was over, true to his word, Mr. Barker cut two players from the ballclub. One was a close friend of mine who had played at Eastern Kentucky and another was a fellow from Morehead State in Kentucky.

We went on about our business of playing the ballgames. We didn't have a very good year in '50-51, and '51-52 was still not a very good year. But there were a couple of things that happened that were exciting. One occurred on January 6, 1951, when the Olympians played the Royals in Rochester. The game went six overtimes and we won 75-73. That is the most number of overtimes ever played in an NBA game to this date. Also, February 6, 1951, was the first time I had taken my daughter Carolyn to a basketball game, dressed in a pink snowsuit, and 18 months old at the time. She may not have known much about basketball, but I know that it was my best game as a professional, scoring 31 points.

One night we were on a plane flying out of Boston after a game when a cowling failed to close and caused a huge backfire. We had several players on the Indianapolis team that were of the Catholic faith. And if you wanted to see something that's funny, when you looked back they all had their rosaries out and were praying to heaven that they were going to live through this experience. As it was, nothing serious happened to the plane. Another time they hadn't closed the door tight enough when we boarded the plane and as a consequence the suction blew the door off the plane and luckily no one was sucked out with it.

One of the experiences that was comical was that we had a pinochle game that went on for months at a time, with players like Cliff Barker, Joe Holland, Bill Tosheff and me. When we got to the location where we were to play a game you'd put your cards in your pocket, go play the game, get dressed, and come back and resume the game on bus or train or plane as if it had never stopped in the first place.

When the next season, '52-53, came along, it was proceeding in an auspicious manner. Then one day, we were on our way to play the Tri-City Blackhawks and stopped in Chicago to watch Chicago play. There was quite a bit of excitement. We were sitting underneath the basket at one end of the court, and people kept moving around, people we had never seen before. And it was unfortunate but it was at this game and at this time that Ralph Beard and Alex Groza were arrested for fixing a game against Loyola of Chicago when they were in college. They both dropped off the team at the time. The rest of the team members vowed to continue with the course of the season, went on to Tri-Cities and continued the schedule that was so horribly interrupted by this tragedy.

It was devastating to me personally. My wife and Ralph Beard's wife had become very close, and we had a few-months-old baby and our future was in jeopardy. But it was a tragedy because everyone associated with the club was affected. Not one other player could understand how those two men could possibly have been involved in anything like that, especially Alex, who was a hardworking team player. Ironically, I had seen that Kentucky-Loyola game because Western Kentucky had played in the first half of that doubleheader, and for the life of me I couldn't remember seeing anything wrong with the way that game was played. But the Olympians club went on to lose an awful lot of money and went bankrupt, I missed out on some much-needed paychecks and they closed the doors at the end of the season in Indianapolis.

At the close of that season I had not completed all of my college work, and I went back to Western Kentucky for the final two courses I needed. That was when I was called by the Milwaukee Hawks and told that they had purchased my contract. Would I like to play for them? Well, not wanting to be hung out to dry, I said, "Yes, I would come provided you pay me fifteen hundred dollars as an advance on my contract." They agreed to do that. Of course, at that time there were no agents. You had no one to talk to. In fact there were few trainers. Some at your home games, but on the road you had to tape your own ankles. Whatever had to be done, the players did it themselves.

Milwaukee was a beautiful place and when we got up there we were elated over the beautiful home we found, a three-bedroom duplex. We got settled down, started practicing and we weren't doing very well. Six weeks after we got there, coming back from Fort Wayne on a train, I was called back to Fuzzy Levane's office, and the owner Ben Kerner told me I had been traded to the Syracuse Nationals. It struck me quite abruptly, and I didn't know what to say except yes, because in my mind I was going from a last-place team to a second-place team.

When the train arrived in Milwaukee, my wife was there to meet us and was told about the trade. And as we rode back in the car along with Ben Kerner and Fuzzy Levane, the things that Jane told that man could not be reprinted, because she told him they had done me a disservice while I was thinking they had done me a favor. The climax was, I had just moved into an apartment with all my things and had to report to Syracuse within 24 hours. I caught a plane out, left my wife and child in Milwaukee, and went to Rochester where the Nationals were playing their next game. I arrived in time to get dressed for the game and scored 14 points. We won that game and went back to Syracuse.

In Syracuse I finally ended up with a basketball team. I am telling you, the difference between that team and the Indianapolis team or the Milwaukee team was night and day. We were blessed with the talents of Paul Seymour, Dolph Schayes,

George King and the first black player to play in the NBA, Earl Lloyd. Al Cervi was the coach of the team and the owner's name was Danny Biasone. Before his death he was the originator of the 24-second rule in the NBA. He passed on a year or two later and has never received proper credit for his contributions by being elected to the Hall of Fame.

Syracuse ended up in the Eastern Division round robin with a game against the Celtics in Boston on St. Patrick's Day. Late in the game, Dolph Schayes was driving toward the basket and he was tunneled by one of the Boston players. He fell to the ground (we later found out he had broken his wrist) and a donnybrook ensued. People from the stands came pouring out on the floor, and fights were going on. We had a fellow from Illinois by the name of Wally Osterkorn, who not only looked and acted and was as big as a bull, but would fight a bull and would take on any of the Boston players that happened to get in his way.

All the players from our team proceeded onto the floor and got involved – except yours truly. I found no one that I could whip. Bob Cousy was being picked on by everybody. I couldn't get to him so I remained on the bench. And you know how the crowds are – when they get excited they're throwing their hands and fists in the air and their watches all came flying onto the court and I kept picking them up. I didn't get involved in that fight but as it turned out we beat the Celtics by one point in overtime in Boston on St. Patrick's Day and went on to win the Eastern Division championship.

We went on to play for the World Championship against the Minneapolis Lakers and lost in the seventh game in Minneapolis by seven points. It was at this time that I decided that I felt no longer capable of playing in the NBA. Chances are I could have hung on but it had never been my intention or my way of life to do something just to be a hanger-onner. So I decided that I would retire from the game and go back to whatever it was that would be my future, whether it was high school coaching or teaching or what it was.

We hope that sooner or later the players that are playing the game today, the players' union whether broken up or together again, that somebody's going to realize that if it hadn't been for players such as myself, there wouldn't be an NBA today. When Pete Rozelle was asked what was his proudest accomplishment as commissioner of the NFL, he stated that it was when he brought *all* of the players into the organization as members of the pension plan. Wouldn't it be nice if the NBA had the same attitude as Pete Rozelle?

Somewhere along the line when they formed the players association in 1965, they forgot about all the players in the early years who were responsible for the NBA in the beginning. We worked for peanuts, played as hard as we could and made the NBA what it is today. And all their complaints about their future and their inability to deal with the salary cap make me upset to my stomach. We had no players union, we had no agents and I'm glad we didn't. We only played because we loved the game of basketball and we gave it all we could.

Bob Lavoy played for Indianapolis, Milwaukee and Syracuse in his four NBA seasons (1950-54). He led the Olympians in shooting percentage in '53 and was second in rebounds to Joe Graboski. He later coached high school teams in Kentucky and Ohio for four years and the University of Tampa for eight. Now retired after 23 years working for Hillsborough County, he hopes to see the arrival of one of his four grandchildren, Tim Fries, as a major-league baseball player.

The Indianapolis Olympians after the departure of the "Fabulous Five" from Kentucky. From left to right: Buckshot O'Brien, Gene Rhodes, Bill Tosheff, Paul Walther, Mel Payton, Leo Barnhorst, Bob Lavoy, Zeke Zawoluk, Joe Graboski and Don Hanrahan. PHOTO COURTESY OF BILL TOSHEFF

Vintage NBA: The Pioneer Era

Bill (Tosh) Tosheff

I'm from the beautiful resort community of Gary, Indiana. They used to say, "Shoot 'em in Gary and dump 'em in Chicago, shoot 'em in Chicago and dump 'em in Gary."

We were not recognized as part of Indiana because we're so far north. Close to Chicago, along with Hammond, East Chicago and Whiting, all the steel mill towns, we used to be called "The Region" or better, "Da Region." Big population of ethnic people. My high school had 41 different nationalities — try that one! When we went down to Indiana University from Da Region and took English, we were credited for a foreign language. Guys who were raised in Gary did two things: we all worked in the steel mills and we played every conceivable sport.

When World War II came along I enlisted in 1943 and served three years in the Army Air Corps. I did a lot of flying. I matured tremendously while I was in service. My body and mind got stronger. I was a kick-ass guy from Gary. I decided I wanted to go to college when I came back. I turned down an offer to join the Chicago Cubs and several other offers from colleges, but entered Indiana as a walk-on at midterm in 1947.

The first year there, I made the first string as a quarterback in football, made the first team in basketball and was a pitcher on the baseball team. My sophomore year I had a 9-1 record and we won the Big Nine baseball championship — it wasn't the Big Ten then. And in basketball I was captain my senior year when we were 19-3, fifth in the AP and seventh in the polls. I set nine free-throw records, starting at 18 and going to 28, during the season, and made All-Big Ten Conference and several published All-America teams.

After my career in Indiana, I was drafted into the NBA by the Indianapolis Olympians for the '51-52 season. The Olympians were then owned by the Kentucky Five — Ralph Beard, Alex Groza, Cliff Barker, Joe Holland and Wah Wah Jones. They had come into the league with their own franchise in 1949. Groza was the Rookie of the Year that year. I was also recruited by the Phillips Oilers and the

Goodyear Wingfoots of the industrial league, but I didn't care to get into industry. I wanted to play pro ball. I took the first contract from Indianapolis over to coach Herm Schaefer, an All-American from Indiana and on the 1940 national championship team.

I said, "Herm, what do you think of this contract?"

He said, "Gosh, it's a damn good contract."

It was for $4,500.

My first year I became the co-Rookie of the Year, along with BYU's Mel Hutchins of the Tri-Cities Blackhawks. That was the year that the big college scandals broke. Just before our season started, two of our stars – Alex Groza and Ralph Beard, who started opposite me at guard – got nailed for point-shaving. They were banned for life from professional basketball. All that happened during their college time. It was a big downfall. Do you think today that something like that would ever occur, that a guy would get banned? Too bad they didn't have the legal representation. They – Beard, Groza and Sherman White of LIU were the sacrificial lambs. Some seven colleges and 34 players were initially named, but the three were truly the sacrificial lambs.

We had a hell of a ballclub. We had just beaten the champion Rochester Royals five times in a row in exhibition games. We saw papers that had the story of Sherman White of LIU being arrested. I looked at Ralph Beard who was my locker partner. I said, "Beard, you guys played all the big arenas. Were you guys ever approached? You guys ever get any of that payoff stuff for dumping?"

Beard said, "Tosh, if I were ever implicated in that stuff, I'd take my wife Marilyn and my son Mikey and we'd disappear to Mexico." It's so vivid in my mind when he said that, even today.

Later that day we took the train up to Chicago to see the Rochester Royals play the College All-Stars. The day after the all-star game we were scheduled to open the season in Tri-Cities against the Milwaukee Hawks. After the game was over, detectives came out with all their badges on, and newspaper guys, and, I mean, I never saw so many in all my life, photographers shooting pictures of the big bust.

They took five of our players down to the South Chicago Police Station. They were Beard, Groza, Barker, Holland and Herm Schaefer, our coach. All night long they grilled Beard alternately with Groza. They had a lot of evidence, especially from New York. The names of gamblers and evidence tabs from the Copacabana nightclub where the two were entertained. Actually Beard was the one that broke down and confessed at about six in the morning. Groza had no other course to take, so he fell in line.

Groza died recently here in San Diego. We used to talk about the situation, and he often told me that if Beard had never said anything, he thought they could have beat the rap. When you look at the money situation, it was reported that Groza made $2,000 to $2,500 a ballgame. He was giving Beard $500 to $750 per game.

Let's hope it doesn't happen again, but, of course, it did happen again – the Connie Hawkins case. I reminded Beard not long ago of his remark about going to Mexico. He didn't like talking about it. He didn't remember saying that to me.

Anyway, it was a big change in our ballclub. We continued to play and we played real hard. I believe we'd have been World Champions for at least five years if we could have stayed together and kept our focus. I'm sure of that. Joe Graboski was on our team, along with Leo Barnhorst, Paul Walther, Wah Wah Jones, Bob Lavoy, Joe Holland and Mel Payton. We just couldn't recover from losing our two stars. By midseason we were in first place, but we faded. We did, however, make the playoffs against the Minneapolis Lakers. I averaged over nine points and was eighth in the league in free-throw percentage. I had the two-handed touch.

As co-Rookie of the Year, I was upped 1,500 bucks for my second year, up to six grand. I thought I was in hog heaven, especially since I supplemented that with baseball for several months, so I made a pretty good living at that time period. Six months of baseball, six months of basketball. My legs were in great shape. In basketball and being a pitcher in pro baseball, my wheels were great. My first pro baseball roommate was Herb Score. We lived together in 1952 and played for the Indianapolis Indians in the American Association. Subsequently, in a six-year span of professional baseball I played Triple A, Double A and A ball for the Texas League and the Southern Association, and spent some time in South America.

My second NBA year I averaged more than 11 points a game and was 10th in the league in free-throw percentage, still over 80 percent. We barely made the playoffs. We were swept by the Lakers. Then we were disbanded. My rights went to the Milwaukee Hawks.

Many funny things happened during our travels. It was by plane, train and we bused around the league. One of the classic exploits was when we traveled on an overnight train from Indianapolis to New York City. All of the guys would go back in the club car. While they were playing poker, gin rummy or hearts, I'd go back into our sleeping car, change all the luggage around, and pull the big plug that feeds the lights. When players went back to their bunks at 12 o'clock or 1 a.m., they wondered where the hell they slept. Much bad language. No one ever found out who did it. I'm not worried about retribution anymore. I was the one who did it.

At various times during the season, two ballclubs would cross paths at an airport or a train station somewhere. If it was at Union Station in Chicago, we usually had a three- or four-hour layover. Invariably we'd go over to a little Rumanian restaurant where we'd join George Mikan and other Minneapolis Lakers. On one occasion I went back to the men's room and I happened to look into the kitchen area. There was the biggest dog I ever saw in my life. It was a Mastiff Great Dane that could not get up on his own because he was so damn big.

I asked the guy who worked there, "How much does the dog weigh?"

He said, "This dog weighs about 305 pounds or more."

"Are you kidding me?"

"Oh, no, we've got a big meat scale back there. We roll him up and put him on the weight platform."

I said, "You sure he weighs that much?"

He said, "Yeah."

I went back to the table where I was sitting with George Mikan and Slater Martin. We were having a little lunch. I said, "George, how much do you weigh?"

George said, "I weigh 285 pounds."

I said, "You know, I've seen dogs bigger than you."

"What the hell you talking about, Tosh?"

I said, "I know a dog right now that outweighs you by at least, I guess, about 10 pounds."

Mikan said, "No way!"

I said, "Yeah, it's true."

We put up 20 bucks. I took Mikan to the kitchen. Two workers put the dog on the platform. So the dog is on the scale. The dog goes to 306 pounds. Mikan hands me the $20 bill and walks out. Yugoslavs – ha!

That dog actually looked like George Mikan. Every time he used to get up to the free-throw line, I'd say to him, "Guro," which means George in Yugoslavian. Then I'd give him the sign. I'd grab my throat with my right hand, like he was going to choke. And he'd always look at me and he'd go, "Naw, naw, naw." He would miss the free throw. He finally got me. He knocked my front tooth out. Maybe that was his retribution.

The referee corps at that time was great. We had Mendy Rudolph, who was a rookie then. We had Sid Borgia. We had Charlie Eckman. We had Arnie Heft. Borgia was a very feisty, little Italian referee. He thought I was Jewish. I accused him of being Jewish one time, and he called a technical foul on me. Every time he called a foul on me, I'd say, "Borgia, you are maudlin – m-a-u-d-l-i-n – maudlin."

This went on for practically the whole season. He'd look at me kind of funny every time I'd say it to him, then walk away after staring at me for a second or two. We happened to be on the same train coming back to Chicago from New York after the season was over, and he walked up and sat next to me.

Sid said, "Tosh, what does 'maudlin' mean?"

I said, "Maudlin means super-sentimental."

Borgia said, "I didn't know whether to call a god damned technical foul on you, or what." Well, he finally found out what the word meant. All the time he thought it was some kind of a curse word, and he didn't have enough sense to look it up in the dictionary. Sid Borgia, along with Heft, Eckman and Rudolph, were players' referees. We got along because they'd call the plays as they saw them, and if there was a technical foul, so be it.

One of the funniest things that happened was in Baltimore. We were in a really tight game with the Bullets. They happened to have "Grocery Night," where they'd give away tons of groceries. Big bags of groceries were raffled to people at halftime. In the third quarter, the game was pretty tight. There was a loose ball. I dove for it along with Bob Houbregs, who was about 6 feet 8 inches tall. Borgia said, "No, no, no, no, no, it's a jump ball."

I knew I couldn't get the jump because he was about a foot taller than me. As the ball went up, I climbed his right hip, went right over him, and I got the tip. Borgia came blasting in, saying, "No, Tosheff, you can't use this as a launching pad. We'll rejump."

At about that time, a guy came out of the stands, kicked me right in the ass and headed for the stands. I went after him. He started up the bleachers. I took the first step on the bleacher stairs in pursuit, but his wife was there. She had a big loaf of Silvercup bread, like a 3-foot package of bread, in both hands. With a baseball swing, she hit me right in the face. There were white bread slices all over the place. TV cameras were zeroed in. I stopped, looked at her, started laughing, grabbed her dress at the front, and pulled down, exposing her mammillaries in full view of the crowd and the cameras. There was almost a riot. The husband never came down from the top of the bleachers to save her dignity. I don't eat Silvercup bread.

The parquet floor at the Boston Garden had to be the worst floor we had to play on. They put it down on top of the ice most of the time. Chasing Cousy and Sharman around in that damn place, you'd hit the floor a lot. It was terrible. You'd get shin splints and a lot of floor burns. The Garden in New York was about the same. It was a makeshift floor. The courts in Baltimore and in Philadelphia were also pieces of work. Old makeshift stuff. You could be dribbling down the court, and all of a sudden the ball would leave you because there'd be a dead spot. Probably one of the best playing floors in NBA history was at the Butler Field House in Indianapolis. It was an elevated floor. When you went down the court to shoot a jumper, the spring in the floor just took you up in the air. It felt beautiful.

Dressing rooms were really brutal places. In Baltimore, for example, you'd dress in a room that had old heating equipment and old carpet and stuff all over the place. After the game, you'd have to hurry up to catch the train or plane, so you took a quick shower and froze your buns off, got dressed and headed for the train station in a taxicab.

Invariably, when we used to go to Minneapolis, it was during the winter months. Minneapolis always had taxicab strikes. We would have to walk from the train station to the hotel. If you played the night before, your uniform was still wet. You'd get to the hotel, open up your satchel, and your clothes were frozen stiff. They were like big ice sheets. We put them on a radiator to thaw them out. So you can imagine how great the guys smelled.

And another thing about smell, which is very important in the NBA, is that you could tell from the smell of his perspiration if a guy drank beer or whiskey the night before. But you could never tell if he drank vodka because it would never give out an odor. One of the classic guys who did a lot of heavy drinking was big Joe Fulks. He'd always sit up in front of the airplane. He'd have about six warm cans of beer in his satchel. Before the airplane took off, you could hear the cans fizzing as he opened them up. He'd drink about three before takeoff. Frankly, I think he was probably afraid of crashing.

I want to relate a truly mind-boggling happening. We had just finished a Sunday ballgame in the Boston Garden against the Celtics. They held the Convair 440 for us at Logan Airport, as we were going to fly to New York and then switch over to a Constellation from New York to Chicago. We got on the airplane still wet from perspiration. We sat up front where we would play pinochle on the floor, altitude about 7,500 feet, much bouncing around because of a lot of thunderstorms in the area with heavy turbulence. They couldn't serve food because it's just too damn rough.

All of a sudden, there was a tremendous explosion. What happens under certain climatic conditions is that the static electricity gathering on the leading edge of the wing, comes down the wing, and injects into the cabin area. It creates a great big ball of gas, very brightly colored and illuminated, all different colors of the spectrum. As it came rolling down the middle of the aisle to the back, seeking to expel itself through the tail of the airplane, a phenomenon called St. Elmo's fire exists. People fainted. The stewardess fainted. There were screams everywhere. Just for one moment — exactly, for one moment — when that explosion happened and the ball of static electricity rolled down the middle of the aisle, I saw the floor of the airplane open up. I saw the clouds below me. As God is my witness, I'll never forget that. When I tell people this, they ask me what I've been smoking.

My third year in the NBA was at Milwaukee with owner Ben Kerner, a classic in his own right. Ben Kerner, 19 coaches in 3 years. That's a record of some kind. I was back to my original salary of $4,500, but I still wanted to play. Fuzzy Levane was the coach.

This was 1953, the year when Maurice Podoloff tried something that made an interesting NBA sidelight. We made a trip to Minneapolis and when we walked in the arena I noticed that the baskets were unusually high. I was told that the baskets were moved up to 12 feet as an experiment for the game that night. I got on the floor, practiced a little bit. It took about a half hour to get used to the extra two feet of height. During the ballgame, George Mikan took his first 19 shots before he even got close to making his first semihook. That was his favorite shot. We, Milwaukee, beat the Lakers that night 76-75. Guys who played in this game don't remember that it even existed. It was the only time in NBA history when they raised the basket to 12 feet. How can one forget?

That same season we had a nationally televised game against the New York Knicks scheduled at 1 o'clock in the Milwaukee Arena. I got a phone call about 9:30 in the morning. It was Al McGuire on the other end. He and his brother Dick and Connie Simmons wanted to borrow my car to see some friends in Milwaukee. I said OK and drove the car down to their hotel. Turned my brand new

Oldsmobile 98 convertible over to the two McGuire brothers and Connie Simmons. They said they'd be bringing it back in about two hours. Two hours came and went. I went back to my apartment in Wauwatosa, about eight miles away, got a ride to the arena. When I showed up for the game my car still wasn't there.

The game started without Dick McGuire, Al McGuire and Connie Simmons. At halftime, two detectives approached me in the dressing room and said that my car was impounded. There had been a high-speed chase through the streets of Milwaukee. I don't know if Al was driving. Probably was. They were trying to elude the cops because they had been speeding. It cost me 165 bucks to get my car out of hock. They showed up at halftime, got dressed and played in the ballgame. They never said thanks or sorry. They just departed. That's the New York Big Apple guys. I think the McGuires' parents ran a carnival in New York at Far Rockaway Beach. Those guys were wild, especially Al. How he became a successful coach is beyond me. Maybe you've got to be in the carnival business to be a successful coach.

In all the NBA games I played in Madison Square Garden, seated around the perimeter of the floor were gamblers. When the point spread was beginning to change a little, especially in the last two minutes of the ballgame, the gamblers would be right behind the basket with their shirts off, waving and trying to make you miss free throws. There was one guy in particular that used to really bug me all the time. He was always on my back. So I made a point that when I got hit on a drive to the basket, I'd always land in his lap, soaking wet, stinking bad as an athlete does, look him in the face and say, "I'll be back."

My third season ended with a game against the Knicks in New York. We were out of the playoffs, our season was over. We left Grand Central about 5 o'clock for the long train ride back to Chicago. Most of us went to the club car to have a few drinks. There was a feisty, little Chinese guy who had set up a bar at one end of the car where he made sandwiches and poured drinks. We got to drinking pretty good, and after a couple of hours we found out somehow that in the next car there were a couple of striptease artists heading for Chicago. So we made a deal with them. If they'd come back to the club car and put on a little show, they could make some money. They were good-looking girls with great bodies. They agreed. The game was on.

We had a ballplayer with us by the name of Charlie Share, a big and really a funny guy. A great guy. We got the girls in the car and shut the door. All was set. As the train was just about to pull out of Utica, Charlie grabs the Chinese guy and virtually tosses him outside the back end of the club car while the train is starting to move out of the station. I broke up laughing. The Chinese guy was running down the tracks, trying to jump on the club car. He didn't make it. Charlie went back to the bar, and started making sandwiches and drinks. He collected the money, put it in the cash drawer, all legit. We moved through a couple of cars where many businessmen were and got the word out that there was going to be a strip show at 8 o'clock. Sure enough, by 8 o'clock all the guys came back and we charged them 5 bucks a head. We must have had 50 guys in there. Turned the radio on to some dance music, and the girls got up on a table doing a strip. The patrons were breaking up. We all were having a blast.

It ended about 9:30. Everybody calmed down by 10 o'clock and departed the club car to sleep. We pulled into Cleveland early in the morning. I heard men talking all over the place. I opened up the curtain in my little compartment, and there were railroad detectives with badges on, trying to find out who in the hell threw the Chinese guy off the club car in Utica. It was like a big investigation. Of course, they never got the right guy, but they kept us there for almost an hour before the train had to depart for Chicago. We're still breaking up. Those business guys had had a blast, throwing money at those gals. They made over 100 bucks apiece. The food was completely gone, the booze, too. Charlie Share made more money for the railroad that night than they did in many a trip. It was a blast.

When I quit the NBA, it was on my terms. I voluntarily retired because I did not like Ben Kerner. I thought the operation was bad. I missed Indiana. We were really focused on having a great ballclub there. I really believed we could have been champions for a long, long time had Groza and Beard not been eliminated. So after my third year, I came back from winter ball in South America, and Kerner asked me to sign a contract for $3,500.

I said, "Give me the pen." I signed my contract and said, "Put me on voluntary retirement."

He said, "You need me, Tosheff."

Three days later I was in South America. I lived there a year just to get the NBA out of my system. It was sad. I cried. I loved the game. I used to say, "Give me the ball. I'll take it home." I loved walking before 20,000 people in Madison Square Garden with all the cameras on you and all the notoriety and stuff. We were really approachable, too. We loved to mix with people. We loved the people in the Big Apple, all over, too.

One funny thing that I used to go through was that some people would come over to say, "Are you Jewish?"

I'd go, "Yeah." Bingo, we're in Lindy's, New York.

In Minneapolis, they'd say, "Are you Lebanese?"

"Yep, I'm Lebanese," and bingo, we go for Lebanese food.

If in Chicago, "Are you Italian?"

"You're damn right, I'm Italian." We go and have Italian food or Greek food or whatever. Anyway, it was a lot of fun doing this. I played the roles of about four different nationalities, and that was my game with people.

Today's basketball game is played above the rim. Our game was played on the floor. We ran a series of patterns, a series of plays, and we helped each other. In our era you could not slam dunk. I could get up there and dunk with two hands, but if you did it, it was a technical foul. It's changed a lot, maybe for the good and maybe not. I personally believe that five fouls would be a lot better than six fouls, because you'd have more guys playing and you wouldn't have so much rough stuff going on the inside. At the time we played, it was more of a finesse game, more of a structured game, with a lot more continuity. Today it's based on speed, a lot of agility and guys who can really score – over the rim. There is more one-on-one, a lot of grabbing, shoving and talking trash. Too much money is being paid to many young men.

Looking back, if asked who I would like to play with in the NBA, besides the pleasure I had playing with my own teammates, my choices would be Jim Pollard, George Mikan, Dolph Schayes, Bobby Davies, Frankie Bryan and Dick Farley. I loved to rattle Bob Cousy's chain. In Indianapolis, on national television, with 12 seconds to go in the game, Cousy was stalling the ball. I reached around his butt, stole the ball, went down and scored, tying the game. He fouled me on the shot.

I stepped up to the free-throw line, winked at Cousy and then sank the free throw. We won the game. One month later we played in Boston. First play downcourt for Boston, Cousy dribbled the ball right up to me, faked a look to the side and with both hands passed the ball right into my nose. Never had so many tears in my eyes. Thought my nose was broken. After a short timeout by the ref, I walked up to Cousy and said, "You're mine." Paul (Lefty) Walther and I loved to guard the great Cousy off switches on defense. I honestly believe we gave him the most trouble in the early 50s. Since the day I stole the ball from him, the man has never spoken to me on the several occasions that I've seen him. Think he remembers?

I've been working really hard, along with guys like Kevin O'Shea, Bob Lavoy and Wally Osterkorn, with the Pre-1955 NBA Players Association, trying to get pensions or remuneration for guys who are now in their 70s. These are the 65 or 70 guys, three- or four-year veterans of the league, who were never brought in on the pension in the 1988 collective bargaining agreement, a big injustice, a big inequity. It's just something that has to be done, and I'm glad to be doing it – for the men of the Pioneer Era.

Bill Tosheff has been a general contractor for many years, but you can hear the voice of the "Tosh" from Boston to Hawaii on his 900-line forecasting all sports with information services. The NBA's co-Rookie of the Year in 1952, he now lives in San Diego and Kanai and is president of the Pre-1955 NBA Players Association.

Zeke Sinicola. PHOTO COURTESY OF ZEKE SINICOLA

Zeke Sinicola

I was a senior at Niagara University when I got drafted for the NBA. My coach said I got drafted by the Fort Wayne Pistons, and I said, "Fort who?" Geographically I knew New York City and Buffalo, and in pro basketball I knew the Knicks and the Celtics, but I didn't know too much about the Midwest or Fort Wayne or the Pistons.

I really felt honored to be drafted, and the next time I was home in New York, I was down in an Italian neighborhood in Manhattan, Little Italy, and my friend Louie had read about the NBA draft in the papers. He approached me and told me, "You know, Zeke, you better be careful, you better go packing."

"Why?"

"You been drafted by Fort Wayne."

"So why do I have to be careful out there?"

"The Sioux, they're still on the warpath there." We laugh to this day, when we greet each other at funerals or weddings or whatever, roll out laughing thinking about what he said then.

Fort Wayne was a beautiful town, a picturesque town. And that Indiana sunset, boy that's something. You have to experience it, it's really nice. But almost as soon as I got out there, I had a mishap, almost became a baked potato. In those days, kids out there used to soup up their cars so much that flames would come out of their exhaust. Well, I was standing too close to a car when they started it and it burned my pants. I was practically on fire. If some kids didn't come to my aid, I'd have been down to my undies.

It was tough to make the pros in those days, because everyone had it locked up on those pro teams. You had to be superman to make it. They just shut you down. Veterans have a way of shutting you down.

The main difference between college and pro ball was that in college ball everybody is smiling. It's a friendlier atmosphere. I could see why it was different in pro ball. Everybody is vying for each other's job. Naturally, the veterans, they form a wall. They don't want to give up their job to rookies. They treat rookies very cold. In Fort Wayne, it was Andy Phillip and his crew there.

Andy was a cold character, never greeted anyone, always looked at you narrow-eyed with his "Gasoline Alley" crew cut. It was like someone was stealing his food or something. I thought he was a bit overrated, even though he was from the Illinois Whiz Kids. He was good but not great. I guess he must have thought the same about me. He never said hello, never gave you a reassuring word when you made a good play. I would love to steal the ball from him. Quite a few times when he was dribbling I'd leave my man just to get that ball away from him. And then I'd be yelled at by the coach for leaving my man. But what could you do? You come in one day and you're a rookie, the lowest thing down there, and you had to play.

I loved playing against Phillip. Even though he was 6-foot-2 or 3, he had a difficult time playing smaller men. You could go around him, and if you got around him he'd go after you in some way, set a hard pick or something. There was one fellow on Fort Wayne, big Charlie Share, 6-11 and about 350 pounds, and he was friends with Phillip. He was like a stooge, a Punjab, and he relished the role. One day when I was playing Phillip, Share stepped out and Phillip ran me into the pick.

Man, it was like getting hit by a truck. He rocked my teeth, my jaw and everything. I vibrated and hurt for two months. I couldn't move, but I wouldn't show I was hurt. I remember Mel Hutchins and Frankie Brian running to my side and telling him, "Share, what the hell did you do that for, you could have killed him." He reminded me of the protector of Tweety Bird and said, with the look of a kid caught with his hand in the cookie jar, "Aw, I didn't mean it." I felt like kicking him in the balls, pardon my language, but what are you gonna do? Some people may be big, but their brains were real small. Besides, I think he got one in for the veteran band.

Hutchins was a great guy, and so was Frankie Brian from LSU. Frank looked like Tyrone Power, a handsome guy and a good player. He'd tell me, "Over here, it's kind of cliquish. Rookies don't have a chance until they're ready to accept them."

The coach was Paul Birch from the Iron Dukes. He looked like he was on Camera 5, always patting his black hair back, looking in a mirror. He had a steady laugh etched on his face like Mortimer Snerd, but he was a little better looking than Snerd. He had one play! I can't believe a coach in the NBA would have just one play. It was get the ball inside, and cut through and fall back on defense.

Fred Scolari was one of the veterans there, the nicest of the group. Larry Foust reminded me of Schultz in *Stalag 17* with his "Philly" accent. "Get the ball inside" was all he kept saying. And if you gave him the ball inside, when you cut off him, forget about it, you never got it back. He had the worst hands of any center I ever knew. I thought Felix of the New York Knicks was bad, or maybe even Ewing, but you'd make a perfect pass to Foust, right on his fingertips, and he'd be catching it off his head. That's how bad he was. Thank God he had a big body so he could get inside and get some layups.

There was one player on the Pistons at that time who was the most snobbish man I ever saw, one of these hotshots from these big schools who looked down on people from small schools – "Golden Eagle" or "Golden Boy" Yardley from Stanford, I believe. I thought he was way overrated and Jack Molinas, who was also a rookie with me, would eat him up alive. I mean eat him up literally "alive." I even think Yardley feigned injuries not to play against Molinas in practice.

We used to play hard against that first team, because me and Molinas were New York boys along with Jack Kiley, and we picked up on their attitude and we really wanted to beat them. I remember Scolari used to tell me, "Zeke, slow down, my feet are burning, I'm hurting, slow down a little."

But Yardley reminded me – I keep saying "they remind me" but maybe I reminded them of a Dead End Kid from the streets of New York, somebody who was gonna steal their pants or their shoes or their wallet, because they certainly looked down on New Yorkers. I guess the whole Midwest looked down on New York at that time. And we're good people, we're honest people. Some people go astray, just like Midwesterners go astray. But I used to go home laughing, chuckling to myself, every time Yardley went against Molinas. Jack could run, his body was strong and he would make Yardley look like he just started to play. But getting back to what Yardley reminded me of, he reminded me of a bluenose, somebody from the English Parliament, how we picture them, wearing a topper, with an umbrella on his wrist and a long tweed coat. And if you opened up his coat he'd have no pants on.

Jack Molinas, to me, would have been a Hall of Famer today, if everything was OK, if he did everything right. Molinas was a bit on the restless side, but he was a good person. Well enough was not good enough for him. He had to be into something. In fact, sometimes he didn't even know his identity. I'm not quite sure. I thought he was Jewish or Russian-Jewish or whatever, but every time you heard him on a radio program out in Fort Wayne, one day he was Irish, one day he was Greek, one day he was Spanish and one day he was Jewish. One day I expected him to say, you know, I'm really a Belgian Congolese. I said, "Jack, tell them who you are." He said, "Nah, I make everybody happy." That seemed like what he wanted to do, make everybody happy.

About Jack Molinas's betting, I used to room with him. Every once in a while he used to come in with a fistful of change. Once I directly asked him. I said, "Jack, you don't bet on this team, do you, or bet against them?" He says, "No, and that's the honest truth." I believed him. I even heard him bet a few times. He was betting football, baseball, whatever he could bet he'd bet. He'd bet two cockroaches hitting the border of Mexico before siesta set in.

He was one of those chronic bettors. It looked like he was restless. He was restless, but he was an arrogant, cocksure ballplayer. When he was playing, he knew what he was doing. He was a pretty good guy – a lot of people didn't like him from the start, because when he was out with them he would say what he had to say. If you didn't like it, be damned. You know, one of those guys. And you had to understand him, but I guess nobody did.

I remember one day, he walked in the locker room and said, "OK, boys, how are we going today?" Man, you could see the terror in everybody's eyes when he said that. I looked at Jack and I got him on the side and I said, "Jack, what the hell?" I didn't say "hell," I said, "What the heck." I was young and trying to be as humble as I could. I was trying to get him to see the seriousness of the situation. He said, "Don't worry about it, everybody bets." He just shrugged it off. I never said another word about it. He did what he had to do.

Before the season started for Fort Wayne, I had to go to Chicago to play against the Rochester Royals, the all-stars against the league champions of the year before. Our coach was the so-called "great" twanging Adolph Rupp. For some reason, when I went there, all he talked about was New Yorkers and how they were not to be trusted. He seemed to hate them. Anybody from the East were like they came out of his bull's behind. He would always make speeches degrading New Yorkers, loud, right in front of you. "We're not like the New York boys." The scandal had broken then with City College. "We're not like those boys there," he'd say, "we teach decency." I remember that speech so vividly.

For some reason, maybe, he didn't like Italians, I don't know, but here we were, me and Sam Ranzino, two New Yorkers, both of Italian descent, and we were playing real good. During the practices we were playing good and suddenly he was taking us out and then we didn't play any more. He sort of held us out against the Royals, and at the end of the game it was me and Ranzino that hit a couple of shots that made the game close. I think we lost by a couple of points. But there he was, him and his stooges, still bragging about how "honest" his team was. They looked like a bunch of guys who would charge you for water, *Oxbow Incident* stuff with their twanging voices. Rupp would have been the one who spurred the horse while he was sitting on him to be hung or carrying the noose, one or the other. We couldn't stand him.

There were a couple of other coaches out there. Phog Allen was another story. He, too, had it against New York boys. Always talkin' about his boys, how good they are, and New York boys were this and that. It was really a knock against New York, and it wasn't true anyway. It was proven not true, because Bradley was in the Midwest and they got involved in it. A lot of teams got involved from the Midwest so it wasn't only limited to New York. But anyway, that day after the game we're sitting down there, Ranzino and me, pissed off and exchanging some hard looks with Mr. Rupp. I felt like telling him off but I held my place. Sometimes you have to count to 10 before you do something – otherwise more trouble might develop. Ranzino felt the same way.

Anyway, while we were dressing, Rupp was in the locker room with a couple of his cohorts. In walked some strange men. Being a New Yorker, I thought they looked like agents. They looked like somebody important. They walk up to Mr. Rupp and I hear them say — we were within earshot — I hear one agent tell him, "Mr. Rupp, we got your boys."

He looked starched. He looked like he'd gotten stepped on by his prize bull, I mean the pain on his face. And then one of the trainers told us they just picked up his boys for dumping. Naturally, we felt bad, some of the players involved were our heroes, Beard and Groza. But here was this man, this hypocrite. You mean to tell me that this guy, who was supposed to be so close to his team, he didn't know what was going on? Come on, he could tell erratic play or whatever. Not only that, he made a lot of money fast from those prize bulls. He probably knew the judges. I heard that he was a shirt salesman or something — he might have been a sheet salesman, sheets with the holes in them that fit the eyes — but we were happy about it because of him.

Clair Bee and Nat Holman in New York, they got a lot of flak, because they were coaches of players who played in dumped games, maybe deserved and maybe undeserved. But this Rupp, nobody said a bad word about him in the Midwest. They were all afraid to, probably had a "Southern mafia" out there or something that kept everything in line.

Anyway, back in Fort Wayne, they treated rookies badly, but there was one good happening I remember. One rainy day, Molinas, myself, Kiley, and a few others, we had a few girls in Molinas's house. I paired off with a girl. They all paired off. This isn't a sex story — I'm telling it because I think it's comic and not revealing. It's about how for the first time in my life I felt like a millionaire, without a dime in my pocket.

I balled with one girl all day, Molinas with somebody else. There were three girls in the house at the time. That night we had to make a trip, to Milwaukee I think. And when you're a rookie, you have to carry their bags on and off the plane. What happened to me was that I was carrying Zollner's suitcase, like a butler. I was there to play ball, and I felt like I was being downgraded, used. I thought, What the hell am I carrying his stuff for, even though he was a millionaire? I'm here to play ball. I wasn't Edward Everett Horton. To help was one thing, but to be ordered was another, and to carry Zollner's suitcase I felt degraded.

A couple of times Molinas had to do it. He told me on the side he was gonna leave that suitcase under the wheels of the plane. Anyway, we balled all day with these girls, and we showered and left to go out to the plane. Suddenly, there's Mr. Zollner at the airport, big zillionaire, kissing all three of these same girls on the lips. The one I was with, he's holding her hand and embracing her like they're long lost lovers, Romeo and Juliet style, and I bust out laughing to myself. Jack and Kiley and I, we laughed. All of a sudden we got a little cockiness in our walk as we strutted up the ramp to the plane. And I remember remarking to Jack, "Hey, Jack, I feel like a millionaire now." I even winked at the girl as we passed. I don't think Mr. Zollner caught me. I don't even think he'd know what it meant. It was a good happenstance. But Mr. Zollner was a good and generous man despite his taste in women.

So there I was in Fort Wayne, where the people were really nice. I loved the people in Fort Wayne. And you know what? – they had great steaks there, great steak restaurants. It was a beautiful community and that sunset ... unforgettable, the sunrise, too. But as far as playing in the NBA, I could play, but if you don't get the chance there's nothing you can do about it. I was a pretty good shooter. I could shoot outside. I wouldn't shoot 22 feet away, I'd shoot from 25 feet, 28 feet, 30 feet. I had a two-hand set, I could drive, I could pass off and I could run pretty well.

I had just gotten off a two-week tour with the Globetrotters, where I led my team in scoring, feeding off, too. To go down to Fort Wayne and just be a robot was kind of a letdown. I played hard anyway but only got in nine games. But I know I could play, and Molinas would have been a Hall of Famer – you could bet on that.

Basketball today seems to me a prison game. In other words, they play prison ball. Some of the coaches, they seem a little timid, afraid to tell people what they really have to do. But I think maybe that's the best way to play the game now, because they can't shackle any of these players. You just have to give them a bit of discipline.

If I was coach, my concept would be to think like you're playing school-yard ball. Why? Because, when you go in the school yard, there's 40 teams lined up to play. And if you lose one game, you gotta wait 40 teams later to play a second game. So what it does in the school yard, sometimes, it brings people together. They don't want to lose, thinking, "We're gonna wait 40 games from now." So what they do, they start concentrating on who should get the ball. Teamwork develops out of the thought of not playing again, and the best player gets the ball inside as it should be. That would be my theory. When we were playing well, we played as a team. We'd give the ball to the hot shooter, and the open man gets the ball. With teamwork and good defense you could beat anybody. You don't need any gimmick stuff.

As far as the centers go today, there's nobody like Chamberlain or Russell or even Mikan. They talk about how Mikan couldn't play today. They gotta be kidding me. Mikan had a huge body, and in today's game that would have been perfect. Mikan might have been a plodder and all, but he could feed and he had a left arm that made a lot of people deaf. His elbow never fit into the eardrums, but bounced off them like a bongo drum. You had to play him with a smaller guy, but he was so huge, what could you do? I remember one time playing against Mikan and an elbow caught me right on my skull. I needed 17 stitches on my head. He didn't mean it, but just the force of that elbow, man oh man, it must have weighed 200 pounds.

There was Mikkelsen and Pollard on the Lakers, too. They were good players, and they could play today with ease. Guys like Walton, Chamberlain and Russell, they would dominate. They were smarter, took no stupid fouls. A guy like Shaquille O'Neal, when he goes to the basket, he's pushing, fouling guys all over the place.

You couldn't do that with Russell or Chamberlain, forget about it, you'd be fouling out. Chamberlain would be smacking the ball off his head, playing ping-pong on his head. That's how good and strong Chamberlain was, when he wanted to be.

Basketball's still exciting to me. I love the playoffs and stay glued to my seat. But these guys in a booming, rich league should remember the pioneers, the people who are left. The top stars were drafted but were never compensated, and most guys who never got a dime for signing deserve some sort of pension, too. We were the pioneers. We put people in the seats. We set it up for these guys to become millionaires today.

Zeke Sinicola is fire safety director in his nephew's security company. He has written poetry and film scripts, and is at work on a novel, False Men.

Paul Seymour

I grew up in Toledo and played at Woodward High along with Johnny Payak and Bob Harrison, two other future pros. After one year at the University of Toledo I turned pro to play for the Toledo Jeeps in the NBL for a hundred dollars a week. I still have a copy of my first check, for $87.10. That first contract was illegal – my mother didn't even sign it. I was 17 years old.

We traveled in a couple of Jeep station wagons, five to a Jeep. We carried all of our own equipment, and as the youngest I had to carry the first aid kit and any other extra stuff, and I always drew the last driving shift after everyone else was too tired on those 12- or 14-hour trips. The guys in the lead Jeep would toss their empty beer cans trying to hit the trailing Jeep. And they'd all be smoking big cigars and I'd be getting sick. I tossed my cookies all over Ohio and Indiana that first season, until finally they suggested I join them smoking those things. As soon as I did, I wasn't sick any more.

We played a 44-game season plus another 60 exhibition games. Once we arrived late in a mountain town in the mining section of Kentucky, I think it was Bellevue, and we climb out of the Jeeps with our legs feeling like potatoes. As soon as we got into the place we were followed in by these two big guys waving press passes. Right behind them come a bunch of cops who arrested them – they were gonna hold us up for the gate receipts. We blew that game and got out of town fast.

We won our first six games, then lost the next seven. We were in Sheboygan after that last loss and Jules Rivlin, our coach then, came in and said, "I don't wanna see a sober player on this squad tonight." And he didn't. He was later coach at Marshall, and it was because of him that I got Hal Greer for Syracuse in '58.

That first year in Toledo went all right. I thought I was being groomed as a kind of protege of Rivlin, who was a player-coach, to take his place in the lineup. In a game against Fort Wayne in Buffalo, I was assigned to guard Leo (Crystal) Klier, a high scorer from Notre Dame. If I shut him down, I was told, I would earn a starting job. I held him to four points, but it didn't get me to start.

One of the best shooters to come to Toledo was little Jackie Goldsmith from LIU. He took one look at me and said, "Hey, kid, why don't you find yourself a job?" He would go by you with the ball and stop to take his two-hand set shot. I learned to let him go by, time his shot and stuff it back in his face, the way Bill Russell would do it later on to a lot of shooters. It was Goldsmith that had to find a job outside pro basketball.

When Harry Boykoff joined the team, he couldn't understand why I got into a fight with Hal Tidrick during practice.

"What's going on?" Harry said. "You're teammates."

"Don't you get it?" I said. "I'm trying to get his job and he knows it."

Instead, the next season, I went to New Orleans to play in a new 17-team United Basketball League, and the league folded after six or seven games. That's when I got a call from Sid Goldberg, who had originally signed me for Toledo and must have thought he owed it to me to make some kind of arrangement for me. Sid said, "If you can get to Chicago there's a ticket waiting for you for Baltimore. You've got a deal to play for the Bullets."

At that point I didn't care where I played, as long as it wasn't Syracuse. I had played there once, and that was enough for me. In Baltimore, Buddy Jeannette didn't play me much, and on my birthday, January 30th, I was told I had been traded back to the NBL, to Syracuse. So I was back in the NBL, playing for Benny Borgmann at $100 a week. I had had five coaches in one year.

I always say I arrived in Syracuse B.C. – that's before Cervi. I played significant minutes the rest of that season, but when Cervi came over from Rochester for the next season, '48-49, I was suddenly down to 12th man on the team. That was also the year that Dolph Schayes arrived in Syracuse, from NYU. They wanted a Jewish player in Syracuse, and they got a great one.

Schayes was a funny guy, but unintentionally. Once, after we had lost five or six in a row, Cervi got us all in the locker room at 9:30 in the morning, not even dressed to practice, and he's screaming and shouting at us for half an hour. Dolph raises his hand and Cervi tells him to put it down and goes on ranting for another 15 minutes. Dolph raises his hand again, and the same thing happens. The third time, Cervi finally says, "What the hell do you want, Dolph?"

Dolph says, in all seriousness, "Don't you think we've heard enough of this shit, Al?" and the rest of us broke up.

Schayes's biggest problem was that when the game got tight, he always wanted the ball. Some big men will disappear when it comes time to take the last decisive shot, but Dolph demanded to take it. Whatever play we wanted to run, he'd get right in the middle and signal for the ball. But he's also the one player in the record books who scored more free throws than field goals in his career.

One of my favorite teammates was Wally "Ox" Osterkorn. He wasn't much of a shooter and he was a bastard size, 6 feet 4 inches or so but with a big man's style.

He got along good with Cervi, who was not easy to play for, and everybody loved Wally, a handsome All-American type guy from Chicago. Above all he was always a hard player.

Everyone asks about the Boston Massacre, when Schayes got hammered and Ox and the rest of us got into it with the Celtics. It was Bob Harris who took Dolph down, bloodied him and broke a bone, and we all thought Red Auerbach had sent him in to do it. We all reacted immediately, and Ed Macauley started to say, "He got what he deser..." and before he could finish the word I had landed a punch on his mouth.

In the '52-53 season, I played in my first of three straight NBA All-Star Games. It was an honor to play in that game. That's why we did it – we didn't get much money for it. But they were trying to promote the game, and we were glad to take part.

The following year we went seven games in the finals, losing the title to the Lakers. Then we won it all in '55, winning the seventh game by a point over Fort Wayne. All seven games were won by the home team. Fort Wayne played its home games in that series in Indianapolis, and in one game there some little guy sitting down front on one of those three-piece folding chairs and threw a chair over our heads onto the court protesting some call. He just sat back down as if nothing had happened, but the sound of that chair hitting the court behind us was pretty scary.

They had us in that seventh game, led by 17 in the first half. But Dick Farley and Billy Kenville came off the bench, replacing George King and me, to start our comeback, and he won it at the end. Fort Wayne had a very strong front line, so we had to win it in the backcourt, which is what we did. When it was over, all I knew was that I was glad it was over. Everyone wanted to celebrate, but all I wanted to do was go home and sleep.

Danny Biasone was a good guy to work for, but cheap. He didn't want to spend a lot of money, but he kept his nose out of the basketball operations. When I came in as coach I made a lot of changes at first, and he didn't say a word. Only twice during my years with Syracuse did he ever call me directly. The first time was 12 games into the season in '56, when we were 4-8. He called me at home at 11 at night and asked me to come into the office. I thought I had either been traded or he wanted me to coach.

When I got there, he told me, "Cervi's out." He asked me if I would take over as coach, and I said I'd let him know. I wanted to get an OK from Dolph Schayes before I accepted.

The other time he called me, it was again at 11 at night. This time, he said, "They're at it again. Kerr and Bianchi are over at Nappy's. They're drunk and raising hell. See if you can get them out of there."

When I got there, Johnny Kerr and Al Bianchi were there, all right, and so were most of the players on my softball team and the rest of that softball league. I didn't say anything to them. I went over to the bartender, bought two rounds for

Kerr and Bianchi, and walked out. The next day at practice I grabbed Kerr by the throat and told him never to embarrass me like that again, that I wasn't gonna be a chaperone for someone my own age. The bartender told me that one of my softball players said to him some time later that I must be a great guy to treat my basketball players like that. "Oh, yeah?" he said. "Have you seen either of those guys in Nappy's since?"

The only time Biasone got mad at me for something that happened on the court also had to do with Johnny Kerr who was our "Iron Man." One night he didn't answer the bell, and with a minute left in the game I told him to stand up and get ready to go in. I wanted to keep his streak alive, but Danny was upset because he thought an Iron Man had to be ready to answer the bell every time the ball was tossed up.

Another record I had in mind had to do with Togo Palazzi who came over from Boston in 1957. We were back in Boston, playing Philadelphia in a double-header game, when Togo came off the bench and was so hot that he had a chance to set an NBA fourth-quarter scoring record. I called timeout to set up a play for a shot that would break the record. We ran the play, freed Togo for a layup, and as he released the shot Joe Graboski came over and blocked the shot. After the game, I said to Joe, "Why'd you do that?"

He said, "That was my record he was gonna break."

In my first year as player-coach, one game I have fixed in my head was against the Lakers in Rochester, Minnesota, home of the Mayo Clinic, when we were trying to get to .500 for the first time that season. Wally Dukes caught me on the top of my head with his elbow, opened up a gash that needed 17 stitches to close. The public address announcer said, "Is there a doctor in the house?" And 500 guys stood up.

Toward the end of the '58-59 season, I traded Ed Conlin for George Yardley, a great player and a great guy. But he was in a cast and Fred Zollner was frustrated about that and the Pistons' poor season. Yardley was making $21,000 and agreed to take a cut to $18,500. Zollner agreed to pay the difference between that salary and what we had been paying Conlin. So the deal was made.

The problem was that Schayes was making $12,500, and we decided to raise his salary to $18,501. Of course, Dolph got mad when he heard what Yardley was making. I said to him, "You oughta kiss that bald-headed guy's head, he just got you a $6,000 raise."

"Oh," he said, "I didn't see it that way."

We should have won another championship that season, should have won the seventh game against Boston in the Eastern finals, but Costello and Greer both blew layups in the final minutes, and the Celtics went on to sweep Minneapolis.

I appeared in just a few games as player-coach the next season, then gave Dick Barnett my uniform. Rookie Wilt Chamberlain and the Warriors took us out of the playoffs, and I was through coaching in the league except for most of one season with the Pistons nine years later.

The refs were lousy back then, and they're still lousy today. I liked some of them, like Sid Borgia and Mumbles Fox. There were two books, the NBA book and the Borgia book. When he was working a game of ours, I'd say, "Sid, what book we playing by tonight, the NBA or the Borgia book?"

I still follow the game, but I don't much like it anymore. I don't like it that they're playing a zone defense, and I don't like making a big deal out of the three-point shot, even moving the line in. That was just a normal set shot in our day. The way they play now they've taken the passing lanes and the cutting lanes away, so it's not as much fun to play or to watch.

Paul Seymour played 15 seasons in the NBL and NBA. In the five-year period 1952-56 he led Syracuse in assists, was second in scoring and free-throw shooting to Dolph Schayes, and was three times an all-star. As an NBA coach, his record was 175-162 and 18-32 in playoffs. Now retired, Seymour was in retail for 35 years, with hardware and liquor stores.

Offical photo of the NBA champion Syracuse Nationals of 1955. Front row (from left to right): Dick Farley, Bill Kenville. Middle row: Earl Lloyd, Captain Paul Seymour, Coach Al Cervi, George King, Jim Tucker. Back row: President Daniel Biasone, Wally Osterkorn, Business Manager Bob Sexton, Dolph Schayes, John Kerr, Billy Gabor, Red Rocha and Trainer Art VanAuken. PHOTO COURTESY OF WALLY OSTERKORN

Vintage NBA: The Pioneer Era

Wally Osterkorn

As long as I remember, I always wanted to play professional basketball. I started out playing before I was 10 years old, and I played and played and played. Sometimes I played so much that my fingers would be raw from handling the ball and dribbling it on the concrete pavement in the alley. I had put up a backboard and basket over the garage, because it was too far to go to the park. My team won the city championship for the grade schools in Chicago, and I also went to the city finals in high school in 1946.

We would have won that championship except for two things: our star forward had been drafted and our coach's contract had not been renewed so the football coach was coaching us. It was a close game. I fouled out and that was the clincher, as I was the leading scorer. I cried after that game, really saddened. Defeat is a big agony for anyone really into his sport, because you want to win with all your heart and soul. And if you don't want to win with all your heart and soul, you won't be good enough to excel in whatever sport you're in. I firmly believe that you've got to give it your all. Anything less does not make a professional in any sport.

I went on to the University of Illinois, which was a major producer of pro basketball players during the '40s and early '50s. I never really counted how many played, but you had people like Stan Patrick, who left there in '44 and played about six years in the professional ranks, and Andy Phillip, Ken Menke, Gene Vance, Jack Smiley, Jack Burmaster, Dike Eddleman and Johnny Kerr. On and on with players in that five- to six-year period. I believe the reason for that, for all of them going to the professional ranks, was that Illinois played a pro-type offense.

You had a pivotman, which I played when I was there, even though I was only 6 feet 5 inches tall. We'd throw it in the pivot, cut off of it and if there was nothing there I'd either try to get a shot or throw it back out and start it all over again. If the fast break was there we'd run and if not we brought the ball up real fast. So it was really a pro-type offense, which suited all these players well. All the original Whiz

Kids – Phillip, Vance, Menke and Smiley – came back from the war in '46, and they were great, great ballplayers, individually and teamwise.

The coaches were topflight, too, Doug Mills and Harry Combes over a 20-year period. Mills became athletic director after the Whiz Kids graduated, and Harry took over. He even had a pro-type offense in high school down in Champaign High School. In '49 we won the Big Ten championship at Illinois and went on to play in the NCAA Tournament where we got crushed by Kentucky. That was a great team where all the players became a pro team in Indianapolis, the Olympians.

The next year, my senior year, I wasn't really trying that hard in the beginning. Harry Combes came to me and said, "Look, Ox," – they called me "Ox" in those days – "you know, if you don't start hustling, we're gonna have to play Fulmer, because he's gonna take over next year." Well, that woke me up. After that, coach Combes said I was probably the best forward, guard or center in the country the last half of the season, and I broke the Illinois scoring record. It just shows what desire can do for you. During the first half of the season I didn't have that enthusiasm for the game and in the second half I really wanted to play and got myself up for every game.

I remember the first game after Harry told me that. We played Minnesota and I had a great game, but I wanted to win so badly that I fouled out. We lost, and after the game I was so disappointed that I just cried my eyes out. Every game after that I would get myself up so much that if we lost I felt very badly.

I remember crying once in the pro ranks, too, but that time it was a game we won. We beat Boston at Boston in a playoff game, and I couldn't stop my tears after the game. I remember Danny Biasone coming up to me and saying, "What's wrong, Wally?" and I said, "I don't know, I'm just so happy that we won I just can't stop crying." And no one thought anything of it.

A funny thing happened at the NCAA Tournament in '49. We were in New York for about a week, and one night all of us went out to this club. We started having a few beers, and someone, I forget who it was, was over there with the dice girl and started to touch her body. He put his hand under her dress and he yells out, "Holy mackerel! She's got balls!" We were in a gay joint and didn't even know it. All the women were men dressed as women and we didn't know it. That's what kind of hicks we were from the sticks. That was the first time that we had flown any significant distance. It was quite unusual for us that we had breakfast in New York, lunch in Chicago, and dinner in Seattle. Seattle was where they had the finals. We beat Oregon State to come in third in the tournament, and Kentucky beat Oklahoma State to win the title.

The Chicago Stags drafted me out of college, but before I could join them they folded. So I signed with the St. Paul Lights and got a $500 signing bonus. I gave them some kind of story that I needed the money to get up there and get an apartment and everything, so they sent me $500 and I signed for $7,500 with them. However, they only lasted one month, so I only got the 500 plus two paychecks out of 'em. After they folded I joined the Sheboygan Redskins.

Sheboygan was very interesting. The only thing you could do there was watch the snow come down during the winter and watch whatever sport was around. So we used to pack them into the old armory there in Sheboygan, but when we played games on the road we used to have to travel in nine-passenger cars. I think they were Chryslers or Lincolns. We had two of 'em, dark green. I remember we had a game in Omaha so we drove there that day. I guess it took about six hours and we played the game and it was snowing. The weather report said there was a snow-storm all the way back to Sheboygan, but we didn't have the money for hotel rooms. So we got in the old nine-passengers and we drove through those snow-drifts. I remember we were the only cars on the highways. Those drifts were some-times four feet tall. They came up to the windshield and we'd plow right through them. Nobody slept that night, it was so harrowing. We didn't get back to Sheboygan till about five in the morning.

It was a nice experience in Sheboygan, one of the most enjoyable times I had in my pro career. There were a lot of nice guys on a good team, like Bob Brannum and Jack Burmaster. Kenny Suesens was a good coach, too, one of the better coaches, and a nice guy besides.

In those days when you played ball you also had to have a job in the off-season. Even if the club didn't fold, you didn't make enough money during the season to live the rest of the year. After the season in Sheboygan I started working in an insurance office with some alumni from Illinois and I sold exactly one policy in two months. I didn't like it at all, just wasn't cut out for insurance. But I got a call from Abe Saperstein, asking me if I wanted to go on tour in Europe with the Globetrotters, playing with the Washington Generals. He offered me $150 a week plus all expenses. I said, "Sure, I'll go for it."

I joined them in June, flew over there and played against them in 145 games all over Europe, North Africa and the Middle East. It was a real heck of an experience. We had a private audience with the Pope, played before 75,000 people in the old Olympic Stadium in Berlin, played in Venice before King Farouk, the deposed king of Egypt, when he had bought out the whole stadium for his own little crowd, and visited the Casbah and the Pyramids. In fact, we did the whole tourists' tour besides playing all those games. We would head out for the next town the morning after a game and arrive early enough to set up the portable baskets on floors that had been set up. Then, if we had two or three games in the town we had two or three days of sight-seeing. You get to see a lot of stuff by driving everywhere in a bus. The one thing I really missed over there was just good old-fashioned water. They only let us drink water in Switzerland and Germany, told us all the other water was contami-nated. It was very beautiful in Switzerland, and I remember we drank tons of water when we got there.

Wherever we played it was before packed houses. Jesse Owens and Sugar Ray Robinson were on the tour with us, and there was always a nice halftime show with the Globetrotters. They always put on quite a show, worth every penny, and the crowds really enjoyed it. The Generals had an eight-man team, including three sets of Clark twins, and I was the only real professional. I would play the whole game, but they had a problem guarding me, first with Goose Tatum, then with others. Goose was phenomenal, though, with his hook shot. He'd hit that thing from 20 or 30 feet out.

Abe Saperstein was one heck of a nice man. My wife and sister traveled with us, and Abe paid for everything. When we got back, he doubled our salary, gave us a bonus of another 150 for each week we were over there. He was probably the reason Syracuse signed me, in that he and Eddie Gottlieb who owned the Philadelphia Warriors were good friends. He told Gottlieb about me, and Gottlieb wanted to get my draft rights. Syracuse must have thought, "Well, if Gottlieb wants him, he must be pretty good." So that's how I wound up with Syracuse because they kept my rights.

I was really in good shape when I came off that trip, even though I had lost a lot of weight. These players nowadays have all these wonderful dietitians and strength coaches and all that, so they don't lose all the weight we did. They take care of themselves much better. We weren't allowed to touch weights in those days. That was really taboo. I think weight training has done a great deal to enhance the skills that these present-day players have.

Another thing, in the old days in the pros we had a general practitioner who was the team doctor. One day in Syracuse he came into the locker room and said, "Try one of these pills, it'll help you." I took one and felt like jumping through the ceiling. I came to find out they were amphetamines. He used to have them there just to help yourself. It got to the point that some of us were taking four or five before a game, and so we stopped that in a hurry. We found out that the more you took, the more you needed. But it was just one of those things that went on in those days. Now I don't know that other teams did it. They could have, I don't know. But I do know that when I had been there two or three years we were introduced to methamphetamines.

Anyway, after we got back from Europe, I joined a group of college all-stars, coached by George Mikan, for a tour against the Trotters. We beat them in our first game, and Abe was quite upset about that. He didn't like that at all, and that's the only time we beat 'em.

I was always short for a center, especially in the pros, 6-foot-5, actually 6-4½ but I said 6-5. And I still played the pivot. What I lacked in my size and abilities I made up for with my drive. In the '53-54 season one magazine writer wrote that I was the spirit of the Syracuse Nationals with my hustle. We weren't that talented a team when I first played with Syracuse, but we did have a bunch of scrapping, hard-playing players. And I had a reputation of being the hatchet man and the enforcer. In fact, Earl Strom, the retired referee, named me to his all-time tough-guy team in the NBA.

The way that started was one of the owners of the Syracuse Nationals had told me before a preseason game that if I were to deck somebody in my first game, the word would get around the league and I'd be safe the rest of my life in the league.

Nobody would bother me and I could do what I wanted. We were playing Minneapolis, and I don't know what occurred, but Jim Pollard was shooting off his mouth and I told him to shut up. He didn't, so I gave him a hard shove and knocked him off his feet, not a real punch. And I told him to keep his mouth shut or I'd really deck him. And word got around and I was never bothered in my whole career. Nobody picked on me or tried to muscle me.

I remember a preseason game against Fort Wayne when Jack Molinas came into the league. He had a great deal of publicity on how great he was. He also had a very cocky air about him and strutted around like a rooster in search of prey. In those days you just didn't do those things. This rookie needed a lesson and who better to do that than the old Ox. He came into the game in the second quarter and I asked Cervi to put me in to guard him. The first time there was a crowd under the basket, one of my teammates got behind him and I got in front of him with another teammate in front of me. The shot missed and I didn't bother to rebound at all but gave him two good elbows in the solar plexus. He turned a little pale and called timeout. As I walked past him, I said, "Welcome to the NBA, Jack." He didn't score a point in the game because he didn't play very much after that. And that was the last time I ever saw him, because he was kicked out of the league.

I used to love playing against the Knicks because they didn't know who to put on me. If they put a big man on me I would go around him. If they put a little man on me I would muscle him into the basket. In Syracuse once, Harry Gallatin got open on a breakaway and I chased him down and fouled him from behind fairly hard so he missed the basket. As soon as I did it I was sorry, since I respected Harry, a real nice guy who played hard but never dirty. After the game I went to their dressing room and apologized to him. He accepted my apology and I left feeling good that I was man enough to admit I was wrong.

A few weeks later we were playing the Knicks in Madison Square Garden and I got loose on a breakaway. All of a sudden I felt a huge shove in my back and I went flying. Next thing I knew, Sweetwater Clifton was helping me up and said, "That was for Harry." The debt was paid and forgotten.

There were no excessive fouls in those days. And not many layups if there was anyone around. When we played Boston we used to dare Cousy to come down the middle. I'd say, "Come on down here, Bobby, 'cause I'm waiting for you." He never did come down there. Now this is not to say we played dirty. But we played hard, real hard. I probably have approximately 40 stitches in my eyebrows and face from elbows. You'd go into the locker room and without Novocain get the stitches and come back out and play.

But I did get into some fights. Once, playing in an exhibition game with Philadelphia, Zeke Zawoluk and I got in a fight and the next thing I knew his mother came out of the stands with an umbrella and started hitting me over the head with it. I didn't know what to do. I couldn't hit a woman, and she started chasing me around the gym, swinging that umbrella. Finally Zeke himself got hold of her and stopped her, and then some security people escorted her back to her seat. But it was one of the funniest things you ever saw, this tiny woman here and I'm running away from her.

I was in the middle of the "Boston Massacre," and you could say I started that one. Dolph Schayes had a broken arm at the time and he was still playing with one arm in a cast. Ed Macauley undercut him while he was going for a basket and I started yelling at Macauley. He yelled back at me, I punched him and knocked him backwards, and as he was going backwards Seymour hit him, and pretty soon, my goodness, the whole stands came out on the floor. The whole crowd was out on the floor.

Fortunately, Bob Brannum, who played for the Celtics, was a good friend of mine, because I had played with him in Sheboygan. He was a big, tough guy, too, an enforcer. He grabbed me from behind and he said, "God damn it, Wally, take it easy, they'll kill ya. Just stay here. I'm gonna hold ya. Don't do anything." And I didn't. The police had to get the crowd back in the stands. They had disrupted the game for 15-20 minutes, and it was all over the TV and everything about the Boston Massacre. And incidentally, we won the game. That was one of the highlights. We used to hate Boston and we used to cream 'em all the time. I think we only lost one series with them the whole time I played in Syracuse.

The first year I played for Syracuse we traveled by train to different games, and that was just terrible. After the game we'd get right on a Pullman car and head back to Syracuse. Whenever the train would stop my feet would hit, and when it started my head would hit. The same was true with some of the taller guys, too. You didn't get much sleep in those days. I remember one time we stopped in one of the towns and one of the players was hungry and saw a guy out there selling hot dogs. He ran out to get some and he missed the train. He's running, trying to catch up and he never did catch up. He had to get a cab and drive the rest of the way to New York.

If we arrived real early in the morning for the Pullman cars, they'd sometimes pull off onto a siding somewhere and just leave it sit, and we'd get some rest that way. Another problem when we went on trains was that we were only on six dollars a day meal money, maybe eight, and the Pullman railroad car diner was expensive for us. We'd spend all our meal money on one meal and that meant we'd have to scrape the rest of the way.

I probably shouldn't say scrape, because it wasn't that bad and we always had enough to eat. We had our favorite restaurants in each town, had a regular ritual we'd go through. Like when we went to Philadelphia to play the Warriors a few of us would go to a place where they had great pork chops. So three or four hours before a game I'd have pork chops. Each one had his own thing he would eat before a game. Some liked chicken, some steak. There was a place in Fort Wayne we used to eat that was a Chinese restaurant but served the most delicious porterhouse steaks that we ever ate around the league. Very reasonable, too, something like two dollars for a big porterhouse steak meal, really marbled beef which you don't get anymore, tastier than heck, and you could cut it with a fork. We made sure that every time we went to Fort Wayne we went to that Chinese restaurant and had those porterhouse steaks. I don't remember the name of it, but it was on the main street and there can't be too many Chinese restaurants on the main street of Fort Wayne, Indiana.

In Minneapolis we would go to Max Winter's bar. He had terrific corned beef sandwiches, piled real thick, and we'd eat them before a game with cole slaw and the works. In New York we'd go to the Stage Door Deli and also have pastrami or corned beef sandwiches. I guess that's one of the most famous delis in the world, and it was only a few blocks from the Paramount Hotel. It was really only a third-class hotel but was within walking distance of the old Madison Square Garden and that's why we stayed there when we were in New York. Everything was planned so we would stay within walking distance of eating facilities and stadiums.

In the early '50s in the arenas and stadiums you were allowed to smoke, and if you played in the second game of a doubleheader, why, you would have to cut your way through the smoke. I remember in New York at Madison Square Garden and in Philadelphia at the Spectrum, why, the smoke would be so thick it would be hanging over the floor like a fog. You wondered how you could breathe in all that. But in all my playing days, smoking was allowed and you just endured it.

Another thing about New York was that they had all these groupies there, quite lovely young ladies, and they would sit underneath the basket and just look pretty all game long. And after the game they'd all be around the dressing room waiting for someone to catch their eye and take 'em out for a good time. I guess that hasn't changed at all, the lure of the sports heroes, and so many have strayed but few have chosen or whatever. There were quite a few guys on the team that never messed around, but then again there were others that did.

At one party, Noble Jorgensen, who was on the team at that time, showed me something I didn't know. If you run out of scotch, what you could do was get warm water and serve it in shot glasses. After you've been drinking scotch, warm water tastes just like the scotch. I guess you have to be drunk or high enough not to notice the difference, but it seemed to work. The ladies at that party were satisfied. Warm water – remember that.

When we played in Syracuse, we'd all go to Danny Biasone's restaurant after a game and have six or seven beers and a big meal. And this would be about 11 o'clock or so. Your hours were all very screwed up. We used to have a big meal before taking a nap from about 2 o'clock till around 4. Nevertheless, we all lost weight, maybe 15-20 pounds during the season.

We would sweat so much during games that, when we started flying or chartering planes from Mohawk Airlines, we'd stop off in a cab on the way to the airport and pick up a case of ice cold beer, put it on the plane, and try to regain some of that fluid. You could drink seven, eight, nine, 10 bottles of beer, and you wouldn't have to urinate at all because of all the water you'd lost from sweating and running and all that. In those days we didn't have sports drinks. Red Rocha, he was very thin to begin with, would keep telling us that his doctor told him to drink a few bottles of beer after a game to keep his weight up. We had hard drinks only occasionally, like when we'd party with some gals after a game, but we did drink a lot of beer.

One time after Danny Biasone started chartering flights from a Syracuse airline, we were on our way to a game in Milwaukee. All of a sudden we had to land on the eastern side of Lake Michigan, right near the lake. There was no way we could land in Milwaukee or Chicago or anywhere in that area, because it was all snowed in. So what we finally did was they arranged for us to go across Lake Michigan in a railroad car ferry boat. The boat was just full of railroad cars that they ferried across the lake, and it was a rough ride. They served a humongous feast, 10-12 courses. Some of the guys ate like horses, but I just barely touched mine. Well, some of the guys got seasick because it was so rough, snowing, wind blowing, waves coming up.

Finally we arrived at the game, and the Milwaukee team was already warming up when we got there. We just made it in time. In those days, if you missed a game, the team was fined $5,000. Heck, $5,000 in those days probably bought a franchise. I remember Danny Biasone telling me he paid $2,500 for the franchise when he started the Syracuse Nationals. That was another harrowing experience but we wound up winning the game.

During my third year with Syracuse I was playing great, starting every game and averaging over 10 points and seven or eight rebounds a game. I didn't realize it at the time but during a game against Philadelphia I got a knee in my thigh. Sitting there watching the second game of the doubleheader, all of a sudden I couldn't get up. My leg hurt terribly, and I couldn't straighten it. The trainer suggested we put ice on it, so I went to the hotel and kept ice on it all night. The next day it felt better, but the day after that my whole leg started to turn black. The entire upper leg, from knee to hip, turned black all around it from the blood vessels that had broken. It was quite painful.

In those days the trainer didn't know very much. He was giving me massage and stretching the muscle, which was the worst thing. Every time he did it, he tore the muscle some more and the hemorrhage would just go on. I was still playing the game, limping up and down the court, because you didn't sit out in those days, you played hurt. I shouldn't have done that, should have gotten off of it and had some deep heat or something to dissolve the blood. The windup was the following season. I had to have the leg operated on. A calcium deposit had formed and attached itself to my bone and my muscle. When the doctor finally operated, he cut out a piece of calcium the size of a cigar out of my leg.

So I only played in 19 games my final year, my fourth year with Syracuse. That drove my average down. I was no longer a starter after that. The doctors said if I continued to play there could be serious consequences if I got hit again in that leg. I wore a thigh pad for the rest of that season and didn't get to play much. But come the finals, no, the semifinals, we were playing Boston at home and we needed to win. Boston was ahead by a lot of points, and we started to catch up. Coach put me in finally. I scored three baskets in a row and pulled us ahead of Boston, and we wound up winning the game. And so I did contribute in that final season, only not as much as I would have liked. That was the year we won the championship against Fort Wayne. It took seven games but we won the NBA championship in 1955, and that was the year I retired from playing, mostly because of my leg.

When people find out I played on an NBA champion team in '54-55, they ask to see my ring. We didn't get any ring in those days. What we did get for winning the championship was a tin ice bucket with an engraved plate on it that measured four by three inches and said "Optimist Club Congratulations on your NBA Championship 1954-55" and then our names. Dolph Schayes says he got a ring with something on it from Danny Biasone, the owner. I never got anything. I know Johnny "Red" Kerr who played with us never got anything. Biasone may have given Schayes a ring out of the kindness of his heart. I don't know where else he would have got it, unless he had it made himself. Who knows?

The fans had a "night" for me in '55, where I was presented different things. That was very nice. And then I retired after that season and it was real hard. I was angry that I couldn't play anymore. It seemed like the same thing had happened when I was in college, that I couldn't get my degree because of someone's oversight or something. Two months before graduation I was called in and told I lacked 10 hours. I made up some of the credits with proficiency exams but when I got out of school I still needed six hours for my degree. I was quite angry, felt that nobody wanted anything to do with me once I was done playing, and so I left Illinois with a bitter taste in my mouth.

And so now I was angry again. I couldn't find a job. All these backslappers when I was playing didn't want to know me after I was through playing. All these guys that had said, "Look me up when you're through, I'll give ya a job." Well, I looked them up but I couldn't get a job. In the early '50s, everyone playing pro ball had to have a summer job to sustain themselves. We had one exception on our team, a guy who never used to get a job. He would file for unemployment insurance, and they'd pay him during the summer because they couldn't find him a job during the summer playing professional basketball. I don't think he ever bought a newspaper either. He'd just go through train stations and airports, picking up papers and magazines to read. But I could never go that route.

I had worked in construction, paving streets and laying sidewalks. I had worked as a pipe coverer in the tunnels of a big factory up in Utica, getting up at 5 in the morning, driving about 60 miles, and then sitting in the dungeons covering pipes with asbestos insulation. Now I couldn't get a job and finally wound up selling pots and pans. That lasted about a month. I wasn't cut out for that or for being an apprentice carpenter, which I also tried.

My life has had a lot of ups and downs, and that was just about the lowest point. But, having fulfilled my legal obligations, having lost my first wife and family, I moved to Arizona and a fresh start. My aunt and uncle owned a motel there and asked me to come out and help them run it while my cousin was in the hospital. When my cousin recovered, I joined the Encyclopedia Britannica in '63, starting as a salesman, and because of the same enthusiasm, drive and desire to succeed that I had when playing ball, I rose to manage the eight western states for the Encyclopedia.

Then, once again, I had to quit something that I enjoyed and was doing well at, so it was like college and the pros again. A near-fatal spinal infection in 1978, with the surgery and sepsis that followed, left me with residual pain and on disability retirement. It was very traumatic, and I was in a deep depression for quite some time. But I decided to go back to school, finally got my degree when I was 55 years old, and went on to get a master's degree in counseling at Arizona State University.

I worked as a volunteer in the Camelback Hospital System, psychiatric hospitals, working in the psychodrama department – 10,000 hours in 8½ years. Through all the constant sharing with patients, I got rid of all my anger, frustrations and depressions. Physically, it's a bit of a struggle. I had taken up bodybuilding, got to where I could bench press 450 pounds when I was 50, and was in quite good shape – but not quite good enough to overcome all the things that had happened to my body in the past. Basketball injuries may have contributed to the weakened spine, the collapsed lung and the total shoulder replacement, not to mention the arthritic ankles.

But now, my wife and I make Southwestern art objects. We have a permanent booth at an indoor swap mart in Phoenix. We're doing fairly well, and life is again rosy.

Wally Osterkorn was known as "Ox" and as a physically dominant basketball enforcer in high school, college and the NBA. Yet even as a starter for Syracuse in 1953-54, when he was third on the club in rebounds behind Dolph Schayes and Earl Lloyd, he also trailed those two in personal fouls.

Dolph Schayes

I went to DeWitt Clinton High School, which was a top school in the Bronx, not just athletically, but for academic and artistic achievement as well. Then I went on to NYU, played in an NCAA final and an NIT final, and began thinking about playing pro ball while I was having a good senior year.

At that time, Ned Irish had instituted a salary cap for BAA rookies of $5,000 and a total team cap of $100,000. When John Goldner called, representing the Knicks, the offer was $5,000. I had also been drafted by Ben Kerner for the Tri-Cities Blackhawks of the NBL. But 1948 was the year that Minneapolis, Rochester, Fort Wayne and Indianapolis all switched leagues, leaving Syracuse as the only team left from the NBL's Eastern Division.

Syracuse claimed territorial rights to draft me, and the offer was $7,500. Goldner called me again and said that Ned Irish wouldn't allow the Knicks to break the rules. They couldn't raise my salary, but they might be able to get me a good job with the Port Authority. "Besides," he said, "that other league's gonna fold."

That job prospect was too iffy, and what I was interested in was playing basket-ball, which I loved, not some bureaucratic job on the side. My father and I met with the Syracuse owner, Danny Biasone, and his general manager, Leo Ferris, at the Paramount Hotel in New York, and I signed on as a member of the Syracuse Nationals.

Teams came into the league in Denver, Detroit, Hammond and Waterloo to join the remaining clubs in Sheboygan, Oshkosh, Tri-Cities, Syracuse and Anderson. The Anderson Packers were a great team, run by Ike Duffy, who bankrolled the league. In midseason, Detroit folded, and the Rens took over their schedule under the name of Dayton. We had Pop Gates on our club and Dolly King from LIU had been in the league, so racial integration was not new to us. The Rens were accepted as a professional basketball team without regard to race. It would be another three years before the NBA had black players.

I was in the NBL because the financial arrangement was superior, but it was also the better league at the time, I believe. When the merger took place for the following season, it would be eight years before the NBA championship was won by a team that hadn't originated in the NBL. And if you look at the 10-man All-NBA squads, it would be 18 years before there was a majority of players from the old BAA franchises.

It was Ike Duffy who precipitated the merger by offering to bankroll the Kentucky team of Groza and Beard into Indianapolis as a new NBL franchise. Even with Mikan's Lakers and the Royals, the BAA was desperate for these new faces. So Duffy's good idea led to the end of his league, and with that Kentucky team in place in Indianapolis we all entered a 17-team NBA for the '49-50 season.

I was lucky to have feisty coaches in Syracuse, first Al Cervi, then Paul Seymour and Alex Hannum. They would get their personalities across to the team, so we always had the feeling that we could out-tough the other guys. We always knew we would come back in the fourth quarter. And, partly because we were put into the Eastern Division with the old BAA teams, we always had a bitter taste for the Bostons, the Phillys and the New Yorks, but especially the Celtics.

The other part of that attitude came from Danny Biasone, who was a perennial underdog. He shared with us the feeling that the big cities wanted to get rid of the Syracuse franchise, that New York, Boston and Philadelphia were too important to want to play in Syracuse. But then we always beat them. Eddie Gottlieb, the Philadelphia owner and coach, was a wonderful man, though you could never win an argument with him. He was the one who really ran the league. But Danny always fought for his rights, always demanded his share of the doubleheader pool, so that those other clubs would have to come to Syracuse not only to play us but to play in the first half of doubleheaders against each other.

Danny was also a wonderful assistant coach, who took an interest in everybody and was always there to talk basketball on the road. What they have now, the shoot-arounds, are a good way to get your mind on the game early. What we had was sitting in hotel coffee shops talking basketball with Danny Biasone. That's how we got our minds on the game.

Paul Seymour was the glue that held that team together, even while Cervi was still coaching. He was smart and a fighter in more ways than one. So was Alex Hannum, who was an NBL rookie with Oshkosh in my rookie year in Syracuse. I remember Hannum one night running all the way across the court to tackle Tommy Heinsohn. Today, no matter how hard we fought each other when we played, we're all friends.

I have practically no memory of that brawl in Boston that began when I was driving for the basket and Bob Harris upended me. I came down on my head and hand, got several cuts on my face and broke a navicular bone in my wrist. I know that Cervi called five consecutive timeouts to keep me in the game, because if someone had to shoot the free throws for me I couldn't come back in. I guess I was out of it, because that's my only memory of it, and I don't remember seeing any of the action going on all around me.

Most people probably remember me for my trademark outside shot, but I went to the basket a lot and drew a lot of fouls. I wasn't very fast but I was constantly moving, going to the ball. I would pass and go to the ball. When a shot went up, I'd go to the ball. My whole game was to get to where the ball was. When my right wrist was broken I learned to play left-handed, so that I could always drive to the basket from either side.

Earl Lloyd, who joined us in '52, played an important part on our '55 championship team as a role player. He was not a great shooter but an excellent rebounder and defensive player. In those days we didn't have a strong forward and small forward or a 3-forward and 4-forward, we had a scoring forward and a defensive forward. Earl was our defensive forward, who would guard the other team's scoring forward. He was a very intelligent player who did his job unselfishly. He was part of the family, too. He mixed well with the team. We all socialized together.

That first all-star game in Boston surprised everyone. I was amazed at how much pride everyone took in it. It was a marvelous game, won by the East, with me playing a lot of minutes with my usual adversaries from Philly and Boston, Joe Fulks, Paul Arizin, Ed Macauley and Bob Cousy. I always enjoyed the all-star game and was sorry to miss it when I was hurt. Toward the end, though, the games developed into run-and-shoot affairs, with no defense at all.

George Yardley, with his great shooting and jumping ability, was probably the most talented player Syracuse ever had. We became instant friends and roommates when he joined us in '59. He helped me financially, too, because he had been making $25,000 in Fort Wayne. He accepted a pay cut, with Fred Zollner of Fort Wayne making up the difference, and Syracuse still had to give me a big raise to bring my salary up to his. He was a magnificent athlete and a wonderful person. I was sorry to see him quit the game early, but he wanted to pursue a career as an engineer.

As I recall, George never once mentioned to me the experience of playing with Jack Molinas at Fort Wayne. I remember Molinas playing against us in Syracuse and scoring 18 points in the fourth quarter. He was such a study, a brilliant person, handsome and talented. He had everything, like Bill Bradley. And I could never figure out how he could throw it all away. The others, too, Groza and Beard. Nobody was quicker than Groza as a big man in the league, and Beard was a player who never got tired, who would go by people on offense and play great defense.

The only thing I could think of that might have contributed to their motivation to do something for themselves in college was that a lot of the college coaches, like Rupp and Holman, were such martinets. Everything with their teams had the coach's name on it, and they used "my" and "mine" to describe what the players did. Whatever it was that made them risk their careers in basketball, it was one of the great tragedies, for the game and for themselves.

With George Yardley and me at forward, that team was a great one, a scoring machine with Larry Costello, Hal Greer and Red Kerr also starting. We should have won the title that year, actually had the Celtics beat in the seventh game of the Eastern Finals. George had 36 points and I had 34, but we ran out of gas. Boston went on to sweep the Lakers in the finals.

Kerr was the kind of guy who always kept us loose. We had a player named Connie Dierking who was afraid of flying, especially on those DC-3s we used for the shorter trips. I remember on one of those bumpy flights, Kerr said to Dierking, "What are you so worried about? More people get killed in train wrecks than plane crashes – 42 people were killed in one just recently."

"What happened?" Connie asked.

"Oh, a plane fell on the train," Red said.

Our other near miss for a title, the one everyone remembers, is the "Havlicek steals the ball" game in 1965. The franchise had moved to Philadelphia after the Warriors went to San Francisco, and I had become coach. But it was yet another seventh game in the Eastern Finals against the Celtics. I understand that in his book, Chet Walker says that he could look into my eyes and see that I was uncertain about what calls to make. But here is the way it really happened.

The Celtics led by one point in the final seconds after we had scored. I sent Chamberlain to cover Bill Russell, who was going to be the inbounds passer. When Russell had to loft the ball over Wilt, the pass hit the guy wires overhead for a turnover. During the timeout it was a wild scene at the bench, everyone screaming. My first thought was to get the ball inside to Chamberlain, but as soon as he got the ball they would foul him. He was shooting about 40 percent from the line in the playoffs and so that wasn't a good percentage play. A better idea, I thought, was to get it into Greer's hands. I set up a play for Greer to pass in to Walker, while Kerr set a pick on whoever was covering Greer on the inbounds pass. I think it would have worked, but Havlicek simply beat Walker to the ball on that first pass. Chet was a good player, but his quiet manner was reflective of a personality that was not aggressive. Havlicek was.

The next year we were even better, with Billy Cunningham's arrival and the emergence of Lucious Jackson and Wally Jones as genuine stars. We won a lot of games and beat Boston by a game in the East. The turning point of the season came when we were on a long road trip and were flying into Cincinnati to play the Royals, when we were forced to land in Cleveland because of snow. Our choice was either to drive the turnpike in the snow or hire some puddle-jumper plane to fly us there. It was my decision to wait it out for weather conditions to permit us to fly, and we never made it.

The club was fined for missing the game, and the owners were angry about it, but the day off seemed to rejuvenate us. The next day in St. Louis we ended the road trip by starting a long winning streak that carried us to the league's best record. That gave us a bye in the playoffs, and ironically that hurt us. I didn't work the guys hard enough. It was always hard to scrimmage with Chamberlain, anyway, because he dominated the court. And after the bye, Boston took us out of the playoffs again.

By some scheduling coincidence, John Vanek officiated most of the games in the winning streak, as he pointed out to me years later. That was a surprise to me. I couldn't remember it. A lot of players and coaches worked the referees, but I always stayed focused on the game, kept blinders on as a player and still as a coach. When I became a coach I remembered how much easier it was to play. Sometimes I think that if I had coached first, I would have been a better player. With the ball I had a nose for the basket, and rebounding I had a nose for the ball. That was my exclusive focus, but as a coach I couldn't be that narrow, had to develop a broader perspective.

The following year the 76ers couldn't be denied. It was one of the greatest teams, went 68-13, winning three playoff series while losing a total of only four playoff games. Alex Hannum had replaced me as coach, and I believe that the biggest difference was that Hannum was able to talk Chamberlain into becoming more of a passer and team player.

It was my love of the game that brought me back to coach the Buffalo Braves in 1970. I still had that flame. But coaching an expansion team was much different from anything I had experienced.

It has been a great joy watching my son Danny play. I'm very, very proud of what he's done, and I hope he can match my 16-year career. Of course, the game is much different. Now the players all seem to be great athletes, while in my time we passed the ball a great deal. Danny's skills are better suited to a passing game, but at least some teams still play that style. But probably the biggest difference has to do with marketing. When I played, the owners had no idea of marketing. All they knew was doubleheaders or getting the Harlem Globetrotters to play a game before the NBA game. And then they'd shake their heads when people left after the 'Trotters' performance. Now, obviously, the NBA is a marketing marvel.

Dolph Schayes was enshrined in the Basketball Hall of Fame in 1972. For 12 straight years (1950-61) he was on the All-NBA team, six times as a first-teamer. He was NBA Coach of the Year in 1966. When the NBA started keeping rebound statistics in 1950-51, he led the league, and was among the top 10 rebounders for the next 11 years, only twice finishing out of the top five. Four times he was among the top 10 in assists, nine straight times among the top seven in scoring average (second to Yardley in '58) and 10 straight times among the top three in free-throw shooting (first in '58, '60 and '62). He has built some apartment buildings in Syracuse and continues to manage about 200 units.

Davage (Dave) Minor

I grew up in Gary, Indiana, but I originally planned to go to LIU. I went to summer school there in '41, but their ballplayers were all getting drafted, so I came back to Toledo. They had a new coach from Fort Wayne Southside High School, and he had seen me play in high school. In fact, he was recruiting all his players from Indiana. Freshmen were eligible because of World War II, and we went all the way to the NIT finals that year before getting beat by St. John's with Harry Boykoff and a guy named Andrew "Fuzzy" Levane, who later became my coach in the pros.

I went into the Army in April 1943, and was assigned to Special Services. That meant I flew all over Europe in a private plane, playing basketball in London, Paris and Switzerland. I played against Whiz Kid Gene Vance in a tournament in Switzerland, and he said to me, "Some day you're gonna be a tremendous basketball player."

I took my discharge in Paris. I intended to stay on there and teach basketball. But I got a telegram from Wilbur Johns who got me to come back to play at UCLA. That's where I first met Don Barksdale in 1946.

I could have gone to Tri-Cities in 1949, but didn't want to go pro. Nobody knew that I had played one game with the Globetrotters in Michigan City, just out of high school. My feeling was that they thought they wanted to give a black player a chance, but then if I got cut I would have lost my amateur standing. So I stayed on to play with the Oakland Bittners, an AAU team. We went on to win the national AAU championship that year, beating Bob Kurland's Phillips Oilers in the finals. In fact we won 67 out of 68 games that season. The only game we lost was by two points to a bunch of doctors and lawyers. Our guys didn't take them seriously, and some of the starters didn't even show up to play, but I was pretty angry about that.

In 1951 I agreed to turn pro because the Bullets offered me $5,000 with enough up front so that it was nearly a guarantee that they'd keep me for the season. At first Don Barksdale wasn't gonna turn pro, either, but he was my team-mate on the Bullets. Our first coach there was Fred Scolari, who could shoot the hell out of that ball.

Scolari said to me, "I have to play you a lot, you're the only one I can depend on." I think he meant that I was the only one who would pass to him, because if you passed the ball to him you might not get it back. The guys felt the same way about Don. The next season they ended up with Clair Bee as coach, who would have been my coach at LIU. He was a hell of a college coach, but he really didn't have anything to teach us as pros.

One game at Fort Wayne that season I'll never forget was when Frank Kudelka, Stan Miasek, Kevin O'Shea, Don and I played the whole 48 minutes. John Steadman made a lot of it in the paper. He was a great guy, who personally took me in when I first hit Baltimore.

It's my theory that when you have one black on a team, the other guys treat you like you're one of them, invite you to parties. It was different with Don there. I was close to him. When I started with the Bittners we had lived with the Barksdales for a time in the Bay Area. He was a good guy, but a loner who never wanted to socialize with the guys. He was a great player, though. On a radio interview in Philadelphia, once, I compared him with Joe Fulks. Joe was a great shooter, but Don could rebound and dribble as well as shoot. Philadelphia also had a great shooter named Paul Arizin.

Things were better for me in Milwaukee, where I played the next season. Bobby Wilson, one of the first blacks in the league, had played there the year before. Ben Kerner was a wonderful guy and super to me. I bought a '52 Cadillac with the advance he gave me, and he and his girlfriend used to ride to games with me in it. I roomed with Mel Hutchins in Milwaukee, and we used to go out with his sister, a former Miss America, who married Knicks player Ernie Vandeweghe.

When he moved the club to St. Louis, Ben Kerner offered me a raise of $2,500, up to $8,000, to come along. But I didn't want to go. I had a job managing a housing complex and I was set. Don't forget I was 31 years old when I turned pro.

Besides, I had had enough of the travel. I wouldn't fly, so I spent a lot of time on trains. I would often leave before the rest of the team to take a train because I wouldn't get on a plane. Here's why. With the Bittners, we did our preseason training in Manila, in the Philippines. Flying home, we developed engine trouble near Guam, but they wouldn't land. "Don't worry," they told us. "Even if we have to ditch they'll get us before we sink."

"Right," I said, "that's what they said about the Titanic." And I said to myself that if I get out of this I'll never fly again. And I haven't.

I met a lot of great people. Jackie Robinson and Larry Doby became personal friends. Sweets Clifton was a good friend, and I remember Bill Calhoun, who was my teammate in both Baltimore and Milwaukee. Of the players I had to match up with, Bob Davies and Bobby Wanzer were very tough, but I think the greatest of them were Jim Pollard and Bob Cousy. With Baltimore, we traveled with the Celtics for a number of preseason games. Bill Sharman I knew from when he was at USC and I was at UCLA, but I never did know what Cousy was gonna do. He was phenomenal, with those big hands, one of the best little men to ever play the game, in my opinion. Cousy and I became good friends, too.

I think I was smart to put all my money into real estate. I learned that population increases but available land does not increase. I was able to retire at 42 with my real estate investments, and I still take care of my buildings.

I still follow basketball very closely. I know the game inside out. In 1989, I was honored by having a street named after me, not in Gary, but in Orlando. Minor Avenue. How about that!

For 16 years and on three continents, Dave Minor devoted his talents as an outstanding player in high school, college, service, AAU and NBA basketball.

Al McGuire

My fourth season in the NBA I was with Baltimore, after three years with the Knickerbockers. I think I was a throw-in in the deal that brought Ray Felix to New York for Connie Simmons. A dozen or so games into the season, I knew the Baltimore franchise was going belly-up, and not just because we played our games in some kind of roller rink.

About a week before it became official, I was in our bus in Baltimore, riding through those white stoops and crab sandwiches, and I was sitting next to our coach, Clair Bee, who was always a nifty dresser. He took his handkerchief out of his breast pocket, wiped his brow, carefully rearranged it in his pocket, and threw his fedora out the window. That's how I knew the end was in sight.

But I had had a pretty good run for a marginal player. And even though I always got paid the minimum in the league, I loved the life. I was a migrant worker. I was swimming the Rio Grande in those days. Those were different times, with different rules, and I don't mean just on the court. There were no training tables and no hair blowers. The showers were about 5 feet 6 inches high and even the smallest basketball players could only get parts of their bodies under them. But it was a great time.

Harry Gallatin was the big man on that Knicks team, a workhorse, a Clydesdale. He was Midwest, very straight and we called him "Farmer" – a nice person but with a lot of competitiveness, a kind of silent assassin. Harry was slow on the court and slow with money, too. He and Vinny Boryla would always sit on the outside in cabs, with a rookie sandwiched in between, because the last one out had to pay. In a game, Harry was always smart enough to keep his eyes on my brother Dick. If you didn't watch out, Dick would take your head off with the ball. But if you got open he'd always get you the ball. When Harry scored, it was off Dick's passes.

Sweetwater Clifton was usually my roommate on the road with the Knicks. It was Sweets who taught me that "aunts" didn't mean you're related. If he told me an aunt was coming to visit, I knew that meant I'd have to make a trifecta and sleep in a room with two other guys. One time that happened was in Boston, after we'd seen, on the plane going up with us, this keeper, an absolutely, unbelievably beautiful keeper. The next night we got blown out by the Celtics, and after the game, Joe Lapchick said to Sweets, "Were you with that girl last night?"

"What girl?" he said.

"The one from the plane."

"No way," he said. "I know her, but I wasn't with her."

Lapchick said, "If I knew her, I'd be with her." That broke the ice after that loss, it was so out of character for the coach to say that.

As strong as he was, Sweets was a very gentle guy. It was hard to get him annoyed. One night, I remember, in an exhibition game against Philly in Hazleton, Pennsylvania, some guy got him annoyed. Sweets just turned around and said "Hey" and that was it, it was all over. You know, traveling by train we'd play cards all night, but we would not allow Sweets into our games. He was so bad, he'd draw two to an inside straight. It was too much like stealing, so we had to try not to let him know if or where there was a game.

A lot of people give me credit for having a special rapport with blacks, especially when I was coaching. But I was no crusader. It was just that racism never came up with me in my life in basketball, as a player, a coach or whatever. At the end of the day I'd go where I lived, and they'd go where they lived. But during the day I can honestly say I was never aware of the color of anyone's skin.

I always thought Carl Braun was a cut above. He came from a gentler background, socially, mentally and financially, like Ernie Vandeweghe and Bud Palmer. He wanted to be one of the boys, and he often was. He was a Jack Armstrong type, the kind that Wheaties would want on a package in those days.

My regular running mate – off the court, I mean – was Connie Simmons, who is co-captain along with Red Rocha on my all-ugly team. Every now and then someone else would come out of the library and join Connie and me at our local watering hole, wherever we were, but usually it was just the two of us.

We were arrested in Syracuse one time after some waiter wouldn't sing "Happy Birthday" to Connie. It was barely a scuffle, no more than a push, but we were both charged with assault, along with my brother Dick, which was a joke because Dick wouldn't hurt a fly. After the season we had to go back to face the charges, and we were fined. Ned Irish paid the fine, which I thought was very nice. I never had very much contact with him at all.

Another incident I've never told publicly before was the time I had my jaw broken. It was three or four in the morning and Connie and I were in some after-hours place under the Third Avenue El. Connie or I said something someone didn't like and I was blindsided with a punch. I knew right away it was bad, the jaw was broken in two places, but I said to Connie, "We gotta get out of this joint before reporters show up."

Connie got me to some hospital with a lot of foreign docs, and I had one from, I think, the Yucatan Peninsula. It was five in the morning, he was probably thinking about some native relics or artifacts, and I'm thinking, "How good can he be?" So my jaw was wired shut, and the story we gave out to the press was that I was hurt in a traffic accident on my way home at 11 the night before. Later in the day I started getting sick, but with my jaw wired shut there was no room to let it out. So I kept regurgitating until an opening was made in my mouth. Anyway, when I showed up at the Garden with that big brace to protect my head, that's when I really earned the name of "Space Cadet."

My role on the Knickerbockers was to go in and disrupt the opposition, to throw off their rhythm, change the game. They called me a scrambler, and that's where I got the idea for "scrambled eggs" at Marquette, a whole unit that would go in to change the rhythm of a game. I remember once Lapchick sent me into a game when we were down 12 points – a huge lead in those days – with about 90 seconds left. "Go in," he told me, "turn this game around, and win it." "How can I save this game?" I said, "Am I Jesus Christ?"

I know that some people called me a designated fouler, but I was more like a tackler. I remember once, when I had had a fight in three games in a row (one of them with Bill Sharman in Boston), Lapchick said to me before the next game in Rochester, "Al, please, no fight tonight." Was I obnoxious, arrogant, surly? I don't know what I was in those days. I guess I was Al McGuire.

Then there was the fight in the 69th Regiment Armory where the Knicks were playing the Celtics, and my brother Johnny got involved. Johnny was a pretty good player himself – basketball, football, track – but he's the usual family person, whose athletic ability keeps getting better with age. By the time Dick and I were with the Knicks, though, Johnny was a cop.

That particular night I was trying to carry out my very public boast that "I can stop Cousy." It was early in the game, and someone was setting a pick for Cousy. It was usually Luscutoff, but it might have been Jack Nichols. Nichols was the second player to wear low-cut shoes. I was the first, because I had broken my ankle high jumping for St. John's and had to have special shoes. Anyway, whoever was picking for Cousy, I ran over him, tackled him really, and that started a brawl.

Now, my rule is always stay close to a bigger guy in a fight. He can't hurt you if you stay in close. In a bar fight or street fight, you never go down, but on a basketball court you go to the floor and grab and you don't get hurt. That's what happened. We went to the floor, grabbed and rolled around a little, and it was over. But here comes my brother Johnny out onto the floor, a cop carrying a gun. I stopped Cousy all right on that possession, because some other guy went to the line. But the fight was stopped when Johnny McGuire came onto the court with his gun.

When the Baltimore club folded, I didn't know what I would do. Connie, Frank Selvy, Bob Houbregs, Paul Hoffman and a couple of other guys were picked up by other clubs. But it was Walter Brown, the owner of the Boston Celtics, who took care of me. Mr. Brown called me and said, "I owe you a favor." I didn't know why but he told me that I was the first to sell out the Boston Garden for basketball with "I can stop Cousy." He told me that Doggie Julian had just lost his assistant coach at Dartmouth, Joe Mullaney, who had taken over another program in New England. If I wanted that job, it was mine.

That was how my coaching career started, and I loved it, as an assistant in Hanover, New Hampshire, with Red Rolfe as athletic director, and all through my years at Marquette. I've never been hurt by anyone in my life. People who might not have liked me before, get to love me when they know me. Now, with Al McGuire Enterprises, it's all toy soldiers and hobbies. Between appearances and broadcasting, what I do is come up with concepts. I sell ideas.

At St. John's, Al McGuire played in three NITs (third place twice) and one NCAA – 1951, losing in the Eastern Regional semis to eventual champion Kentucky. In three-plus NBA seasons (1951-54), he had an impressive personal-fouls-to-minutes-played ratio (highest on the Knicks). He climaxed his 13-year coaching career at Marquette with the 1977 NCAA championship, his 404th win. As one historian says, "McGuire coached with relish, flair and unique style. The free-wheeling, off-court openness and colorful copy he provided lent an aura of deceptive casualness to his players. In truth, they played with great discipline while appearing to enjoy what they were doing. McGuire communicated well, both his system and his joy."

Arnie Heft

Baseball was my game. I always thought I was gonna be a big-league ball-player. I never played basketball, and of course in later years many of the players would say that I refereed like I played. I was a midyear high school graduate and went right to Washington and Lee to play baseball. There was no scholarship, but the deal they offered me was that I would have a bus available to me and tickets so that I could take 40 or 50 people to five or six W&L football games on the road. Well, it never got to that because I didn't go back to school after playing that freshman season there.

I signed with the Orioles of the International League in 1938. I was a left-handed pitcher, 5 feet 10 inches, about 125 pounds and wet behind the ears. At spring training I was assigned to Thomasville, Georgia, but I was brought up to Baltimore for the last month of the season. I really didn't belong there. The Orioles were an independent club, the highest paid minor-league team at the time, but hopelessly mired in the cellar. So they unloaded their high-paid ballplayers, and brought me and others up for $100 a month. I had been making 75 in Thomasville.

I didn't even look like I belonged. At two ballparks, in Montreal and Rochester, they didn't even want to let me in until someone vouched for me. Two highlights were pitching complete seven-inning games against the Buffalo Bisons and the Newark Bears, losing both by the same 2-0 score. Another vivid memory was giving up a grand slam to Charlie Keller of Newark. My aunt in Baltimore, who had never seen a game before, thought I was sensational. "When the other pitcher was in there, nobody was running," she said, "but when you went in everyone was running."

I was with Portsmouth in 1939, but had a groin injury in midseason and was released, then finished the season with the Durham Bulls. In 1940 I was out of organized ball. That was the year I got married and played in a semipro league in Baltimore. Out of that league I was signed by scout Fred Hunter for the Boston Red Sox, sent to Scranton in the Eastern League, and optioned to Owensboro in the

Kitty League. We were a seventh-place team in an eight-team league. I won 22 and lost 14, leading the league in innings pitched and strikeouts, and was the winning pitcher in the all-star game. In 1942, when I spent some time with Evansville in the Three-I League and Wilmington in the Interstate League, I hurt my arm. By 1943 I was out of organized baseball and into the U.S. Navy.

It was Curly White who got me into reffing basketball, not long before I went into the service. Because of my baseball background they put me into the Gene Tunney program, training recruits at Bainbridge. They had a fantastic basketball program with a team so good they substituted five players at a time. Five of those players played pro ball in Baltimore, five others in Trenton. Not being an introvert I walked down and asked, "I've been refereeing basketball, can I help?" I worked their practices, and it was the best training experience I had. When the BAA started, I swear, of the 25 guys at Bainbridge 15 or 20 were in the league, Herm Schaefer, for example, who played at Fort Wayne, Indianapolis and Minneapolis.

After P.I. school I was shipped to Sampson Naval Base, a recruiting station at Geneva, New York, and they had the same sort of thing going. The team was so good, Max Zaslofsky, one of my all-time greats, was on the second team. I reffed practice sessions there, and then one day they had a tremendous snowstorm, not unusual for the Syracuse-Rochester area. Ten minutes before the scheduled game against the Brooklyn Armed Guard, only one referee had showed up. I offered to flip a coin with my buddy in the stands to see who would go down, but he said, "Not me." So I went down, reffed the first half, and then the guy from Syracuse showed up for the second half. Fortunately for me, he did not do a good job, and they had appreciated my acting – I was a real ham. Both coaches in that game recommended me to Asa Bushnell, the head of the Eastern Collegiate Basketball Association as well as chairman of the U.S. Olympic Committee, to give me a try when I got out of service.

I picked up some high school games in late '45, and I probably looked better than maybe I was because a lot of guys were still in service. I wasn't leaving home, was working in my father's meat market and worked a couple of Mason-Dixon games. My big break was in a Southern Conference game, where I filled in for someone who got sick and got the greatest compliment a ref can get. The losing coach, Gummy Proctor of VPI, said it was the best-reffed game he'd seen, sent my ego through the ceiling. That earned me the Southern Conference Tournament, where I replaced Paul Menton, who had worked that tournament for 19 years, and who also had to release me from a commitment to work the Mason-Dixon Tournament. Well, I had a great tournament and got good clippings.

The following year when the BAA started, each city submitted names of two referees. I was not one of those selected from this area – they chose Phil Fox from Washington and J. Dallas Shirley – but a month or two after the season started I was invited to ref a game.

In early times in the NBA, we had the fans sitting right on the floor. In Fort Wayne they played in a high school gym, with one row of seats on the floor. They usually played a slow, deliberate style in the West and Midwest, while the East played give-and-go, and that difference in style lasted a long time. In my last couple of years I kept a pedometer with me. When I caught a New York, Philadelphia, Syracuse or Boston game, I'd run as much as 6½, seven or 7½ miles. If I caught a Fort Wayne, Minneapolis or St. Louis game, I'd run 5½ or six. Even Minneapolis had a narrow court, while Fort Wayne had three animals who if they stretched their arms out they covered the width of the floor.

Now people sitting on the floor or people in Syracuse, yes, they may try to intimidate you. One referee refused to go out on the floor for the second half of a game because of that. There may have been some fear on occasion, though most of the places had pretty good police protection. But if a referee can be intimidated, he doesn't belong on the floor. If you're intimidated or if you don't hustle at all times, then you should not be an official, and that refers to any league – high school, college or pro.

Yes, we've had police escorting us off at times. In fact, I'm surprised we haven't had more of that today, with the instant replay in some of the arenas, with a call at the end of the game. If I make a call at the end of a game that you think is the difference in the game, you forget the 10, 12, 14 free throws that they missed, you forget the seven or eight passes that they threw out of bounds. But that particular play, because it was one point, in your mind it made a difference, not in my mind. You really shouldn't have a guy around who makes the call at the end of a game just because it favors the home team. It's as simple as that. So whenever I hear that the home court advantage has to do with officiating, I defend myself wholeheartedly. If anything, I'd try to lean the other way. That was my feeling, and the best compliments I ever got were from losing coaches or a guy like Bob Feerick who used to say he loved to see me on the road.

I think we were better referees back then because we traveled more together. I was always talking basketball with Sid Borgia, Norm Drucker, Louie Eisenstein, Mendy Rudolph, Earl Strom, Jim Duffy, any one of the guys. If we were on a train or plane going from Washington to Minneapolis or New York to Boston, whatever, invariably, no matter what else we talked about, we'd say, "I had a play the other night, it was this, this and this, and this is what I called," and he'd say, "Well, I had one...."

In those days, yes, we acted, yes, we were hams, yes. A lot of us knew when to put it on and when not to put it on. When I say put it on, I mean that there are certain plays where you have to come out of the woodwork and be strong or you look like a nothing out there. Pat Kennedy was great. I learned a lot from him. And that's where Sid Borgia got all his learning, traveling with Pat Kennedy. He refereed a hell of a lot like Pat. We all had our shtick. I took pieces from Pat Kennedy, Chuck Solodare, Dallas Shirley and Curly White. I took a piece of everybody I knew and made Arnold Heft.

Sid Borgia never blew the whistle and yet he controlled the game as well as anyone. Lots of times he made up rules as he went along, yet he had full control of the game and those guys had as much respect for Sid Borgia as they did for Arnold Heft and the way he refereed. We didn't referee together often after the first few years, because our styles were different and you can't screw up the ballplayers with inconsistencies. Consistency is what we're striving for, but nobody will believe that.

I did things that we were told in those days not to do. I think it hurts the game a little bit if you don't talk to the players. I even talked to the fans, found that I was able to get 'em on my side, not necessarily to agree with me but to get off my back. If a guy yelled at me, "Where's your seeing eye dog?" I'd say, "How did you get in here – I thought I tied you outside." I think I had an easier time refereeing by talking to the players. Why? Because if you referee according to the rules and make every call, you aren't gonna have a ball game. Keeping from blowing the whistle makes you a better ref.

I'd talk to the big guys, saying, "Open it up, you're backing in, get out of there, quit pushing." You want to try to get the first foul, not the retaliation. I hate the three-second call. Unless a guy anchors himself in the lane I don't want to call it, and I'd count loud and slow. You could make a wrong call if you're not in position, and the question is who got there first, because that's who's entitled to the spot. Another thing I don't agree with is the idea that there are different rules for stars and non-stars. I agree that the game has gotten away a little bit with the extra step, but it's not for one or a few players but for all players.

When I started they still had a lot of player-coaches in pro basketball. Paul Birch was at the end of his playing days with the Pittsburgh Ironmen when I came into the league. He would have had a lot of problems in today's world because of supposedly racist remarks. Today he'd be hung. For an official it didn't really make a difference if there was a player-coach. Buddy Jeannette, for example, was a great player. And I remember Al Cervi because he had what we call in Yiddish the most shticklach or idiosyncrasies.

Cervi, Red Auerbach and Eddie Gottlieb knew the rules better'n anyone in the league. When they called a timeout, you would have a second or two before they confronted you, and in that time I'd be ready with an answer. With those three guys my answer better be right. Eddie was probably the real brain among the owner-coaches, the pepper pot, in Yiddish we say kuchleffel. He could give you all kinds of hell but was the fairest guy. As soon as there was a new rule in place I guarantee you Red Auerbach would have a way to get around it, not necessarily to cheat, but a play that would work around it. Cervi was like that, too, a street guy who never went to college.

The referees weren't out there to hurt anybody. I remember one game I worked with Normy Drucker, when Boston played the Bullets at the University of Maryland. Normy called a technical foul on Tommy Heinsohn early in the game, and when you know this you're a little reluctant to call a second one. At least I was, because I knew people didn't come to see the referee. With about five minutes to go in the game I called a technical on Tommy. Heinsohn was always a little more loquacious than other players, but fining a player 50 or 100 dollars in those days would get them to keep their mouths shut. All I had to say was, "Another word and you're gone," and they knew "gone" meant another tech and expulsion and a fine.

Well, Heinsohn was on me for something, and I called a T. The horn sounded from the table and they signaled, "second T." I thought, "Oh no." I wouldn't have called it if I had remembered the first one, but he had to go. Tommy was a great guy. Just because I say he was talkative doesn't mean he was looking for anything he could get. After the game, I told him, "If I don't get in trouble, I'm not gonna turn it in for you to get fined — on the condition that you buy a hundred-dollar bond in your kid's name."

I was aware that there was gambling on basketball games. It was pretty hard not to be. All you had to do was go into Philadelphia, go into Syracuse, go into the schools for that matter, and the first time someone goes driving for the basket and you blow the whistle, you know who everybody behind you is betting on. I remember in Philadelphia, if Tommy Gola or Joe Fulks or any of 'em would go driving for the basket and you don't blow the whistle, boy, the roof came down. Then you'd go down to the other end and the other team comes down and you blow the whistle, they'd yell, "What's he in, a glass cage or something?" Anybody who says they don't hear what's being said … But I never saw anything suspicious in any game I worked.

I never saw anything suspicious to me, but maybe I was naive for thinking that nobody would fix games or shave points. But one time I had a game at North Carolina State, and when I got there about three or four in the afternoon for the game that night, Butter Anderson, the assistant coach who was Everett Case's hatchet man — you know, all the coaches had someone sitting next to them to do the bitching and moaning — called me aside and said, "Arnie, I want you to come in and see a film and tell me what you think."

I didn't know what he was gonna show me, but it was a game film, N.C. State versus LIU. Now Case and Anderson were from Indiana and the guys they recruited from there didn't know anything about passing the ball. As soon as they got it, boom, they shot. It was run, run, shoot. And LIU played the same style. When I saw about four or five minutes of the game, to my eyes there was an obvious difference. I picked up right away that they didn't shoot, they were holding the ball. They had some of the leading scorers in the country in those days and they weren't shooting. N.C. State jumped out to a 10-point lead and then held the ball in a possession-type game. LIU, favored by about 10 points, seemed to think they could catch them any time they wanted, but it never happened. Apparently what had happened, as we later found out, was that it had been one of the point-shaving games. That's the only game that I could recall that I noticed anything, and it was on film where I was looking for something, not refereeing.

I refereed the first game with the 24-second clock, by the way. That was an innovation instigated by Danny Biasone, a fantastic guy in my mind. And I agree with Maurice Podoloff's decision to put it in, that it helped save the game.

Mr. Podoloff was a real intelligent guy. A lot of people didn't give him credit for it. He was about five feet tall and heavy, a butterball. He inherited basketball. I don't think he knew anything about it to start with, but any question you wanted answered, Podoloff would reach into that side pocket and pull out a handful of papers – whether it was the schedule, whether it was the rules, whatever it was, there it was.

I probably set him back more than anyone else because of my flying, although I only missed one game in my history of basketball. I was the first official that started flying to games. When they first had the league, the rule was you had to be in the city the night before a game, and your games were spaced out in those days.

Well, for a three o'clock Saturday game in Syracuse that was to be televised on Dumont, I could get there easily on a 10:00 a.m. flight on Colonial Airlines from National Airport in Washington. Unfortunately, there was bad weather, and I decided to charter a flight and take my two kids with me. We never made it to Syracuse, had to sit down in the snow in Elmira, New York. At game time, Podoloff was undergoing surgery in Philadelphia, but not because I missed that game. He recovered nicely, and I got a $300 fine and was not reimbursed for the cost of the charter. I was also "fined" by my wife – carpeting for our home. It was bad enough when Mr. Podoloff didn't see me on the floor, but when Sylvia didn't see me, knowing I had the kids with me in a small plane flying in the snow belt, the question "Where are the kids?" took precedence over "Where's the referee?"

Arnold Heft has been active in commercial real estate, has been a part owner of the Washington Bullets and Capitals, and is a one-third owner/partner in the Capital Centre (Largo, Maryland) now known as USAir Arena. He also owns a stable of thoroughbred racehorses – athletes, he says, who never ask to renegotiate their contracts after winning a race.

Norm Drucker

I played high school basketball at Erasmus, for coach Al Badain, and at City College, for Nat Holman. In 1943, during my third year at CCNY, I entered the Army and was discharged in 1946 as a first lieutenant. I played professional ball with Trenton, Troy and Elizabeth in the American Pro League. All the games in this league were played on Friday, Saturday and Sunday. I'll never forget what many people were saying about the BAA, that it wouldn't last because they were playing games during the week and wouldn't draw.

I started officiating in 1949 and began working some college ball in 1950 and 1951, when I received a call from Mr. Podoloff asking me if I could get to Baltimore immediately for an 8 p.m. game. He told me he got my name from Haskell Cohen, the PR director. Can you imagine David Stern doing that today? In 1951 the commissioner did many of those chores. In fact, one year, Podoloff did not have a supervisor of officials. He did the assigning.

I told him I would be there and he told me the home team would have a referee's shirt for me and the other referee would brief me before I went out on the court. I arrived at the arena about 6:30 and waited for the other official to arrive. At about 7:55, Baltimore's business manager urged me to start the game promptly, even if I had to work alone, as there was a nice house of about 2,000 people. Both teams had player-coaches, Al Cervi for Syracuse and Chick Reiser for Baltimore. In the basketball world they were best described as "animals."

Just before the scheduled tip-off, Max Tabacci shows up at midcourt, takes off his topcoat, with his uniform on underneath, and says to me, "This is the pros – keep the whistle in your pocket." Which means – let them play. So they play the first half and it's brutal, blood all over the floor and both coaches were complaining. This irritated Max and for the second half he told me, "Blow everything." You can imagine how frustrated the players were, and of course, right after the game Max put on his topcoat and beat the crowd out of the arena. This was my first BAA game – what an introduction!

After that first game in 1951 I entered the league during the '52-53 season. I started at $40 a game, and if you were rehired for the following season, you would receive an automatic $5 per game raise. After two seasons I would automatically go to $50 a game. I decided to ask for a $10 raise for the '56-57 season. I called the office and arranged for a meeting with Mr. Podoloff. The office was in the Empire State Building and staffed by Connie Maroselli, Haskell Cohen (PR) and Mr. Podoloff. A far cry from the hundreds of staff and two floors of offices on Fifth Avenue.

Mr. Podoloff was five feet tall, rotund, brilliant and had the gift of gab. He sat behind a big brown desk, and when he sank down in his plush seat it was difficult for me to see his head from the other side of the desk. He told me that he had very satisfactory reports about my work and that he had great expectations for my future. After all these compliments I nearly changed my mind about asking for the $10 raise.

"What's on your mind, referee?" he said, indicating to me that he didn't know my name.

As soon as I had given him my pitch for a $10 raise, he jumped up out of his seat, pounded the desk, and said in an anguished voice, "Are you trying to bankrupt the NBA?"

So it's clear, at least to me, that the financial success of the NBA today is due to my settling for a $5 raise in 1956.

During my first season I worked a Rochester game in Fort Wayne that Rochester won. After the game I passed Les Harrison, coach and owner of the Royals, and he said to me "Good game – you have the potential of Pat Kennedy." Being a rookie I accepted the compliment. A few days later I had another Rochester game, and they won again. This time, as we passed, he said, "Good game – you're on your way." But the third time I had a Royals game, they lost at home to their rivals, Minneapolis, and after the game he knocked on the dressing room door and said, "Drucker, forget what I told you after the last two games." There's a lesson to be learned here about how coaches react. It's much easier to be complimentary after a win than after a loss.

The owners were at all home games and most of them went on the road with the team. Harrison, like Eddie Gottlieb in Philadelphia, was his own coach. In Syracuse, Danny Biasone acted as an assistant coach. Fred Zollner in Fort Wayne and Ned Irish in New York sat up in the stands, but Ben Kerner of the St. Louis Hawks would sit in the first row, with his wife and mother, and shout at the referees. His mother would make comments after a call against the Hawks, such as, "This is the last NBA game you will work in St. Louis."

It isn't fair to compare the owners of yesteryear with those of today. One thing is certain, the NBA today owes a historical debt of gratitude to men like Podoloff, Brown, Gottlieb, Biasone, Zollner and Irish.

Norm Drucker overrules Bob Cousy's objection to a technical foul. Bill Russell and Tom Heinsohn look on, while Sam Jones looks ahead. PHOTO COURTESY OF NORM DRUCKER

During those years most trainers did not travel with the team. Visiting teams would hire a local college trainer to tape ankles and attend to the players during the game. The Knicks and the Pistons were the only teams to travel with a trainer.

The league was constantly in money trouble and it took great owner imagination to keep the franchises afloat. Rumor had it that Ned Irish of New York lent the league money to make the referees' payroll. Gottlieb ran his club from his vest pocket – rules, schedule, finances – everything was in his vest pocket. Eddie didn't throw money around. In the American League, Eddie owned the Philadelphia SPHAs, the forerunner of the Warriors. Butch Schwartz, who played for the SPHAs, was shocked when Eddie gave him $5 to purchase a $4.95 round-trip ticket to New York and told him to keep the change.

The arenas were old, dirty and had the smell of a locker room. The crowds were predominantly male, cigar- and cigarette-smoking, and of course beer-drinking. I always thought the Rochester court was not regulation. In Boston, the Celtics players knew where the dead spots were on the parquet floor. Many an opponent lost the ball dribbling over these spots. In Baltimore the team benches were under the basket instead of on the side of the court. The baskets were not standard and players thought Fort Wayne had very soft rims, which made it easier to score. The backboards had guide wires, to hold them in place, and they were extended to the stands for support. In many places fans would get to these wires and pull on them so as to shake the basket. Eventually, guards were stationed to protect against this type of action.

The locker rooms for the referees were not so clean and usually the poorest room in the building. In New York and Boston we dressed in the hockey team's locker room. Usually the hockey uniforms were being dried and there was not much room. However, the typical smelly atmosphere was the same in every locker room. If we needed some assistance we would have to go looking for the home team trainer. They were overworked but always accommodating. The common practice would be for referees to bring soap and towels from the hotel as we would never know when they would be needed. I remember a game in Minneapolis when someone shut off the hot water valve and we had to take cold showers.

In the Cincinnati Gardens and the Syracuse War Memorial you had to go through the stands to get to the locker room. The fans were wild in most cities but especially so in Syracuse. They saw a loss at home as the end of the world and usually blamed the officials. As we walked off the floor we'd take off our belts and wrap them around our fists with the buckles obvious to everyone. This was going to be our protection. We hoped this would be a warning that we were ready to protect ourselves. Earl Strom and I had several physical encounters with fans, and in a playoff game in Baltimore Earl broke his thumb punching a fan. Sid Borgia was involved in a fistfight in Syracuse and the fan sued Sid. Podoloff, I understand, wouldn't back Sid because he had thrown a punch at the fan. The policy of the referees was, you are on your own – take care of yourself.

Syracuse also had a character known as "The Strangler," who roamed the sidelines and harassed the visiting team. Once he got too close to the Celtics huddle when Boston was in town. They pulled him into the huddle, and he came out bruised and bleeding.

At first there was no security for the officials, and then Podoloff decided that security was necessary. He ordered each home club to provide a uniformed guard or someone who looked like official security to escort the officials on and off the court. Ben Kerner of St. Louis hired a guy who looked like he was 95 years old, and we told him to stay in the locker room, as we reckoned it was safer not to have security.

In my early years in the league, with eight, nine or 10 teams, you saw each team a dozen times a season and developed a familiarity with team personnel. Mostly, we stayed in the same hotels with teams, and we'd often travel with them when two teams played home-and-home games back-to-back. It must be hard to identify with players today, because officials only see teams two or three times a season.

All the refs back then somehow had both a learning and a teaching experience. It seemed as if we were all dedicated to a mentoring relationship as a normal part of our activities. Of course, we had a lot of time together, seven-hour train rides to get to a city for a game. The best official I ever saw was Mendy Rudolph. He had good judgment, he had a flair that made him popular and both players and coaches respected his ability – a perfect trifecta for a referee.

Sid Borgia, Mendy Rudolph and Arnie Heft were great teachers and communicators. Sid was a great admirer of the "let them play" theory. He was a great official and helped develop the NBA's personality in the early years. Many players would facetiously ask, "Are we playing by the NBA's rules or Sid's rules?"

Right from the start I had a thing going with Red Auerbach. He'd get on me, I'd chase him and he'd scream all the more. It was the same with Red and Sid Borgia. Among the players, two that often gave me trouble were Rick Barry and Alex Hannum. But as a coach, Hannum was one of those I had most respect for, along with John Kundla, Jack McMahon, Dick Motta, Jack Ramsey, Doug Moe, K.C. Jones and Lenny Wilkens.

Players often would complain that there were different rules for stars. Earl Strom had the best answer to whoever said that. He'd say, "Sure we do, so why don't you become a star?" But it seems to me fair to say that the standard of play is, in the natural course of events, set by stars.

An interesting complainer was Walt Bellamy, because he always spoke about himself in the third person. "Why is that a foul on Walter?" he'd say. "Bill wouldn't get a foul for that" (meaning Bill Russell).

I'd call another one on him, and he'd say, "Sure, Walter doesn't get that call."

When I'd heard enough, I'd tell him to keep quiet. And one time, when he didn't, I said, "Bellamy, tell Walter he's got a technical."

Norm Drucker presents the game ball to Wilt Chamberlain after Chamberlain scored his 25,000th point with it. PHOTO COURTESY OF NORM DRUCKER

I believe that Wilt Chamberlain was the strongest man ever to play basketball. I saw him block Bellamy's first 10 shots in a row once. Another time, against the Celtics, big Clyde Lovellette was playing in relief of Russell and trying to muscle Wilt, who asked him to cut it out. Then there was a commotion in front of the Warriors' bench and Clyde took a fighter's stance and taunted Wilt, who dropped him with a quick, short right to the chin. George Lee jumped up from the bench and yelled, "Clyde, take the full eight count, don't get up."

Chamberlain was not only a great player of the older era, but a classy guy who was easy to work for. The others I put into that category are George Mikan, Slater Martin, Paul Arizin, Tom Gola, Frank Ramsey, Bob Pettit, Bill Russell, George Yardley, Jerry West, Oscar Robertson, Bob Cousy and Bob Wanzer. One of the great big-men matchups was the Russell-Chamberlain confrontation. They played hard but never dirty or extremely vicious. Mutual respect was always there. Russell had the better players surrounding him, but I think that Chamberlain was the greatest player of that era. In fact, he still holds it against me that I ejected him from a game in Los Angeles — the only game he was ejected from. He never fouled out.

At first, when there was a televised game of the week on Saturday afternoons, they were paying $5,000 for the game, which didn't make it worthwhile for the better teams, who didn't want to give up their profitable, popular Saturday night games. As a result, the TV audience saw only the poor teams, which I always thought was shortsighted planning. All teams scheduled doubleheaders to help draw more fans. This reduced traveling expenses. But I loved to work the first game of a doubleheader at Madison Square Garden because I'd be home by 9:30. Even if I had the first game of a doubleheader in Boston, I could catch a plane and be home by 11:30.

The Boston-Philadelphia rivalry was fierce, especially the Russell-Chamberlain rivalry. In Boston and Philadelphia there was a custom for fans to throw eggs at the other team. The referees learned to stand close to the home team during timeouts. Some of the writers at that time used to identify closely with the home teams they covered. One of the worst was Jack "Poison Pen" Kaiser in Philly. He sat at the press table (the first row) and yelled like a fan. I was working one game in Philadelphia against Boston, and I could hear him clearly directing his remarks at me personally. "You're dumping, you're shaving points, Norm." Finally I blew the whistle and told him, "You're out of here."

I don't think I had the right to throw a writer out, but I told him to go. Philadelphia's owner Eddie Gottlieb came rushing out, saying, "What's wrong, what's going on?"

I told him and said, "If he doesn't leave, I'm going to forfeit the game."

I didn't know if I had the right to do that, either. But Gottlieb looked around, saw a full house of paying customers, and because he feared he'd have to refund the gate if there was a forfeit, he personally ordered Jack Kaiser off the press table.

That wasn't the only time I heard about gambling on basketball and people's suspicions. You had to be aware of it, working a game where one team held a 12-point lead at the very end of a game and guys in the stands are going wild over two free throws that made no difference to anything but the point spread or to anyone but bettors. For a long time, the gambling was so open in Madison Square Garden, that we'd never walk in through the lobby where gamblers were always doing business. The NBA is keenly aware of this problem. When I became supervisor of officials we had Jack Joyce, an ex-FBI man, in the league office, and every franchise city had a retired agent keeping his ear to the ground for rumors of any kind dealing with the integrity of the game.

During the playoffs, I believe, clubs were asked to write down the names of the officials they wanted. After 1956 the league devised a rating system. Another difference was that back then none of the officials was wholly dependent on the league. We all had regular day jobs – mine with the school system, Mendy Rudolph worked for WGN-TV, Arnie Heft was in real estate, Jim Duffy was a car salesman, Jim Gaffney a golf pro, Sid Borgia a salesman. But I really like the game now. Every year, back then, they'd put in new rules, trying to change the boring nature of the closing minutes of play. Now, with the clock and the team fouls, every game can be interesting right to the end.

Norm Drucker left the NBA to be an ABA referee and supervisor of officials from 1969 to 1976. He returned to the NBA to referee in 1976-77 and then served as supervisor of officials from 1977-81. He was operations director of the World Basketball League from 1987-92, and he was elected to the New York City Basketball Hall of Fame in 1994. His son Jim was commissioner of the Continental Basketball Association for eight years and is presently commissioner of the Arena Football League.

Vintage NBA: The Pioneer Era

Maurice Podoloff

In 1946, when there were discussions about forming a new basketball league, and I was under consideration for the job of running it. I knew absolutely nothing about basketball. In fact, as I told the organizers, I had seen only one basketball game in my life, a Yale game in the Payne-Whitney Gymnasium, starring accordionist Tony Lavelli.

At the time, I had been president of the American Hockey League, originally the Canadian American League, since 1935, a position I had accepted without knowing anything about hockey. To understand how these events came about, I must be somewhat autobiographical.

I was born in August 1890 in a little settlement about 75 miles from Kiev, Russia. As soon as my parents thought I was old enough to travel, they left for the golden land where the streets were paved with gold. We lived for a year on the east side of New York and then for three or four years in Setauket, a suburb of Port Jefferson, where my brothers David and Jacob were born. My father worked in a shop making sneakers.

Of course, Jews, wherever they are, do not just respect learning, they reverence it, and when my folks heard about a school of learning called Yale, they traveled by ferry, with their three sons, to New Haven. My father was through with shops. He wanted to become a businessman, so when the family arrived in New Haven he went looking for a business, leaving his family in the steamship office. The business he found was selling kerosene, the source of all cooking and illumination at that time. The equipment he acquired included an antiquated horse, a covered wagon containing five gallon cans and a residence on DeWitt Street.

Now I will jump over a number of years. In 1909 I became a member of the Yale Academy. As soon as my folks planned to send me to Yale, they decided that I was to be a lawyer. In my junior year an announcement was made that all members of the Academy who wanted to enter the law school could combine their senior year with the freshman year of law, so on June 15, 1915, I was a graduate of the Yale Law School with two degrees, B.A. and L.L.B. On the same day I was sworn in as a member of the Connecticut State Bar and could describe myself as attorney at law.

By that time my father had gotten into the real estate business and shared a suite of offices with Samuel J. Nathanson, a lawyer who immediately on my arrival made me his partner. I did not like the practice of law, but it was not without any advantage. The time I spent in New Haven's City Hall made it possible for me in later years to work out a complicated deal for Yale to purchase the city square on which the Yale-New Haven Hospital now stands.

After some four or five years practicing law, I joined my father in the real estate business, moving from one side of the suite to the other. A. Podoloff and Sons, Real Estate and Insurance, was really quite successful. My father was semiretired, my brother Jacob took care of the insurance and I did a land office business in the care of 22 apartment buildings.

And now a completely different tale. Originally every household had an ice box in the kitchen or back hall. The ice for the ice boxes was supplied by a resident of Bridgeport, Harry Walker, who was called the "Ice King." There were a number of freshwater lakes surrounding New Haven, the most prominent being Lake Whitney. When the lakes were frozen sufficiently to support a pair of horses and a truck fitted with circular saws, the ice was cut and stored in storehouses to wait for spring and summer demand.

This practice continued until the York Ice Company of York, Pennsylvania, began making machinery to freeze artificial ice. Some entrepreneurs of New Haven heard about this, acquired the machinery, formed the Center Ice Company, and purchased a square block of land in New Haven on which the Arena was finally built. The company started to make the ice and sell the product all over New Haven. When the hot weather arrived and the demand for ice was its greatest, Harry Walker flooded the city with ice at one-half the cost of the artificial ice. Well, the results were predictable. The Center Ice Company went bankrupt, and Walker purchased the property.

Some of the buildings in which ice was being manufactured for home use also had arenas constructed where there could be skating and hockey. The Ice King decided to do the same and started to build what was later called The New Haven Hockey Arena and also an ice house in one corner of the lot for the storage of 65 tons of ice for places where there was no artificial ice machinery. One day, when the arena was only partially built, Harry Walker drove to New Haven and put a revolver to his head.

While I had been watching that red-painted steel skeleton slowly rising to the heavens, I had been only mildly curious about the building. I had heard that it was to have an ice rink with Yale as possible tenant for ice hockey, but I had no interest in any sport, especially hockey. Well, one day we had two surprise visitors from Bridgeport, the Schnee brothers, who were settling the Walker estate. They kept talking in generalities, until they played their trump card. They informed us that

Walker had negotiated a seven-year lease with Yale for practices and to play varsity games on some Saturday nights. For this he would be paid $20,000 a year. Well, that did it – $20,000 a year from a solid tenant. So we agreed to buy the arena project from the estate and the purchase price was simple. We would pay the outstanding bills for the construction, which were not too much.

There is an old saying, "Fools rush in where angels fear to tread." Well, I was the biggest fool. Walker's contractor would not do business with us, so I called on my brother Nathan to leave his job in New York and become the manager of the Arena proposition. He had himself a real job. He had to install the ice floor in the Arena and the seats, get the garage under the Arena ready for use, and install all the ice-making machinery outside the building. This machinery froze the ice floor in the Arena Building and made artificial ice for buildings needing air-conditioning during the summer.

As the winter approached, we started to plan. Yale had Saturday night, the best night for spectator interest. Sunday was unavailable because New Haven, settled by Puritans in 1638, still had blue laws forbidding any activity other than religious on Sunday. My next task, as oldest of the brothers and president of the Arena, was to secure the withdrawal of the blue laws. Now all sports could be played on Sunday, but the only sport we were interested in was hockey, which was an almost unknown proposition to us.

We learned that there was a National Hockey League which played in the larger cities of Canada and the United States, and there was a minor hockey league, the Canadian American League which played in Providence, Springfield and some other small cities. We received a franchise just for the asking, and now where were we to get a team? Almost all the teams in the C.A. League were farm teams for the NHL. At that time, there were two teams playing in New York, the Rangers and the Americans. We managed to make a deal with the Americans, and I as the oldest of the four brothers became the governor for New Haven in the Canadian American League.

At that time Cleveland was also a member of the league and there I met one of the ablest promoters in the country, Al Sutphin. I rank him with Tex Rickard and Bill Veeck. In 1935, almost entirely through Sutphin's help, I became president of the league. That was the year that Ned Irish began staging college basketball doubleheaders in Madison Square Garden. He had a choice of the best teams in the country, and their players really put on a great show. These were the days before TV, but the AP and the UP really did a great job of covering the games.

The people who read the game stories most avidly were the arena owners who had hockey teams. They had many dark nights with no event to present. Basketball would be a perfect audience attraction. Also, the basketball floor was smaller than the ice floor and it could be built in small rectangular sections and easily stored. In New Haven, while my brother Nathan was the Arena manager, he laid a floor in 35 minutes.

Of all those interested, Al Sutphin was the most eager. In 1932, during the Depression, he had built a 10,000-seat arena on Euclid Avenue and he had to have events, especially since he had devised a financial strategy of paying interest on mortgage notes with tickets to hockey, basketball, ice shows and other events, instead of cash. Early in 1946 Sutphin started to work on the basketball proposition, and he called a meeting in New York for the purpose of starting a professional basketball league.

After the meeting was over he took a plane to Chicago to talk to Arthur Wirtz, another great promoter. Wirtz and the Norris family owned the Chicago Stadium, the Detroit Olympia and the St. Louis Arena. Al gave him a long talk, knowing that if the Wirtz-Norris teams came in, he was on his way to success, for Al was also a member of the Arena Managers Association.

Wirtz asked him who would run the pro team. Al told him Asa Bushnell, who was then boss of the Eastern College Athletic Conference. But Wirtz asked how much Bushnell wanted. Al told him $25,000 and a term contract. That's when Wirtz asked, "What kind of job is Maurice Podoloff doing in the AHL?" And Al told him, "He's doing a good job." Wirtz told him that if I would take the job his teams would go in. The next day Al and I met in New York, and even though I told him that I knew absolutely nothing about basketball, they hired me for $8,000 or $9,000 a year, I forget exactly.

I had already prepared a constitution patterned after the hockey constitution, and it was adopted along with the name I suggested, the Basketball Association of America. Later, before the 1949-50 season, threatened with some kind of a lawsuit, I changed the name to the National Basketball Association. There was no discussion of basketball rules at our first meeting. However, the length of the BAA game was slightly increased, the idea being to give spectators as long a game of basketball as was taken up by Irish's college doubleheaders.

As soon as I was elected to the presidency I started the preparation of a schedule. I was instructed to move both league offices to New York. In 1946 I first moved to a suite of rooms on Madison Avenue. I stayed there for two years and then moved to the 80th floor of the Empire State Building where I stayed until my retirement in 1963.

As our publicity man I picked Walter Kennedy. At the meeting in New York City, Chicago was represented by Arthur Morse, who was in charge of college basketball games in the Chicago Stadium. While Kennedy was attending Notre Dame, he was in charge of the Notre Dame team whenever it played in Chicago, and Morse recommended him highly. Another advantage was that Kennedy lived in Stamford, Connecticut, easy commuting distance from New York. When I resigned the presidency of the NBA in 1963, Kennedy took over and changed his title to commissioner. I didn't know why but I thought it had nothing to do with feeling inadequate to be president. To me, "commissioner" sounds too much like "commissar."

Vintage NBA: The Pioneer Era

The first game was scheduled at Toronto on November 1, 1946. The reports I received about the game were hardly encouraging, but that was the first game and I thought things would improve as the schedule would bring more teams into play. But that did not happen and there were talks about rules and almost everything else. And there were meetings and discussions, without end and without any ideas as to what the cure should be.

If the 1946-47 season was bad, the next season was worse, two disastrous seasons. I got the idea that the trouble lay in the team personnel. I began to think people would buy tickets to see the famous players we lacked, but I'm not sure I'd have bought a ticket to see a player perform, not even Bob Cousy when he came along a few years later, not just a great player but a brilliant showman. To me, at the time, the most famous player was George Mikan, who was playing on a team that was a member of Ike Duffy's league.

So I started a little bit of proselytizing. I approached Max Winter and Ben Berger, the owners of the Minneapolis Lakers. I got nowhere, so I started around the back way with Paul Walk of Indianapolis and Carl Bennett of Fort Wayne. I called a meeting of the Governors of the BAA and the individuals who had an interest in teams in Ike Duffy's league. This was not a merger. If it had been a merger, I would have invited Ike Duffy.

For this special meeting in 1948 I had engaged a large room in the Morrison Hotel in Chicago, and I had a large desk brought into the room with a chair for me, and I had placed a large briefcase on the desk filled with newspapers. All this was to impress those people gathered – which my height did not. When they had all assembled, I asked who was interested in a franchise in the BAA. When the first one spoke up, I told him he had to resign his position in the other league before he could become a member of our league. I believe each one went somewhere below and he came back and advised me he had resigned. And the fastest moving man was Max Winter.

I had started this move in desperation. I believed that the only way I could save our league was the addition of what I considered star players. I knew full well that some of the teams that joined could not last beyond one season, but to me it seemed that this was the only way we could last another season or two. That wasn't a merger, it was a raid. That night I slept the sleep of the just.

Our dreams of glory turned to nightmare. Soon I had a rude awakening. The games were just as lackluster as they had been. Games dragged on and on. Stalling by a team ahead and in possession of the ball and deliberate fouling to gain possession made for a constant parade to the foul line.

In 1951, one important event occurred when a young woman, Connie Maroselli, came to work in the NBA. She was a valuable assistant, who took such good care of the NBA books that there was never an error in the checkbook. Later on, she and her sister Grace would prepare all the information that Haskell Cohen would need for the preparation of the news for early newspapers, often working until the wee hours. I still consider Connie and Grace among my most wonderful and valuable friends.

At the end of the 1951 season I resigned the presidency of the hockey league. That was the year Haskell Cohen, our publicity director, introduced the all-star game to the NBA. In time, he also accomplished something else which was even more important. He negotiated the first TV deal with Tom McMahon of Dumont. Dumont lasted one year, that is the company itself. The original contract was $3,000 per game for 13 games – a total of $39,000. That was for the '53-54 season.

Tom Gallery of NBC was in charge of "Friday Night Fights" at Madison Square Garden. He had watched our NBA games, so when I approached him for TV for the NBA, we made a deal in minutes. It started with the next season, 1954-55. The fees were simple. $3,000 for a regular-season game and $5,000 for a playoff game. Originally, the games on TV were only on Sundays. In 1959 Saturday afternoon games were added. There was only one stipulation. I had to attend all the TV games to make sure that two properly spaced timeouts would be called in each quarter for commercials.

The result of this was simple. I never watched a game. My eyes were glued to the clock. When games were played on Sunday only that was easy, but when Saturday games were added there was a travel problem, especially when the Saturday game was in L.A. and the Sunday game in the East. But most fortunately, I had no travel problems.

At one of our meetings, Max Winter described a particular game. The Lakers were beaten by Fort Wayne by a score of 19-18. The game lasted over three hours and 8,000 spectators were reduced to 500 diehards. Then came a playoff game of March 20, 1954, between Minneapolis and Syracuse. It lasted over three hours. The spectators left and the TV crew was disgusted. I already had scheduled our annual meeting for April 24th at The New Yorker Hotel in New York. To me everything was threatened with death. The NBA, the TV deal and me also. I was 64 years old. Where could I get a job?

The man who came to the rescue was Danny Biasone. The first time I met him was at the meeting that brought the NBL teams into the NBA, when he inquired about me in tones that could be heard a block away, "Who the hell is he?" Now he told me he had a rule which he thought would help the NBA. He didn't tell me what the rule was. Just like a drowning man grabs a rope thrown to him, I began to view the meeting with hope but not conviction.

So when the meeting started, I called on him first to speak and he told us about his brainchild, the 24-second rule. No one seemed to be impressed. However, the rule was adopted on a provisional basis, and I was given strict instructions that, if the rule did not accomplish the desired results when tried out during the summer, I was to cancel it immediately.

It was apparent to everyone that some kind of clock had to be built. At this point, Walter Brown, the owner of the Boston Celtics, said he had an electrical contractor in Boston who could build a clock. I did not know what to do, so I returned to New Haven for help from my brother Nathan who was the manager of the Arena. He referred me to a Robert Roston in New York. I gave him the job and then spent many anxious weeks waiting for some word from him. Finally it came. I phoned Brown in Boston, and we agreed to try out the clocks on August 11 in the Blodgett School in Syracuse where Danny assembled two teams. The school was actually his alma mater.

The Roston clock cost $200, while the Brown clock was to cost $1,200. I gave Brown the first opportunity to try his clock out. It wouldn't even start. However, Roston's clock worked perfectly. I still was not perfectly satisfied, so I had it tried out in every preseason game, and it worked perfectly. There were a great many preseason games, because in 1954 the regular season started later than it did in later years.

What were the long-term benefits? Franchise holders almost tripled. Franchise fees jumped from $10,000 to some millions. TV fees jumped from $100,000 to $18 million. Millions of dollars flowed into the league and team treasuries. So how did the NBA acknowledge its debt? They had a big dinner in Washington and gave Danny a gold watch which he needed as much as he needed a hole in his head. What he should have is a gold niche in the Hall of Fame.

When I heard another owner question Danny's credentials as the league's 24-second savior, I felt like taking a dull hatchet to his neck. The failure to get Danny Biasone into the Basketball Hall of Fame is one of my two major regrets. The other concerns Red Auerbach. He was an able coach, always the quickest to see the faults of any suggested changes in rules. But he was an abrasive man. When he'd light his victory cigar in those televised games, I always wished someone would shove it down his throat.

Until shortly before his death, at 95, Maurice Podoloff could recall, in great and specific detail whole transactions and conversations from throughout his career. As a graduate of Yale and the Yale Law School and an experienced real estate investor, he was central to the negotiations that provided the site for the Yale-New Haven Hospital. As co-owner, with his brothers, of the New Haven Arena, he became involved in professional sports, becoming president of the American Hockey League and first president of the NBA. He often gave credit for the eventual success of the NBA to contributions of Danny Biasone and Haskell Cohen, while others credit Mr. Podoloff himself for his business acumen and the summary judgments he made to dismiss and ban for life anyone found to be involved in gambling on basketball.